Bullfight The Pas de Deux

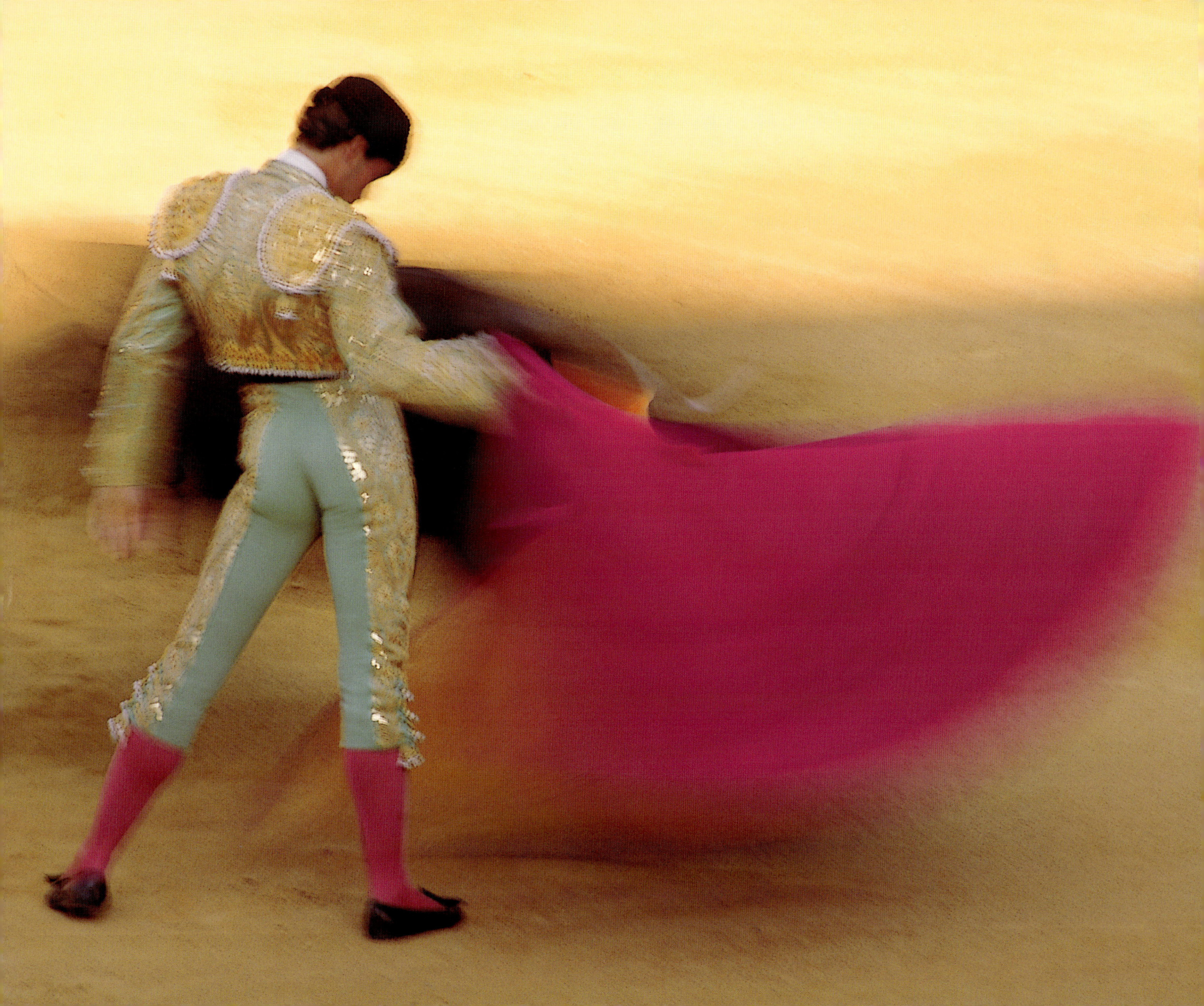

Bullfight The Pas de Deux

RICARDO B. SANCHEZ

COMMENT BY JOSEPH CAMPBELL
FOREWORD BY ROSA OLIVARES

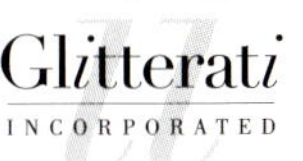

Glitterati
INCORPORATED

NEW YORK

First published in the United States of America in 2011 by

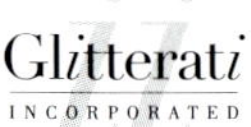

Glitterati
INCORPORATED

225 Central Park West
New York, New York 10024
www.GlitteratiIncorporated.com
Telephone: 212 362 9119
info@glitteratiincorporated.com

First edition, 2011

Design by Lynne Yeamans

Library of Congress Cataloging-in-Publication data
is available from the publisher

Hardcover ISBN 13: 978-0-9832702-1-8

Printed and bound in China

10 9 8 7 6 5 4 3 2 1

To Diane and Bartolome, my mother and father; to Alexandra and Ricardo,
my daughter and son; and to my soulmate, Zulema.

ACKNOWLEDGMENTS

My gratitude goes to all the bullfighters who appear in these photographs: Their performances in this ritualized dance between light and shadow and life and death made these images possible. To the late Humberto Gomez Osorio and to Juan de Muga, who made this project see the light of day. To my good friend Rosa Olivares, who has spent countless hours talking with me about how seduction, deception, illusion and truth are so fundamental to the way our society and culture function. To Monica Sevil, for her advice and support in making this project viable for all concerned. To Belen Moreno, for our special connection, and support for what I do. To Marta Hallett, who proves that passion and faith in what we do is essential to creating the art of living; I thank her especially for believing in the value of my efforts. To the entire Gitterati team that has made my dream come true. To all those whose name is not mentioned, but assisted me in creating and promoting BULLIGHT: THE PAS DE DEUX. Thank you. R.B.S.

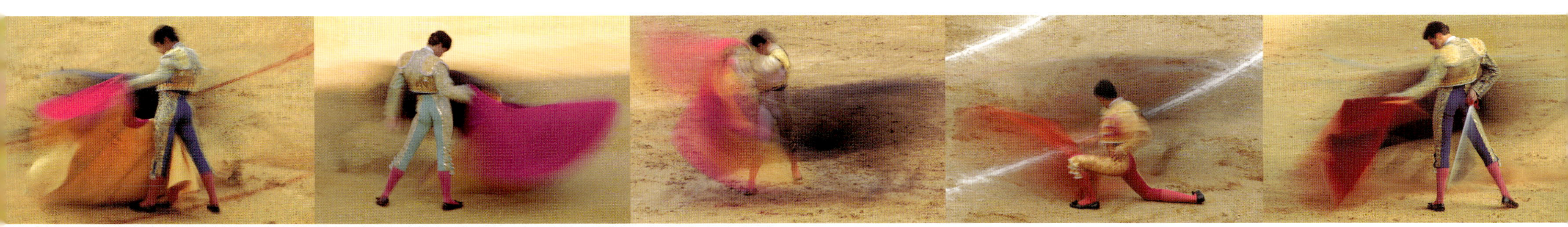

CONTENTS

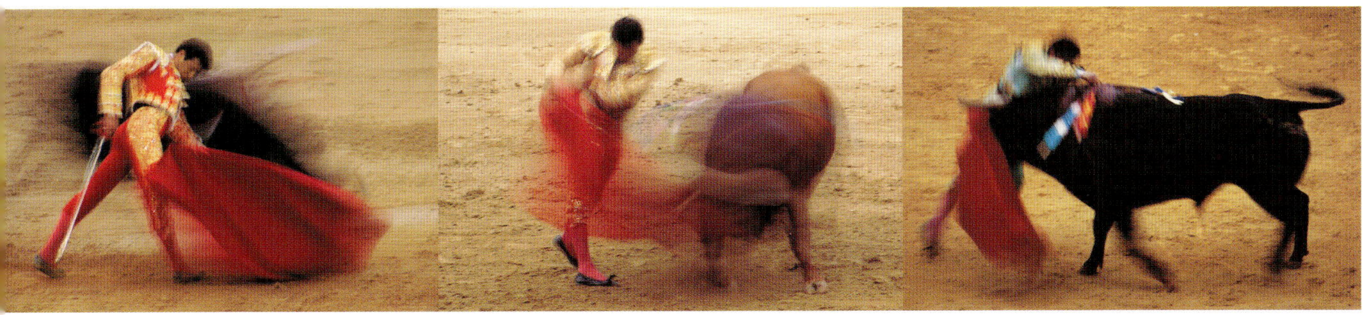

9

COMMENT

JOSEPH CAMPBELL

11

FOREWORD

The Art of Passing and Leaving Traces

ROSA OLIVARES

25

INTRODUCTION

RICARDO B. SANCHEZ

35

SEDUCTION, DECEPTION, ILLUSION AND TRUTH:

The Photographs of Ricardo B. Sanchez

174

INDEX

Considering the myth of sun, moon, serpent and bull, just look at the bullfight: The bullfighter—who is wearing a brilliant shining dynamic garment. He is the solar power and the bull is the moon power. Going in over the horns of the bull is the point of ultimate danger to the coup de grace, where the bull is knocked out.

Similar rituals appear in relation to serpents and sacrifice. In the bullfight there is the sacrifice of the bull so that there should be a "new period." The past must be killed so that there can be a future; this is the bull sacrifice. This is a fantastic thing to see….the calming and then the fixing of the bull—three times—the struggle between the consciousness principle of the individual and his transformation to becoming part of a larger entity, which is a death to the earlier primary existence of the individual.

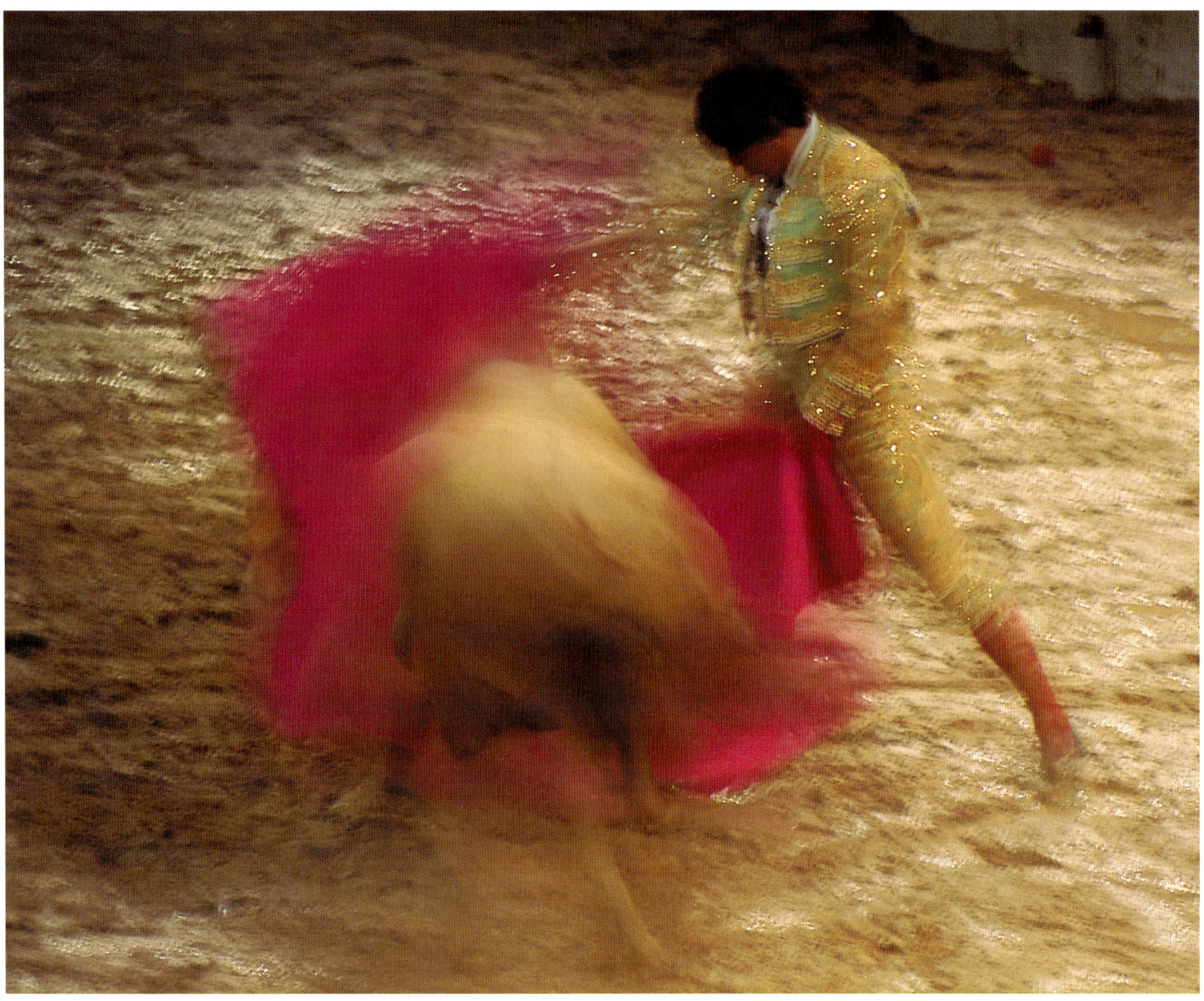

Verónica
Chamaco; Las Ventas, Madrid; May 17, 1993

THE ART OF PASSING AND LEAVING TRACES

What the Eye Cannot See

ROSA OLIVARES

Between the certain and the uncertain, between certainty and doubt, there is a strange territory in which the senses are unable to guide us, in which light and darkness merge to create a blinding chiaroscuro. It is in this territory that intuition, desire, dream and illusion produce what are sometimes monsters, sometimes gods. It is also in this nameless place — and those who come so far and are not afraid to continue, despite the unstable terrain, know this — where art grows, where man justifies his existence, where we want to return in order to continue believing in innocence and truth.

We rely on our senses and we rely increasingly on technics and technology, a prolongation of our senses, of our body. What the eye cannot see can be captured by a camera. In situations where time is incalculably fast and events succeed each other without becoming defined as images, the lens may capture the beam of light that produces a gesture. Our trust in our senses as the only possible way to trap existence is now a theme for poets only. The definition of reality, of certainty, has changed to the point where it fades into thin air. Technology, the machine, exists to perfect perception, to go beyond what a man can reach with his hearing, with his sight. There are machines that can portray what we cannot see, not only making us doubt our own sensorial capacity but also altering the limits of what we consider real. There are cameras that, apparently, are able to capture the aura, that halo of heat all living bodies emit which has always been a symbol of holiness, the golden ring that religious painting has immortalized. But the aura as symbol, as the manifestation of the idea of saintliness is no longer; now it is something completely different because we know that every living body has one. Furthermore, it is something that can be given visual form in a photograph. This knowledge may change our concept of what is real, make us doubt what we believe because we see it and what we do not believe because we cannot see or perceive it with our senses. Today we know that even DNA has a recognizable form, a photographically reproducable image. Suddenly, between what we can see and what we cannot see, barriers emerge not of truth, but of illusion.

Photography has transformed our concept of reality. Through its images we have reconstructed the idea of what is true and what is false, finally to realize that it is merely an extension of man's ability to create illusion. As a part of art, that cultural game that emerges from man's atavistic need to search for truth and to hide and disguise it to continue seeking it, in order not to find it, photography began with this search for truth to eventually collaborate in the construction of an illusion. For while in its origins photography was the documentation of objective reality, having evolved into a cultural tool it has reached the same point as all the other artistic languages: an illusion, a game of seduction and deceit that man himself constructs. Every photograph is undoubtedly a document of something; at least it is proof that the exact moment it preserves for posterity actually existed: that it happened, and that there was someone there with a camera to show that it happened. But what do these photographs by Ricardo Sanchez prove? They give no face to this man, this bullfighter who risks his life, or to that other who makes a long, elegant *pase*. Naturally, some aficionados would be able to identify the *diestro*, or matador, by his body, by his gesture ... but this is not what the photographer is after. These images may be proof that once again the ritual, the game of life and death, occurred and that, once again, the man defeated the animal. But no, what these photographs document is these images' ability to seduce, like beauty, color and movement deceive the animal, like the sheen on a surface, a fleeting beauty, deceives us. Through our capacity to deceive we may even replace the natural with the artifical, nature with an indoor plant.

Light is the origin of color, the essence of painting, the basis of photography. And deceit converges in light. These photographs are simply documenting deceit. The deceit that is produced around life and death in the *fiesta* of the bulls. That absurd deceit that leads the bull to death chained to a blood-colored muleta. It is the document of an abstraction that becomes tangible in real life and which fades away between light and movement in these photographs. An abstraction that is also a symbol. And this is what differentiates these photographs from so many othhers that highlight courage, ferocity, art, the body, the bullfight (as the Anglo-Saxons call it, an inadequate translation that nonetheless defines the *fiesta de los toros*). For this reason also, these photographs are far removed from the usual document to become a testimony, although still a document, that comes from somewhere else. It is also for this reason that the fascination of these works lies in a more conceptual than visual terrain. Ricardo Sanchez employs the very art of seduction that he reveals in his photographs. He also deceives us, makes us enter the cape, and it is here that we return to the bullfight, to the intimate struggle between the images we see and the ideas that occur to us as we contemplate them.

What attracts us about these photographs is not horror. It is their beauty that catches our eye, their color, the fleeting presence of the shadow of death, that vertigo produced when someone risks his life, or even something more. We have already been deceived. Seduced by illusion, deceived by appearances, attracted by beauty, we come to a place that was not announced. We thought we were looking at bullfight photographs, and suddenly we realize that there is no bullfighter and no bull, that what we were staring at and believed we were seeing, almost with the background noise of a bullring, is a deep well in which lights lead us to the density of a black stain. Caught up in a dance of colors we are guided, we discover that the gold and the lights are life, that the ring does not exist since its dimesions are infinite and therefore beyond the scope of the lens. We realize that there is no blood, nor words, that there are no spectators and that only rarely is there tragedy. There is only the shadow of death, the presence of danger like an aroma, like a color. And looking at these photographs we come to think of bullfighting as a collective performance, we realize that this magic ritual is what now, without religion, or sin, or blood, or death, surrounds certain artistic actions. Those in which the body is used as a work field, in which the idea of action is centered on the sublimity of existence, on the infinite vulgarity of the things that make us revolve and move. We are reaching the point of searching for an explanation for what has no meaning other than the terrain of sensations, of rituals and of tragedies.

The idea of seduction is linked to illusion and deceit, like truth to lies, like good to bad, like bad to worse. The illusion of appearances, the illusion of the desired, of what we do not have, the deceit of appearances, of beauty, of youth. Eternal youth, the postponment of death to a later time. While young men dress as dancers and enter the ring to kill black bulls ten times their weight, risking their lives in

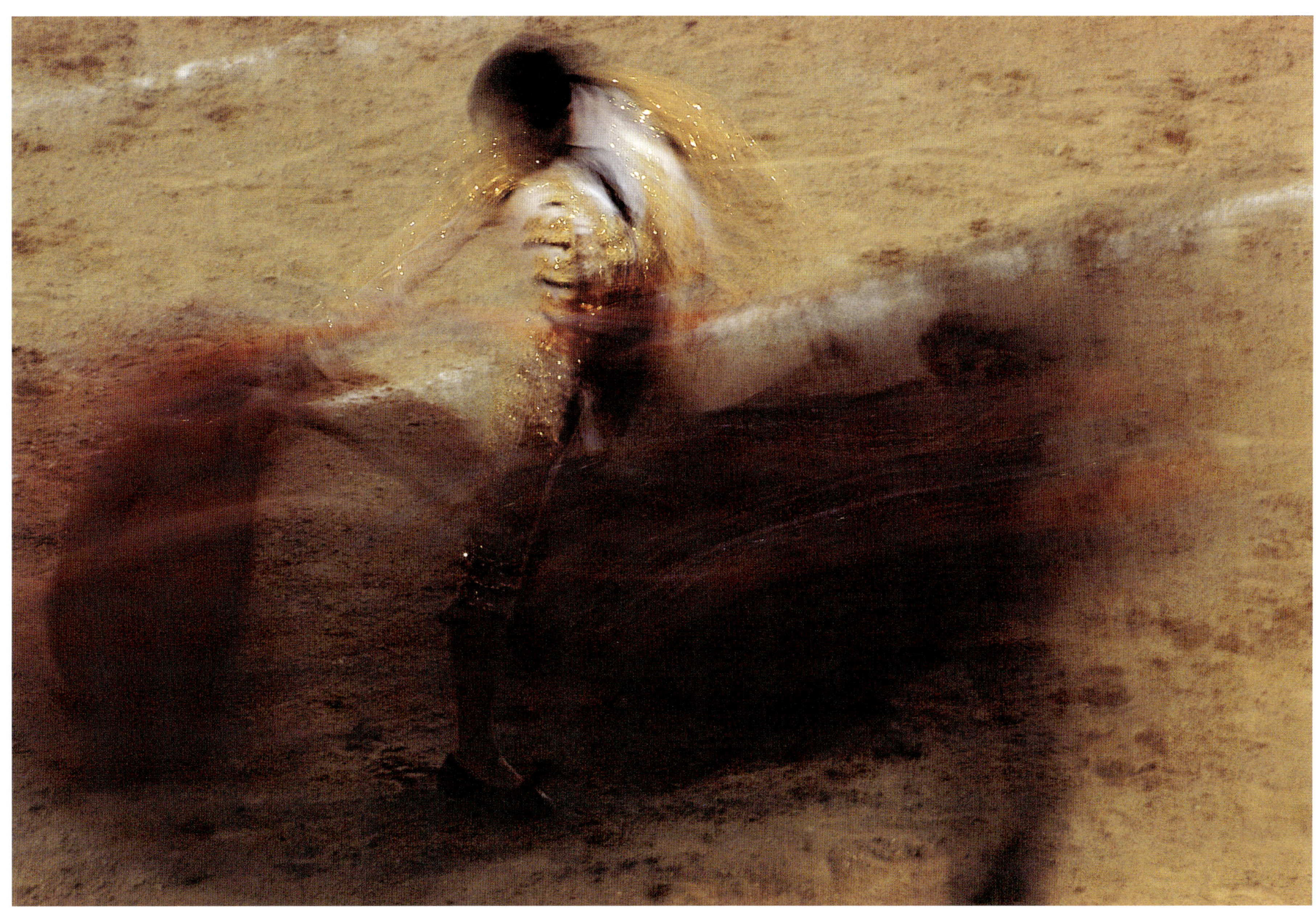

RIGHT-HANDED PASS/ *Derechazo*
César Rincón; Las Ventas, Madrid; June 6, 1991

an ancestral rite. Neither the fastest race track, nor the tallest mountain, nor the darkest chasm compares. It is not the same thing. Not the same thing?

We are speaking of deceit, and art is undoubtedly the territory that best represents it. The art of bullfighting does so symbolically. On the other hand, literature does so in a mathematical, logical way: "What is life? An illusion, a shadow, a fiction. Everything in life is a dream and dreams … are no more than dreams," said Calderón de la Barca. Others deceive themselves in other ways, by swearing eternal love beyond the grave, perhaps as proof of absolute devotion or perhaps like that red cape with which the bullfighter deceives the bull, like the lover who seduces his loved one. Beyond life we shall merely be dust, "but enamored dust," promised Francisco de Quevedo. Illusion and deceit come together, and there is no illusion like the one art produces. Painting, full of representation, of stories that substitute for others, and then photography, the great deceit of appearances in the name of the purest truth, of the truth which is the product of technology, as nobody today would question.

Photography is true because everything that has been photographed existed. But everything that serves to speak the truth serves equally to speak the oppostie, such as words. And fiction, that is, illusion, dream, comes with the word. Photography, like all the media that man has invented to express himself, was born from the intention of transmitting experiences and sensations, of giving form to dreams and desires. But these methods have evolved rapidly and have adapted to form, to the nature of the human race, and they have become new forms of deceit, of creating illusion, of concealing and transforming, to deceive and lie with what has always been a principle of credibility. Photography is the paradigm of the reliable document, and it is also a technique that may be manipulated, assembled, deprived of meaning to produce something that is not real despite its appearance of reality. Art is approached in this way, through a magic device with which man tells his own tale, deceives and ennobles himself, turns defects into virtues, analyzes and delves into every recess of the concious and unconcious mind. If we expect truth from photography, we are deceiving ourselves. The truth can only be in our gaze. If from photography we expect explanations, the perfect image that clarifies the situation, we must look in another way or perhaps elsewhere. Deceit, the game of illusions, appearances, these are all the subject matter of art. For this reason, art has developed its vast symbolic capacity, its psychological depth, because man deceives and seduces, but eventually even in his forms of deceiving flashes of truth may appear—at least the truth of his being, of his way of wanting to be. Intention and intuition invariable emerge from behind a more or less successful act of deceit. Illusion always becomes truth. Or perhaps it is another illusion.

When photography has taken the bullfight as its subject, the resulting works have been very disparate, although most of them eulogize the magic and beauty of a pagan festival beyond time and place. The colors, the bodies, sex, death and danger and, above all, beauty and spectacle. Only few have seen anything else, perhaps because they did not want to see anything else. Between relating what is outside and investigating what remains inside there exists the same difference as between art and the graphic document; between speaking about what is private and establishing universal principles there lies the development of artistic creation.

The series *Pases*, which Ricardo Sanchez has been compiling for years all over Spain, attending bullfights in all the rings and following individual bullfighters over entire seasons is not, curiously, a series of photographs of bulls, about bulls. Or rather, it is much more than that. Ricardo Sanchez has constructed a beautiful metaphor of life and, above all, of deceit. In his previous work the idea of deceit, of the seduction that external forms exercise on us by concealing with their sheen, with their outward appearance the true reality of their essence, constitutes the guideline; it is in this series on the bullfight that he reveals, perhaps unexpectedly, the most complete and the most spectacular form of this deceit. A deceit that in the case of the bullfight leads straight to death, even as risk and the pure game of seduction insist on life, with its permanent games of deceit, of seduction, of adornment of appearances, that double public and private stance. Life leads inevitably to death, but who cares about this when in the middle of a game of seduction? Just like the bullfighter who does not stop to think about death when he makes a brilliant *pase* with his muleta, nobody wants to stop to see what lies behind that shining surface, apparent beauty, morning glory, perfect deceit by which we are taken in like the bull, blinded by the shine of blood, overcome by the yearnings of desire.

Magic and religion fill our memory with illusion, with rituals, and with deceits of seduction. The history of mankind, of culture, is marked by attempts at and achievement of deceit and seduction– fables, legends, fragments of history whose intention is to create an illusion, characters who seduce us with deceit, with the ignorance that time and lack of information reinforce, magic rites whose origins are lost in memory and which survive as game, spectacle. Of all the primitive rituals of the West only the bullfight, the art of *el toreo*, is still alive in the twenty-first century. And only in those few areas where the bull, this mythical animal, symbol of strength and virility, is still bred exclusively for the *fiesta*.

In Spain, the bullfight is more than a spectacle, more than a tradition. It is part of a culture rooted in the deepest of all places: language. Bullfighting terms impregnate a language that contains words that cannot be translated into any other tongue, words that tell of feelings and situations that can be understood only from a special perspective, from the ability to see the other side of appearances. And this needs time, time to sit down and watch how a man dressed in red and gold performs a dance of sex and death with a black animal ten times his weight. Time to understand that this is no macabre spectacle, that the bull is not martyred, for in the fight, in which it is given the chance to reveal its courage, its strength the animal is administered the noblest of deaths. Time to feel that we are spectators of a symbolic dance, a duet not just of man and bull but something more, a metaphor of life, a masked ball in which we do not know who is disguised. Time to realize that everything is a deceit, and that with what we see we can construct only half a reality, a reality that needs the two sides, light and shade, life and death, joy and pain.

In life, as the poet said, "everything passes and everything remains, but we are doomed to pass...." In the bullfight, the *faena is built up on the basis of pases*. The verb *pasar* is a curious verb in Spanish. It is charged with innuendoes and it would be impossible to list all its possibilities here (something that no translator would forgive me for), but it is an essential term in the bullfight, just as it is essential to know the two basic laws: command and moderation. One must know how to command the bull and to firmly withstand its charges. It is a conflict of characters rather than of bodies. And although we know that life is full of *cornadas* (horn thrusts), we strive to believe that the bullfight is something else, merely a spectacle. We forget that in life, too, we must remain firm, show moderation, "withstand the charges" of all kinds.

Those who have seen a bullfight first hand will not easily forget the anxiety of the spectators: the color of the arena, the red blood, the gaze of the torero, the impression we get that the bull is an innocent victim, and though it is a foreseeable death—that of the bull—something else is in the air. It is life

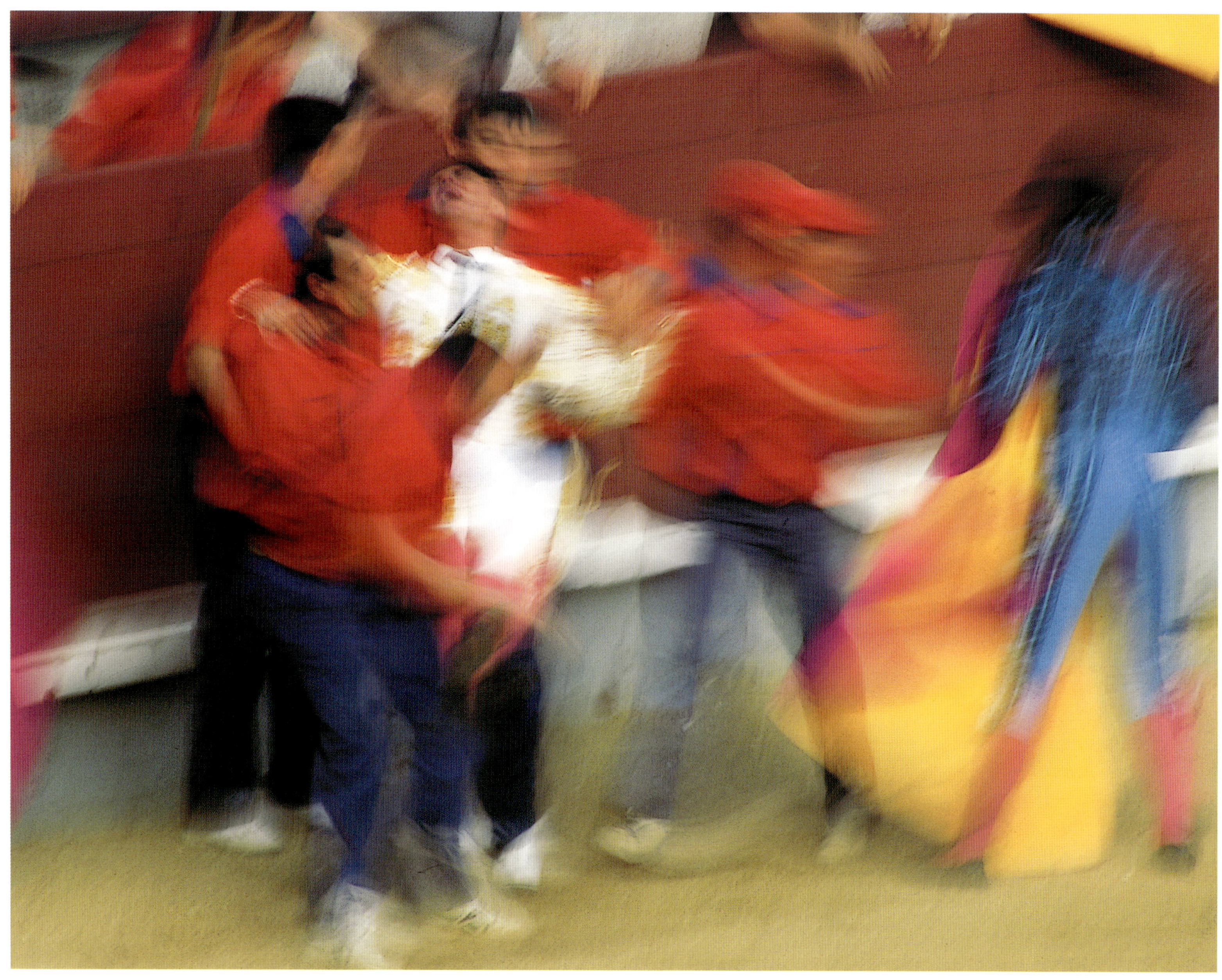

GORED OR TOSSED / *Cogida*
José Luis Bote; Las Ventas, Madrid; May 17, 1992

that parades before us, in those young, tense bodies—life as a game. An afternoon at the bullfight is a compendium of the life we lead, however unaware we are of this. It is an abbreviated catalogue of so many things in our lives that we never think about. Most probably because we do not have the time.

In Spain, language unwittingly returns time and time again to the ritual of the bulls, and not only in puns and aphorisms. It is the essence that persists, and in the background of the bullfight, as in the background of myths, what remains is deceit. The bull is deceived from the very moment it enters the ring: the running, the colors, the punishment, the noise, the body of the bull, so fragile and yet so imposing, involve the bull in a continuous dance until it meets its final suerte, its fate, its destiny. *Suerte*! The *suertes* in bullfighting are the different phases of the *faena*, the series of passes with the muleta. Before he enters the ring, everybody wishes the torero *suerte,* luck. And if the fight goes badly, it is because *suerte* abandoned him. In life, too, if things go well or badly this apparently has more to do with *suerte* than with anything else. But the truth is elsewhere, and it has more to do with the permanent deceit with which we adorn our lives, our private *faenas*. Just as the bull is deceived, until it is killed, with a seduction of colors and blood in which apparently it always has a chance of salvation, in life everything may be an illusion, a shadow, fiction.

It is said that in the bullfight everything is deceit, except the courage of the bullfighter, and the strength and danger of the bull: except that life and death are at stake. The man, the torero, looks like a woman: the color of the muleta and the cape is not blood red, it is another color we see in them. Today, even the torero's braid is false. The bull practically never kills the bullfighter (although this sometimes happens), and it is practically impossible that the bull's life will be spared and the animal allowed to return to the meadow with the wounds received in a struggle far more noble than the miserable, automated death of the abattoir. The horses are heavily protected and they cannot pursue the bull, the sword the bullfighter carries as he engages in the *faena* is almost invariably sham… until the end. Until the end, nobody knows for certain what is true and what is false. It is said that the bullfight is a dance, a sexual dance, but this is another deceit. The thrill is one of pure illusion, or perhaps it is the thrill one feels in the face of maximum risk. It is true that the man-woman, the torero, dressed in sequins, dances before the bull, almost invariably black, serious and armed, to deceive the beast, like an odalisque that leads it to the slaughter.

But the bullfight is much more than a road to death. It is the symbol of many things, not only of life as an absolute. It is also a parody of masculinity, the mass of disguised appearances.

We must know how to look in order to see beyond what the eye registers. Beyond the possibilities of our gaze lie not only the origin of light but also a world of impossible images. Since its invention, photography has become a witness of reality, of that moment that undoubtedly existed because we have its image, a photograph, the document of its reality, its existence. And this photograph is also proof that the moment no longer exists, that it passed. Photography thus becomes a document of the passage of time and, inexorably, of the reality of death. How many photographs confront us with those who are gone forever, with the feeling that they are no longer with us, and even with ourselves, in photographs that show us not the way we are today but the way we were and will never be again. It is like the image of a body without a shadow, a document that preserves something of the magic of its creation, of the impossibility of stopping time forever, even if only on a fragment of paper.

The photographs that Ricardo Sanchez has taken on so many afternoons of *fiesta*, of glory and of blood, are not the record of anything concrete in itself. On the one hand, they are a catalogue of the almost infinite types of *pases* in the bullfight, but this is merely a justification. In these photographs there is no anecdote, there is nothing more than the confrontation between light and darkness. In these images, like flashes of a fleeting existence, we are offered the fragment we never managed to see, that line of death hanging from the bull's horn. We see the black shadow, a formless stain, which is the bull as it charged, and we see the sequins of the *traje de luces* like little bells that almost chime. Unlike what we see in most bullfight photographs, here there is no flesh—what there is is spirit. Behind these stains of color lies something more than an imagined body behind a shadow. In these photographs we see danger, we see deceit as if it were something physical, embodied. It may be glimpsed behind a flash of color, of light that makes the reddish yellow of the arena the perfect backdrop to the black of a bull that for an instant was death. And between life and death *pases* succeed each other, the afternoon passes and the game of deceit comes to an end once again in the bullring. But outside, in that other spectacle in which we are all toreros, although some would prefer to see the bulls behind the barriers, the risk of finding life continues. Deceit continues, but this time there are no elegant *pases* nor graceful gestures.

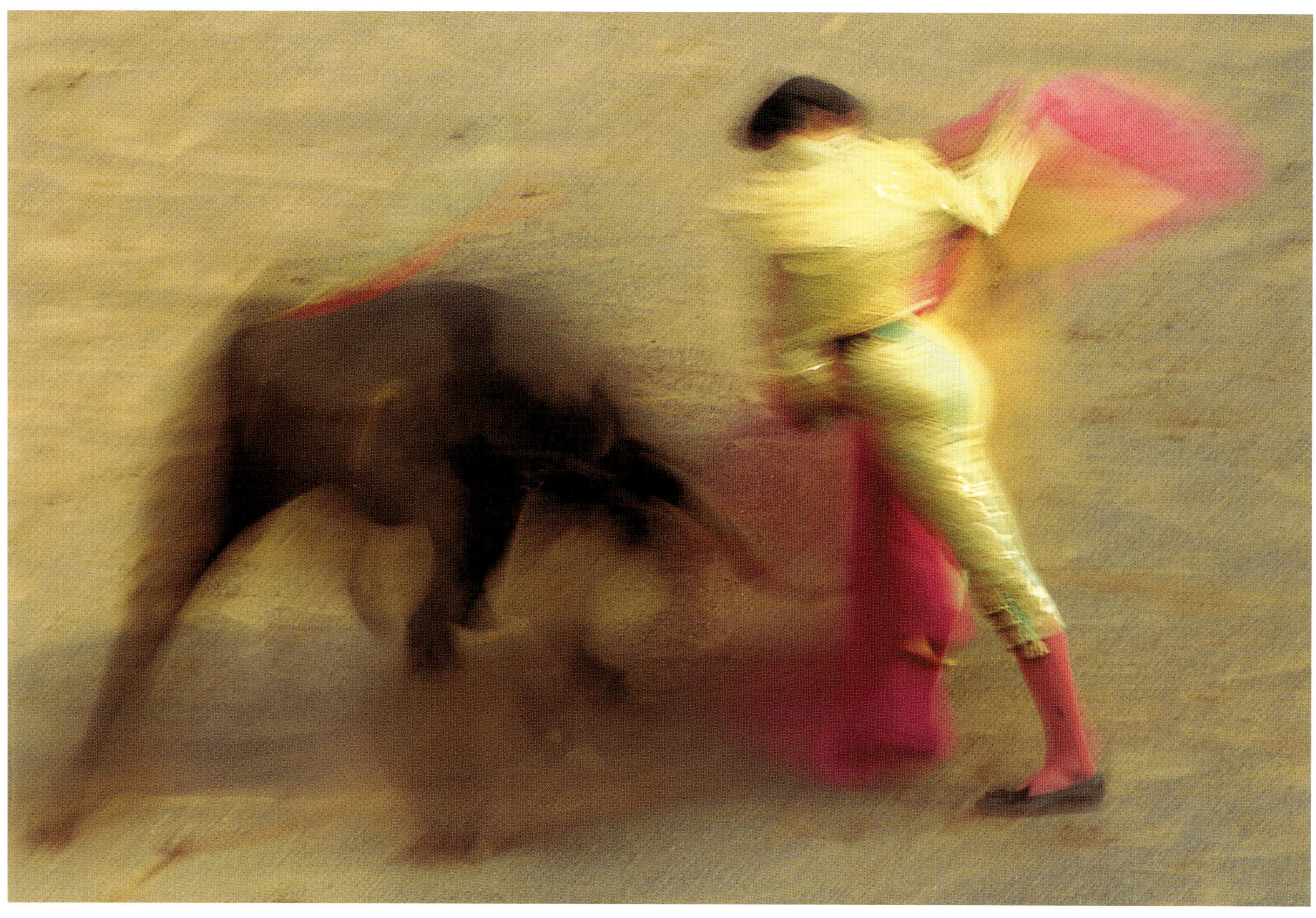

Verónica
Enrique Ponce; Vista Alegre, Bilbao; June 7, 1992

RICARDO B. SANCHEZ

"To transmute the threatening and dangerous existence of a beast into something as gossamer as a dancer's veil is the great marvel of bullfighting" (Manuel Chaves Nogales). Combining the knowledge of his craft with intelligence, willpower, courage and art, a bullfighter uses two cloths (the cape and the muleta) to lead, dominate, pass and kill a charging bull. The pass as it occurs in a bullfight can be regarded as a metaphoric representation of life as it occurs outside of the ring. My photographs illustrate how though all passes are the same—the bull must always pass—they are never equal. Like fingerprints and the steps we take in our lives, there are no two that are identical; the pass is that which forever comes and goes, without ever repeating itself.

We are the result of what we have been. In Western theology, when God created Adam and Eve and placed them in paradise, nature and the human being were one and the same: good and immortal. Unfortunately, in this story, evil manifested in the form of a snake and an apple tree, both representing nature; thereby, Eve was seduced and Adam deceived. Paradise was lost and we were condemned to mortality and its consequent fears. Ever since, and leaving theological considerations aside, our relationship with nature has been ambiguous at best. Western culture has been involved in a power struggle with nature ever since we recognized it as the giver and taker of life..

Today, an ancient ritual continues wherein the human being plays the character of good and evil, female and male, predator and victim. The bullfighter, dressed effeminately with a costume suitable for a snake and using a red cloth (apple) to deceive the bull, creates a powerful drama of life and death. The bull, symbol both of the male and of nature, is irrationally seduced and deceived by the cloth. While it pursues the illusion of a target, the beast is condemned because it is powerful and physically superior.

As I understand it, energy is action. Energy by nature tends to be chaotic and unpredictable; the world often acts in ways that escape our control—through our own actions we can attempt to create order. We are obligated to act without guarantees even as we seek the widest possible margin of safety for our actions. The bullfighter, in his solitary confrontation with the bull, seems always to ask this eternal question—what is it that happens or comes to pass in our lives, in death? With each pass, he attempts to demonstrate his ability to dominate, to control the measure of time and space as they converge with the energy of the bull. Confronted by the magic and the mystery of his existence, the bullfighter requires answers as to how to act in each pass; he must estimate the precise distance that separates life from death. What meaning can one find in life as death passes so near? Perhaps, in fact, one only finds truth in life when death is so close at hand.

There are five fundamental elements to the bullfight and each has a very particular function. The bull is received into the ring with a cape, he is thus led to the horse, then the banderillas are placed and finally we have the passes executed with the muleta, which set up the bull for the kill. The maneuvers with the vara (the horseman's pic used to damage and weaken the bull's neck and shoulder muscles) and the banderillas (rounded dowels, 70 cm– just over two feet– long with a harpoon-shaped steel tip, placed in a pair on top of the withers of thc bull) are used to sap the bull of his strength thereby transforming the practice of their art into physical punishment. The movements with the capes, the red muleta and the final kill or suerte suprema are those maneuvers that represent deception and illusion as an art form. With the cape and the muleta, the bull is punished with nothing but a cloth to lead and touch it. Deceived in his spirited charge, he is thus dominated and eventually killed. I am more interested in the use of deception and illusion as an extension of our culture than in the art of physical punishment. Therefore, all my attention has been dedicated to the passes and what they mean. It is the paradox of the pass that it never ceases to deceive as it reveals its truth.

If we think of the pass both as a series of ordered steps and as something that happens upon which the bullfighter's very life depends, we see in it analogies to power and its absence, luck and destiny, what happens with our emotions, what happens when we take risks, both rationally and irrationally, what happens when our courage is demanded, our fears confronted, what happens when we face the magic of the unknown. Eventually, in the bullfight, as in our lives, death will be the end. What happens before we reach that end is what makes life and the bullfight fascinating. Life and its intimate relationship with fate involve a continuous questioning of that which appears to be and that which really is. Is it really me or does it simply look like me? Fact or enigma.

To admit the fragile and vulnerable nature of the human body when exposed to danger, and to recognize the immensity of the risk whereby the unpredictable becomes predictable, is part of the essence and seduction of bullfighting. The bullfight explains the inexplicable just as passion for someone or something, or seduction by a magic incomprehensible but real at the same time, heightens and stimulates our desire to live. Only rarely do the bull, bullfighter, spectators and weather synchronize in such a way that the ritual flows harmoniously, transporting the experience of the bullfight to the limits of the unknown. Contemplation of the sublime is a profoundly emotional and moving experience. However, for the most part, man kills the beast with a colorful spectacle for an excuse. It is a lust for conquest, consummated in the kill; the beauty of the fight is a means to an end, or is it?

In the bullfighting pass, the contrast between doubt and certainty is extreme. The bullfighter doubts his pass will deceive the bull, and is certain of safety only once the bull has passed. This process, repeated time and time again by the bullfighter, is a metaphor for the risk all human beings take in each step of our lives. Some of our actions are obviously more dangerous than others, so the balance of doubt and certainty regarding the outcome of our actions is proportionate to the risk involved. We are afraid of that which is unknown, of that which is apparently uncontrollable, ultimately, of death—the final unknowable. A bullfighter can feel great fear before he faces the bull. He is judging what he is going to do and whether he will be able to dominate and control the bull. This doubt is a fundamental part of the bullfighter's life and it illustrates the uncertainty of our existence. What happens when, in spite of what you want to happen, things happen as they will? In order to balance the fear produced by the doubt and uncertainty of our actions, we find the willpower and the courage to determine that our actions are correct. The bullfighter does this by projecting his sense of self to the point of a radiant conviction that allows him to dominate and conquer the bull. The selfish role of "me first," which we are all capable of playing, becomes a catalyst to overcome fear and motivate the courage needed to survive. Me first: this is a rule imposed by a society, which is made up of more or less self-interested individuals. We think of satisfying our needs, wants and pleasures, and as long as we get what we want, we waste little time thinking about how our actions may affect others. Even though our evolution has been shaped by the power of our intelligence, for the most part our culture has manipulated the materials necessary for our survival without considering the consequences of such manipulation. We live under the collective illusion that we have achieved the height of civilization; we are often easily deceived and seduced by the comforts and security of our lifestyles. Individually and socially we act from a selfish perspective, and we consider the concepts of living in harmony with nature, of environmental balance, as utopia. Though we are realizing that our behavior must be modified for the benefit of the planet and the future survival of our own species, we are still the great predators. No human being interprets this role better than the bullfighter. All good bullfighters must be very selfish; only in this way can they generate the necessary courage to face simultaneously the possible roles of hero or tragic victim of their unfortunate egotistical valor.

When a bullfighter enters the ring, he defies both the existential solitude of his life and his fear of dying. His actions in the bullring are a reflection of the solitude each human being encounters in confronting his existence. In his extreme, almost tragic isolation, the bullfighter knows that the spectators are all anxiously looking at him and yet none are capable of aiding him if he is suddenly helpless before the bull. Alone, he is willing to overcome the fear of dying in order to feel the power and glory of his victory over death. It is for this reason that he is so admired, well paid and revered, for he is a bullfighter, confronting his solitude and fear, willing to risk his life for the glory of all men. Last of the courageous hunters who risks all in order to kill, he is a salvational figure, who by possibly sacrificing his existence, redeems the rest of us mortals from the sin of fear.

The creation of form, that which perpetuates our memory and endures, is a cultural attribute particular to the human species. Matter is manipulated to secure our survival and to glorify the memory of our existence. If death is the most visible and immediate expression of the disintegration of form, the desire to create form celebrates the will to live. In the process of creating a civilized world, mankind has used deception, seduction, illusion, and truth. This is especially so when it comes to establishing the codes that control and condition human behavior; codes such as religion, law, politics, economics and social status. The fine arts also dwell in the ambiguous terrain of deception, seduction, illusion, and truth, for they lead us to believe that by manipulating matter or concepts, we can create a concrete representation of life's multiple realities. Through our intelligence, knowledge and wisdom, we are capable of shaping the form of life itself. We are seduced by our ability to create form and regard judging the true or illusionary value of such a capability as a secondary consideration. If we consider an art form as something created by the human being, and we recognize our ability to shape life itself, then I believe that the most important art is the art of knowing how to live. Because we must deal with reality before contemplating its interpretation, the art of living focuses on the immediacy of what we do with

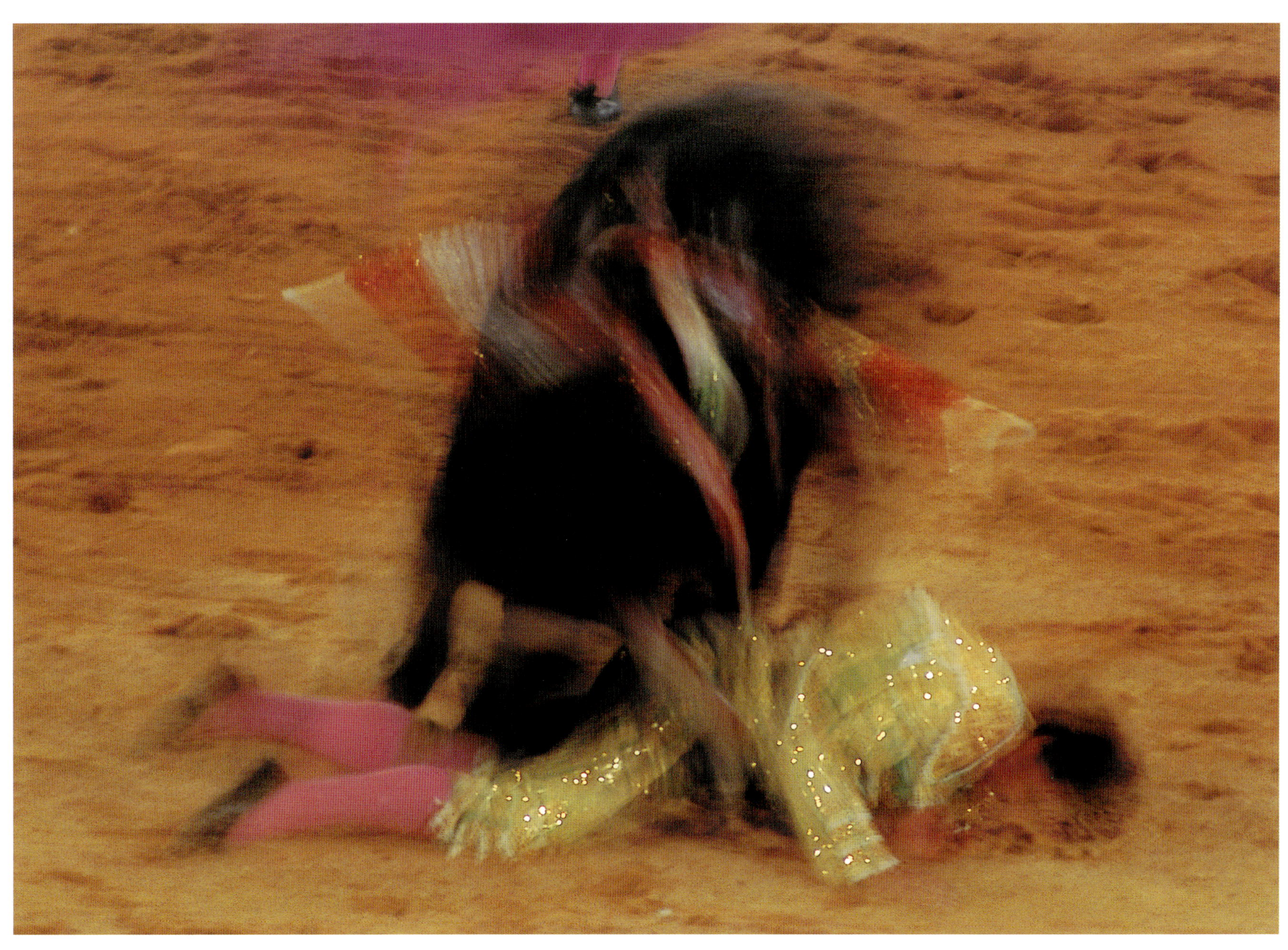

GORED OR TOSSED / *Cogida*
Víctor Mendes; Plaza Mayor, Salamanca; June 13, 1992

our lives. The fine arts on the other hand are a sophisticated medium through which we express our feelings, thoughts and the implicit mysteries of our existence. Because it is so all encompassing, the art of living is the most difficult of all artistic disciplines.

Photography, as an extension of what we see and as a fine art, is a sophisticated expression and an extension of the art of living. The photographer chooses that which is important to him or her, thereby establishing a peculiar relationship between fascination with and conflict with what is being photographed in order to stimulate a worthy reflection of our existence. It seems evident that someone who photographs the tragedy of war, poverty or any other subject that is being personally investigated can be both attracted to and confused by what he or she photographs. In photography, as in life, there are many paths and each person must follow his own; thus seeing what I have seen and seeing what others have seen, I may learn to live a better life.

Bullfighting celebrates the domination and conquest of the fighting bull. It is a real and vital blood rite regardless of whether it is judged as good or evil. I am interested in the idea that we, as predators, kill to live and live to kill. Our intelligence allows us to manipulate, control and pretentiously attempt to dominate what we consider to be "nature," a "nature" that Western culture has always feared and admired because it is the giver and taker of life. Bullfighting is a ritual with a strict order imposed to simulate the principles of the eternal conflicts between life and death. The bull and bullfighter create a dance in which time, space and energy converge between light and darkness. My photographs record a reflection of this incomprehensible and passionate pas de deux, where the bull and bullfighter trace the lines and forms of their existence with each pass, confronting their lives with their destiny. As an investigation of the photographic language, these photographs are clearly a combination of what the eye can see as apparently real, and what can only be seen as a product of photographic technology. I have photographed the extensive variety of passes portraying the dialogue that occurs between that which moves and that which stays still. These photographs strive to illustrate the proper execution of the passes performed in the arena. These are images that suggest a relationship between the controllable and the uncontrollable, between what is apparently static and what is constantly moving.

From the beginning of my investigation into this subject, I have combined abstraction as a representation of the unknown with realism to represent what we recognize in order to suggest metaphors about the passing of our lives. The bullfighter creates that which instantly disappears in time; I have created photographs of that which we are incapable of seeing to celebrate his magic. Using the knowledge of how light can be reproduced, the photographer can create an illusion that represents an instant of reality frozen in time and defined in space by the boundaries of its own frame. My photographic process transforms the vision of what I see into a mirror from which I want to learn. This constant looking and reflecting reminds me how difficult it is to see beyond the obvious, and how easily we are deceived and seduced by the illusion of what we think is real and true. While I do not condone or condemn bullfighting as a spectacle, I hope this book will reflect on the bullfighting passes as metaphors of the broader relationship between nature and us. I selected these photographs to reveal the essence of a sublime pass, to reflect the passing of light and darkness, which is the soul of this ritual.

"In the duration of a bullfight--these are 20 minutes of absolute truth."

—LUPITA LOPEZ, ONE OF FOUR PROFESSIONAL FEMALE MATADORAS IN THE WORLD

THE PHOTOGRAPHS OF RICARDO B. SANCHEZ

About the Bullfight: Pas de Deux

A bullfight is above all about the demonstration of style, technique and courage displayed by its participants. While there is usually little doubt about the outcome, the bull is not viewed as a sacrificial victim—it is instead seen by the audience as a worthy adversary, deserving of respect in its own right. In this public spectacle, highly trained men known as bullfighters (in exceptional cases, women), perform with, and ceremonially kill, selectively bred bulls. Identified as a "corrida de toros" in Spanish, the bullfight takes place in a large outdoor arena or bullring known as the "plaza de toros."

In the cultures of Spain, southern France, Mexico, Venezuela, Colombia, Ecuador and Peru, bullfighting is an integral part of national culture. The aesthetic of bullfighting is based on the interaction of the man and the bull. Rather than a competitive sport, the bullfight is considered a ritual to be judged by aficionados, based on artistic impression and command. Ernest Hemingway astutely observed in his book, *Death in the Afternoon*: "Bullfighting is the only art in which the artist is in danger of death and in which the degree of brilliance in the performance is left to the fighter's honor."

The modern bullfight is highly ceremonial and ritualized, involving three distinct stages or "tercios" (thirds); the start of each "tercio" is announced by the playing of a bugle. In a traditional "corrida," three bullfighters will each fight two bulls. The senior bullfighter will fight the first and fourth bull to enter the ring, and the less veteran fighter will perform with the third and sixth bull, leaving the second and fifth bull to the middle man. If a bullfighter is wounded during his performance, and cannot continue in the ring, the senior fighter will take his place, finish the performance, and kill the bull.

The bulls bred for bullfighting are the product of centuries of cross-breeding to provide the most suitable specimens. Over the past 50 years, the bulls have changed from lighter weight and faster movement, to heavier and more predictable in their charge. This allows for a more artistic performance on the part of the bullfighter, although some argue that the ferocity of the bull has been undermined. In contemporary bullfighting, the bulls are bigger, slower and are drawn closer to the bullfighter's body than ever before. Each bull is in the ring for approximately 20 minutes, and unsuitable bulls (if a bull is wounded or appears too weak to fight) will be replaced by others prior to the last "tercio."

Fighting bulls are between four and six years old and weigh no less than 1,014 pounds and usually no more than1650 pounds. Each matador has six assistants—two "picadores" (lancers on horseback) mounted on horseback, three "banderilleros"—who, along with the matadors, are collectively known as "toreros" (bullfighters). These participants all perform inside the ring; a "mozo de espadas" (sword page) is in the protected side of the ring, and provides the "matador" with the different cloths and swords needed for each part of the performance. Collectively they comprise a "cuadrilla" (entourage). The word "matador" is used in Spain and, when the bullfighter is highly respected, he is usually referred to as a "maestro."

After the announcement that the bullfight is about to begin, the performers enter the arena led by the "maestros," followed by their assistants. This ceremony is identified as "el paseillo;" a parade to salute the presiding dignitaries and public, accompanied by band music. Andalusian fashion that originated in the eighteenth century still dictates bullfighting clothing and attire, and matadors are easily distinguished by the gold sequins of their "traje de luces" (suit of lights) as opposed to the lesser banderilleros, who are also called "toreros de plata" (bullfighters in silver).

A curious fact about a bullfight: it invariably starts on time. Once the first bull enters the ring, the "maestro" and his caping assistants test it. This is the first stage, the "tercio de varas" ("the lancing third"), and the matador confronts the bull with the cape, performing a series of passes and observing the behavior and quirks of the bull. Once the "maestro" has fixed the bull's attention to the cape, he will perform the first traditional pass in a bullfight; the "Veronica." On rare occasions the bullfighter will kneel approximately 15 yards in front of the bull's exit door and wait for the bull to charge into the ring. The pass performed at this point is called "Larga a porta Gayola," and it is considered of high risk because the bull's behavior is untested.

In the following photographs the extensive variety of passes used by bullfighters in the course of a modern day bullfight are to be seen. Though these photographs do not portray images in the traditional way of freezing the action, they do display in very accurate and suggestive terms how a multitude of passes are enacted, and the complex choreography of the ballet of man and bull.

A pass, or "un pase" in Spanish, is a delineated maneuver by which the bull is enticed to charge and follow a cloth, with which the bullfighter moves the bull from one side of the bullfighters body to the other while maintaining his feet fixed to the ground. Here, these passes are each identified in a caption to the photograph by name; each demonstrating a calculated move that entails an almost geometrical precision in execution. These passes represent the repertoire of choreographed steps performed in the centuries of bullfighting history. Passes are executed at two distinct stages of the bullfight. In the first, the bullfighter uses a heavy and large cloth with a different color on each side—traditionally yellow-gold and magenta, though that can vary slightly with the taste of the bullfighter—and this cloth is called "capote" a reminder that it is as large as a cape.

These photographs present four distinct sequences of passes, and are organized to display what occurs in a bullring with both the full cape and the "muleta," which is the smaller red flannel cloth draped over a stick and manipulated by the matador in his passes. They illustrate the "maestros" movements from the moment the bull enters the ring, until the last pass is executed and the order maintains a recognizable choreography; the photographs portray the bullfight as a *pas de deux*, and each step is interpreted by a different bullfighter, which brings the exquisiteness of their particular art to this book. In the following photographs, the name of the pass, the bullfighter, the bullring, and the date of the performance are given to identify the pass, the bullfighter, and to provide historical record.

Cape passes, as well as those performed with a "muleta," offer a variety of formal moves interpreted according to traditions that vary, according to the bullfighter's creative capacity, style and school. The invention of a new pass is a rare occasion in bullfighting, and only when it has been performed repeatedly with convincing authority and artistic merit, will it be included in the repertoire of recognized "passes." These intricate "dancing steps with a cloth and bull" are performed at close range.

Once the bullfighter has tested the bull's charge on both the left and right horn, he will lead the bull to face the "picador." A picador enters the arena on horseback armed with a "vara" (lance). To protect the horse from the bull's horns, a protective, padded covering called "peto" surrounds the horse. The manner in which the bull charges the horse provides important clues to the matador about which side the bull favors.

The picador thrusts a lance into the bull's back, just behind the "morrillo," a mound of muscle on the fighting bull's neck, weakening the neck muscles and leading to the animal's first loss of blood. If the picador is successful, the bull will hold its head and horns slightly lower during the following stages of the fight. This ultimately enables the matador to perform the final thrust later in the performance with more ease.

The only time the bullfighters will engage each other's bulls and compete for bravery and artistry using the same bull is when the bull is led away from the horse. At this point all the bullfighters in the ring may perform what are known as "quites" (literally meaning, "take away," as the bull is taken away from one bullfighter to the next). The "quites,"are more elaborate and somewhat riskier passes with the cape than the traditional beginning ("Veronica") or the finishing passes (the "Media Veronica," "Revolera," and "Larga"). The "quites" include those passes such as the "Chicuelinas," "Gaoneras," "Saltilleras," "Brionesa," "Tafallera," and "Faroles."

Finally, during the "tercio de banderillas" (the third of banderillas), the matadors' assistants will plant two sharp barbed sticks between the bull's shoulder blades. Each bull may have up to six banderillas placed on his back. These placements anger and invigorate, but further weaken the bull, who has lost strength by the previous attacks on the horse. Sometimes a "matador" will place his own "banderillas."

In the final stage of the performance, (the "tercio de muerte"), the matador re-enters the ring alone with a "muleta" in one hand, and a sword in the other. The passes performed with the "muleta" are almost all single-handed, though in some cases, both hands will be used. It is a common misconception that the color red is supposed to anger the bull, because bulls, in fact, are colorblind. The matador uses his "muleta" to attract the bull in a series of passes that serve the dual purpose of wearing the animal down for the eventual "suerte suprema" (supreme luck) and producing a beautiful display of passes or "faena" (act of labor). He may also demonstrate his domination over the bull by passing it especially close to his body. The "faena" is the entire performance with the "muleta" and it is usually broken down into "tandas," a series of passes, usually no more than four or five at a given time. A "faena" consists of five to ten "tandas" which eventually lead up to "la suerte suprema."

The "natural" or left-handed pass, is the one aficionados most highly revere and respect. Unlike the "derechazo," or right-handed pass, the natural pass does not enjoy the benefit of expanding the cloth with the aid of the sword to make it a bigger target for the bull. When a "natural" is performed, the sword is in the right hand and the "muleta" is in the left. When a "derechazo" is used, the left hand is free and the right holds both sword and "muleta." For this reason, most swords used by the "matadors" are made of light but strong wood. The weight of a steel sword is substantial, and the cloth is already heavy enough, so combining the two requires a significant effort which most bullfighters prefer to forgo for the majority of the "faena."

"Muleta" passes performed on the knees or in a lower than standing position are usually either used at the beginning or ending of a "faena," their purpose being to force the bull to bring its head down, preparing it for either the "faena" or the final thrust kill. Though most "tandas" in a "faena" are performed as "derechazos" or "naturales," towards the middle and end of the "faena" other linking or decorative passes are employed, such as the "Pase de Pecho," "Trincherazo," "Capeina," "Ayudado por Bajo y por Alto," "Circular," "Manoletina," "Pedresina," "Molinete," "Doblon con Rodilla en Tierra," "Cambio de Manos." to name just a few.

The "faena" ends with a final series of passes in which the matador with a "muleta" attempts to maneuver the bull into a position to lance it between the shoulder blades and through the aorta or heart and make the final kill. Killing the bull is called "la suerte suprema," supreme luck as it were—and it is. Most bullfighters that get seriously injured do so performing "la suerte suprema;" it is the ultimate moment, also known as "el momento de la verdad," or the moment of truth.

The images in this book portray four sequences of passes executed with the cape and the "muleta," a man, bull and sand—the elements of the bullfight that most represent, to the photographer, the ballet that takes places during the essential sparring of bull and man. These photographs are about the *pas de deux*.

Sequence One

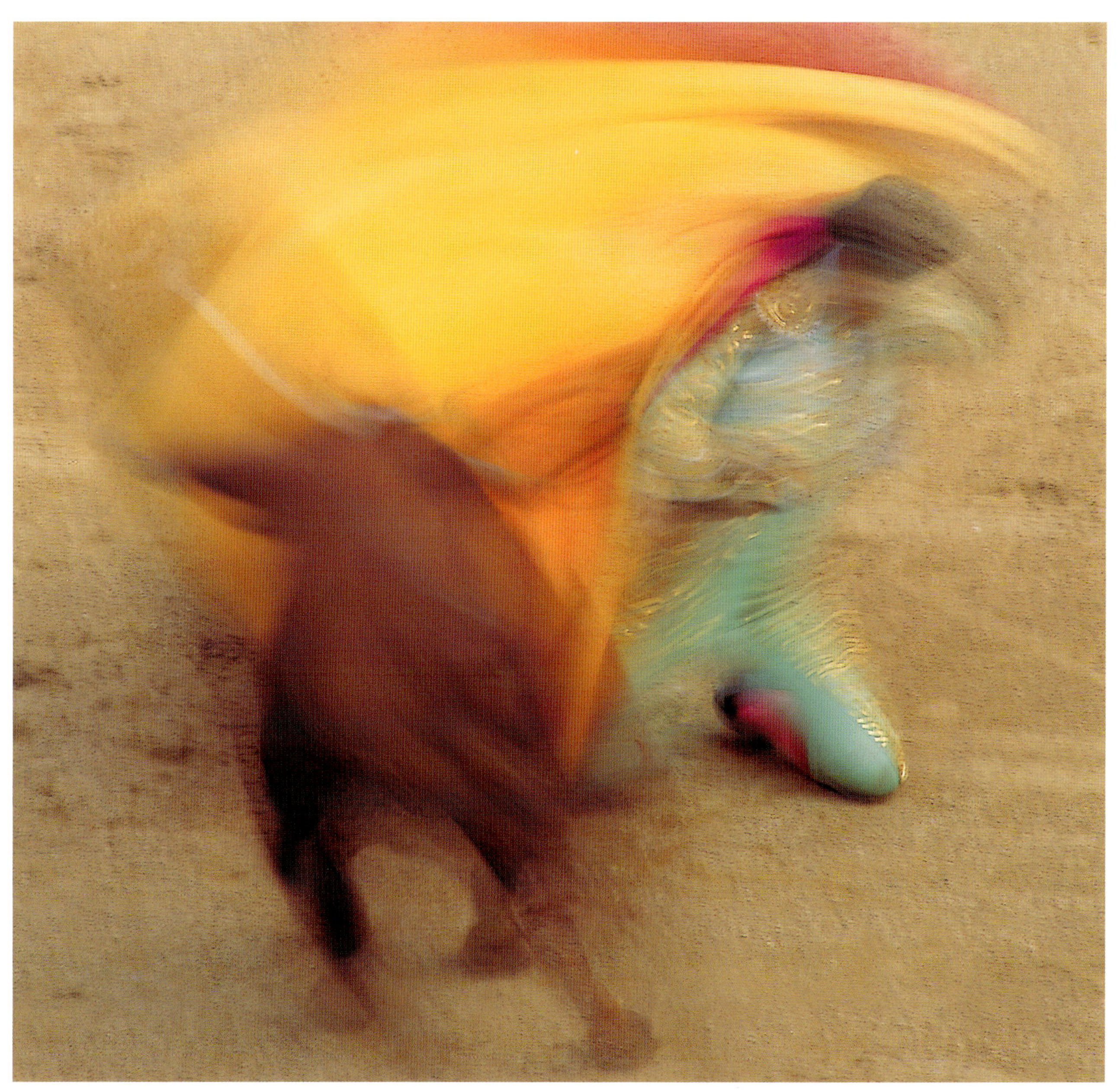

Larga a porta gayola
Javier Vázquez; Las Ventas, Madrid; May 11, 1992

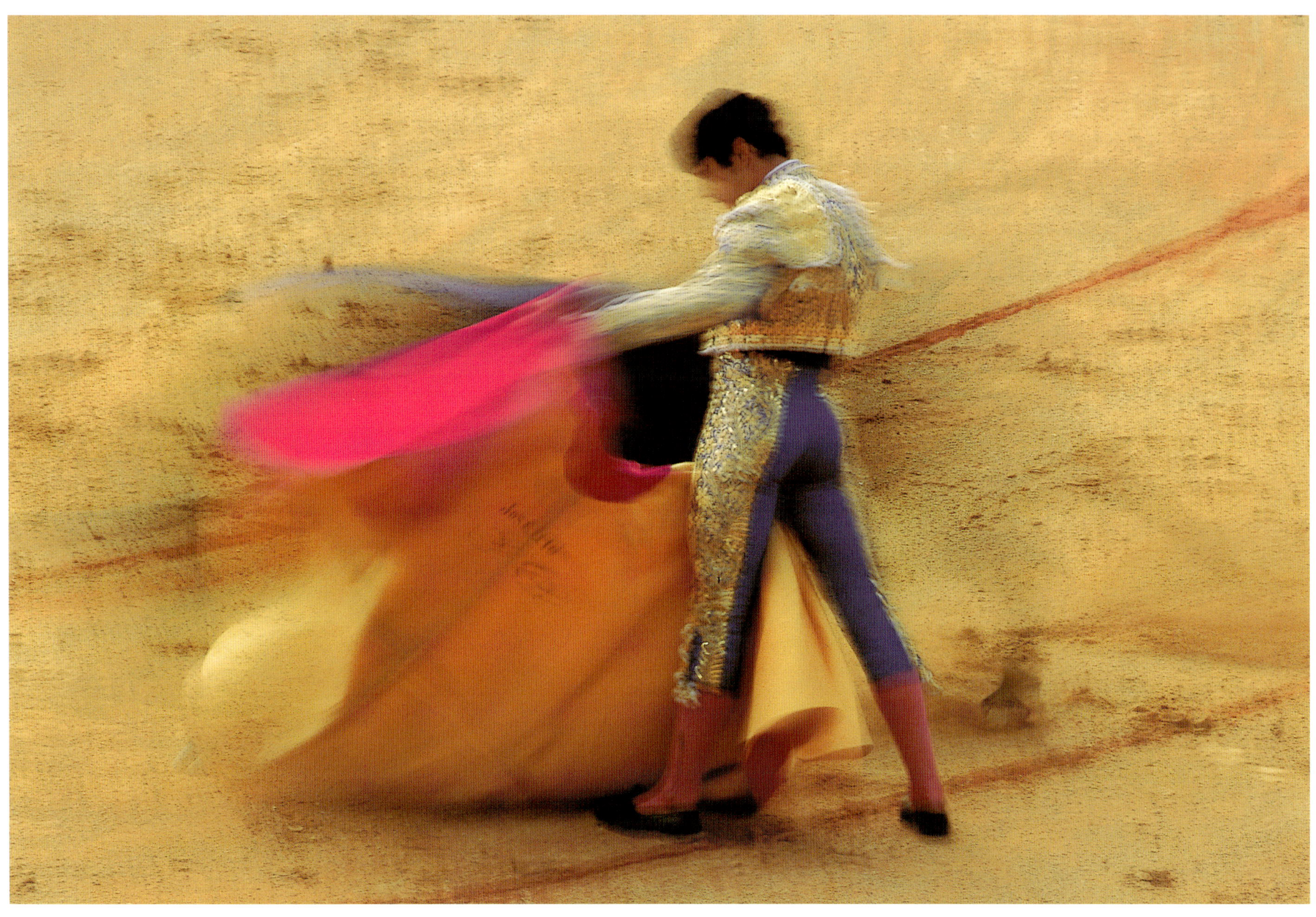

Verónica
Joselito; Real Maestranza, Sevilla; May 11, 1993

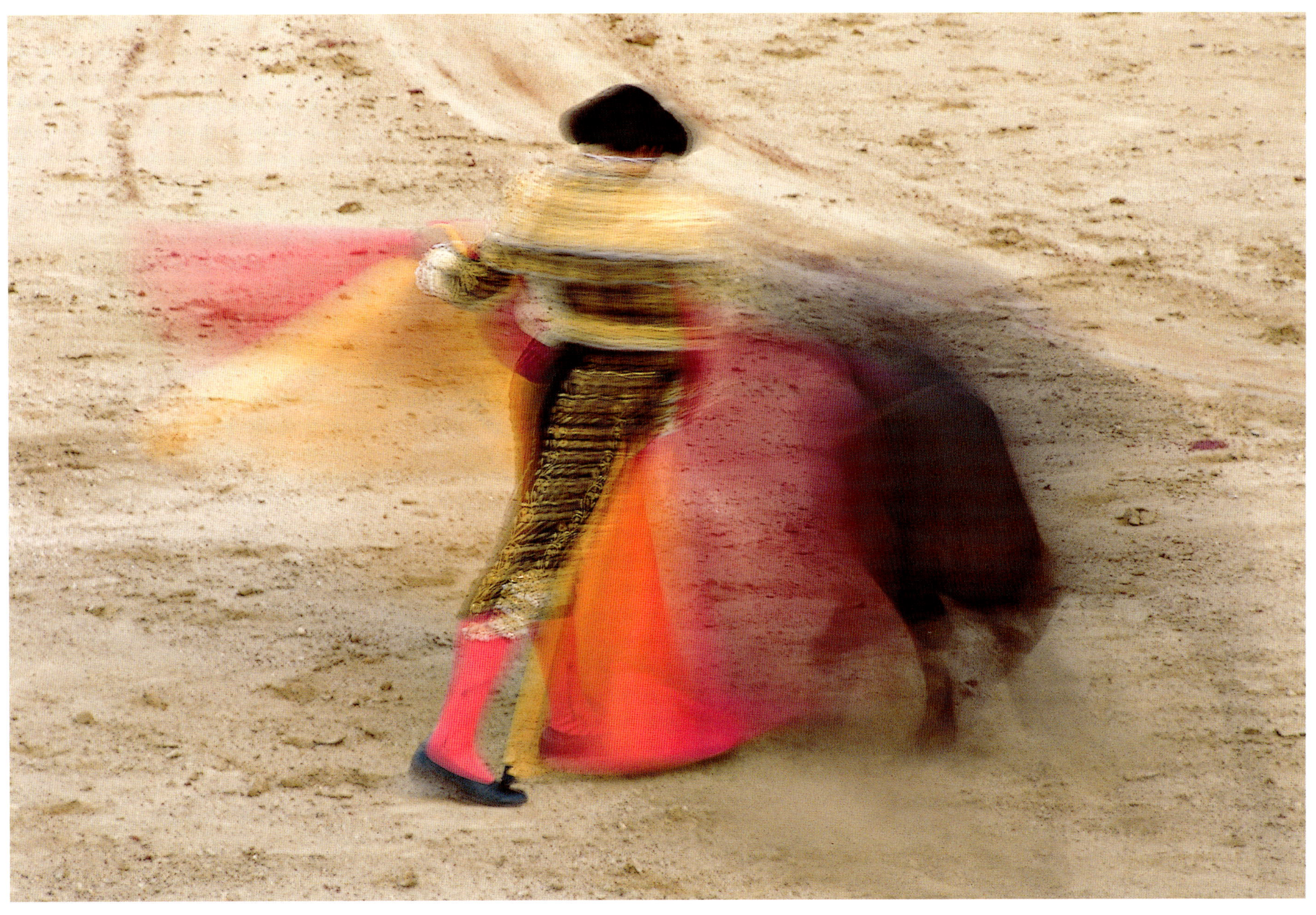

Verónica
Juan Mora; La Caprichosa, Talavera de la Reina, Toledo: September 22, 1991

"If hunting is a sport, then bullfighting is the pinnacle of such athleticism."

—Ricardo B. Sanchez

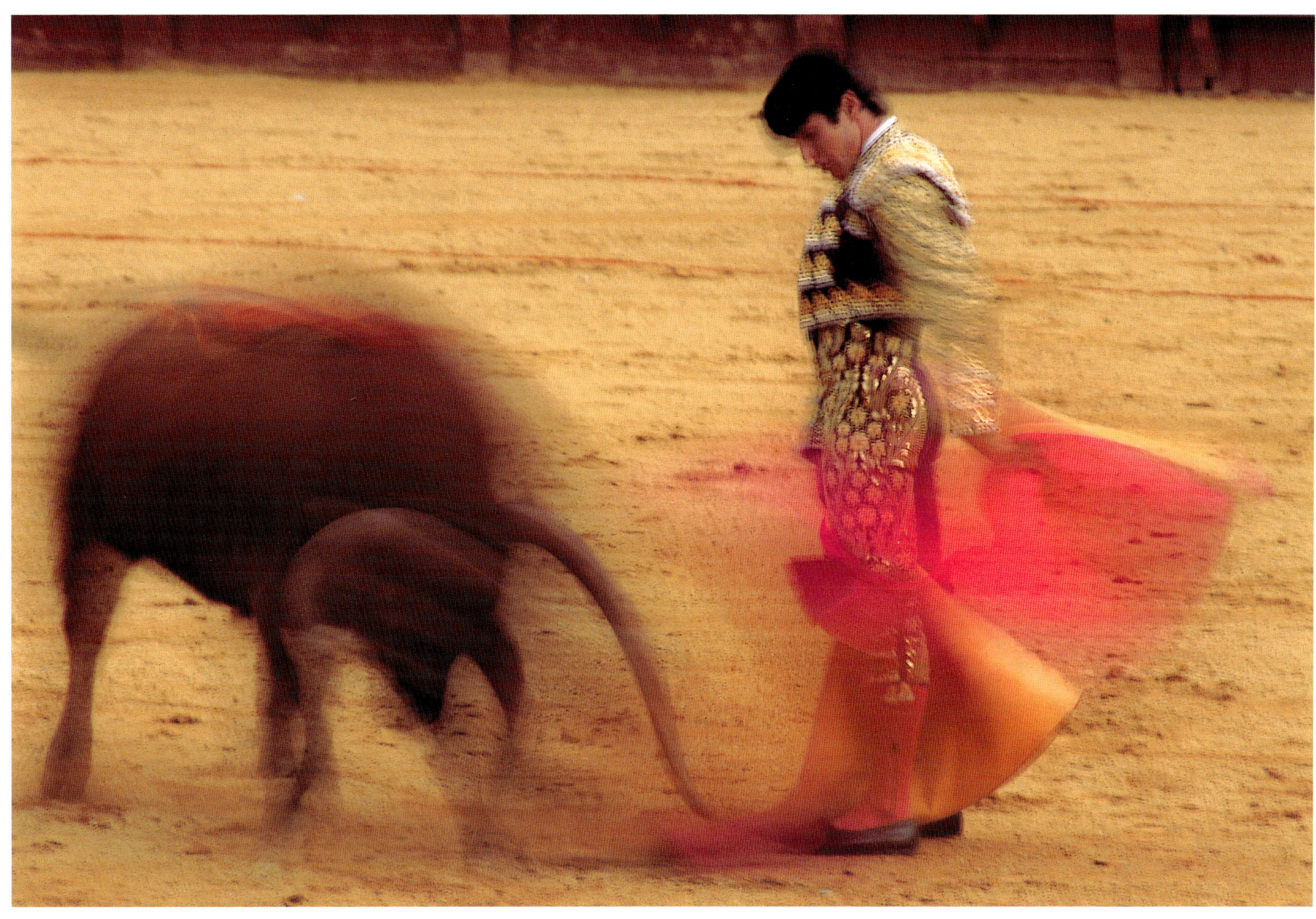

MEDIA VERONICA WITH FEET TOGETHER / *Media Verónica a pies juntos*
Joselito; Real Maestranza, Sevilla; April 30, 1993

"Bullfighting is a mysterious art, half vice, and half ballet. It is a multi-colored world, its characters

like caricatures, alive, intimate, where those of us who dream of one day being bullfighters, live."

—Camilo José Cela, Nobel Prize Recipient for Literature, 1989

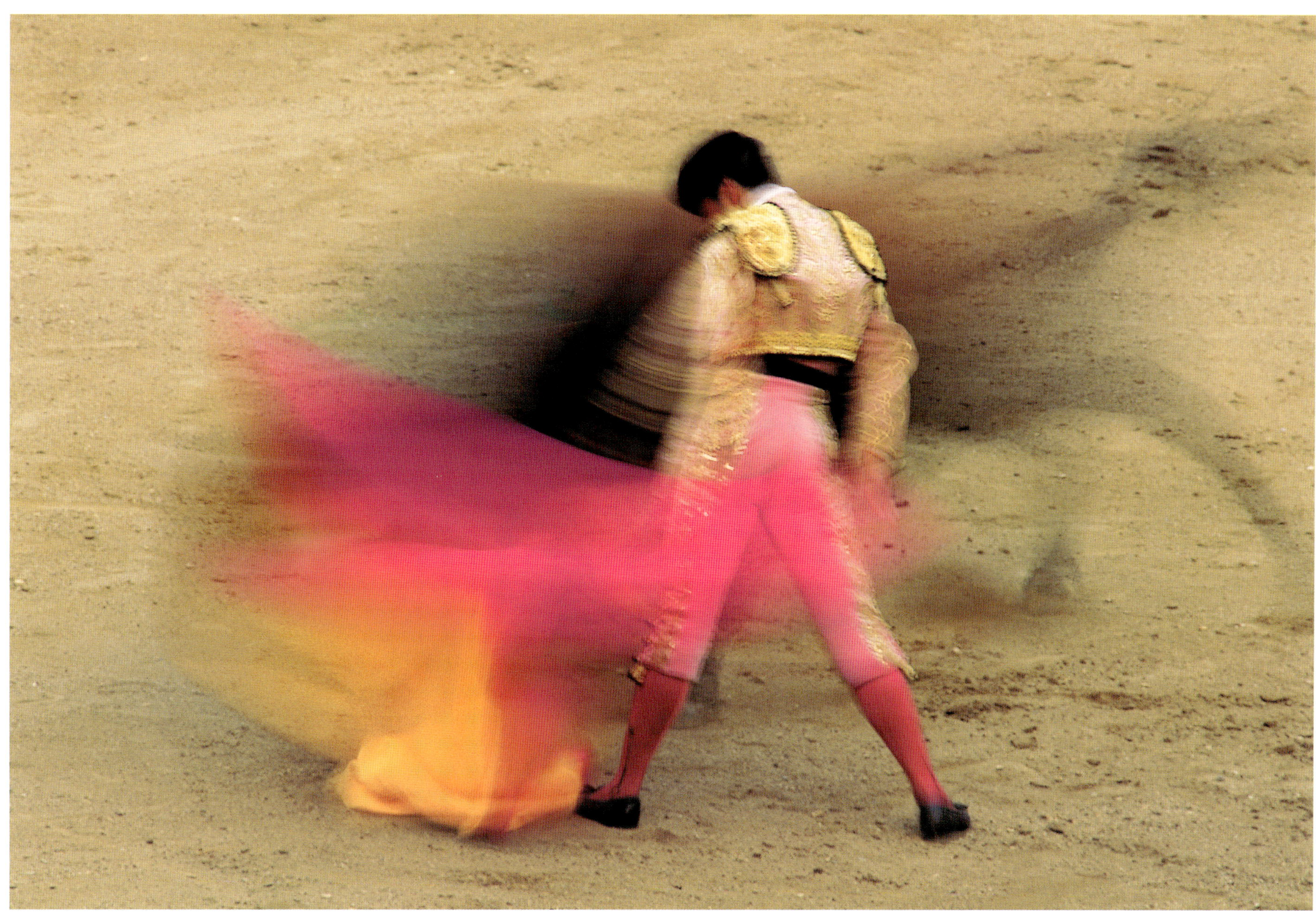

Revolera
César Rincón; Las Ventas, Madrid; October 1, 1991

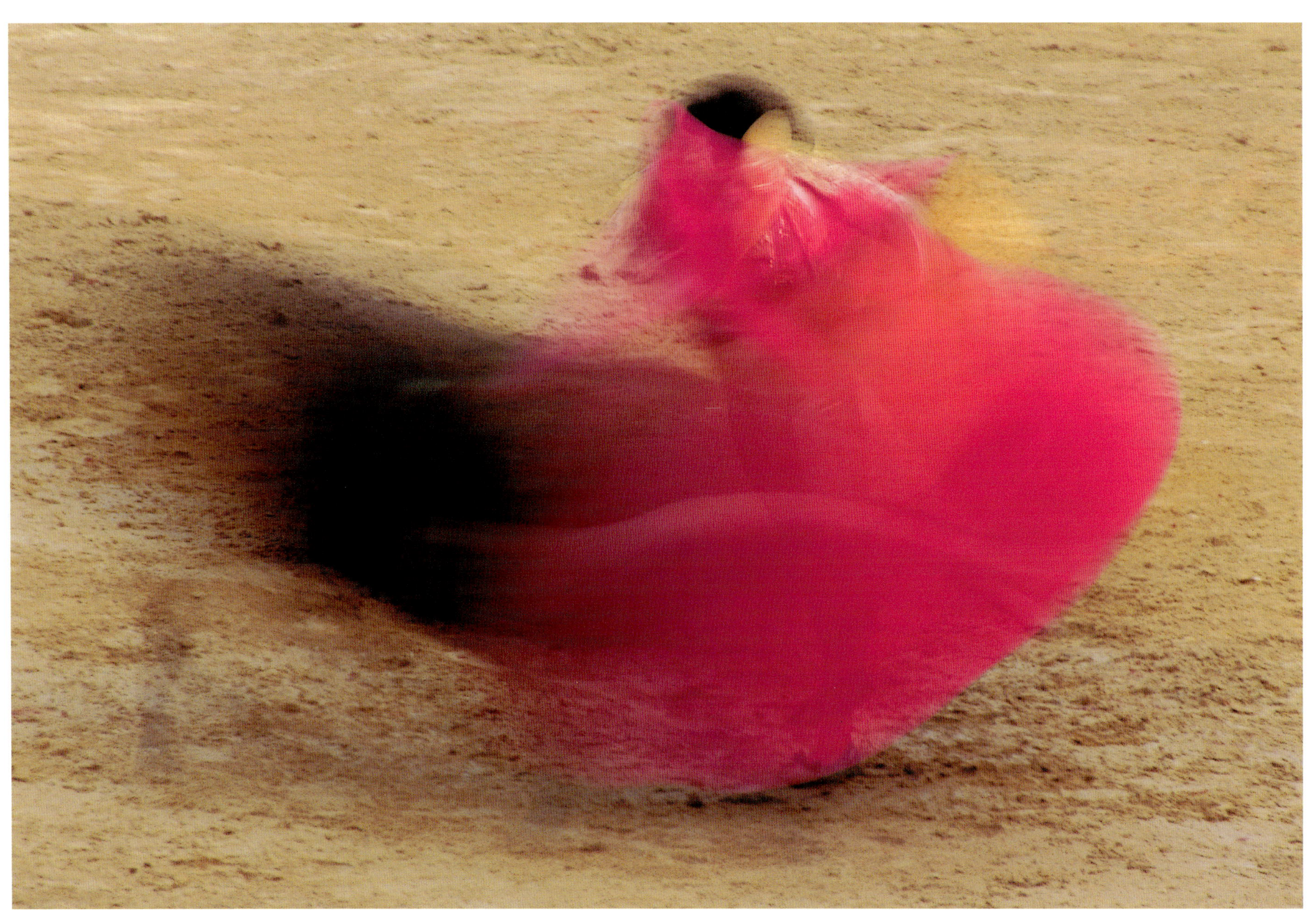

Brionesa
César Rincón; Las Ventas, Madrid; June 1, 1992

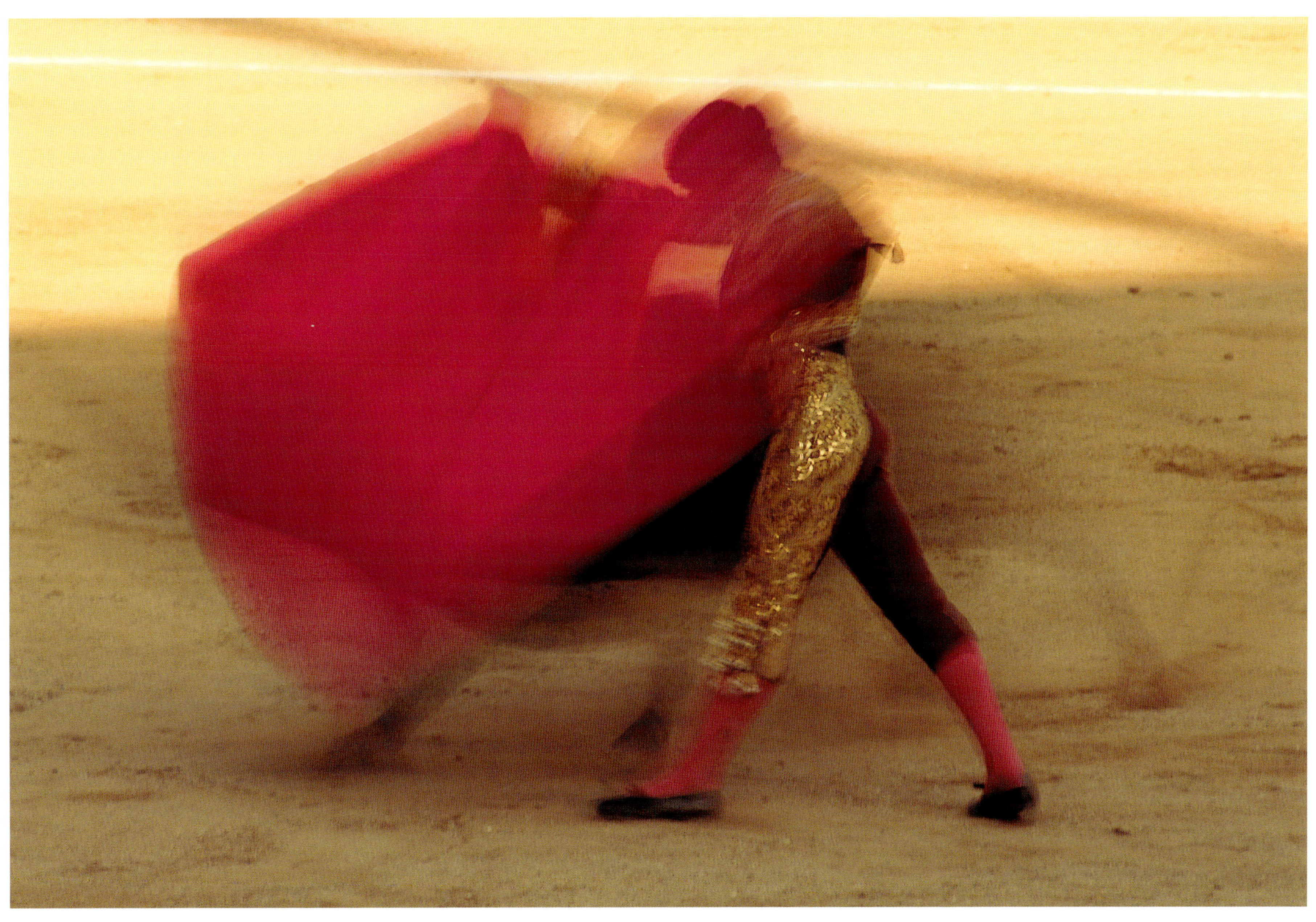

Tafallera
Joselito; Las Ventas, Madrid; June 17, 1993

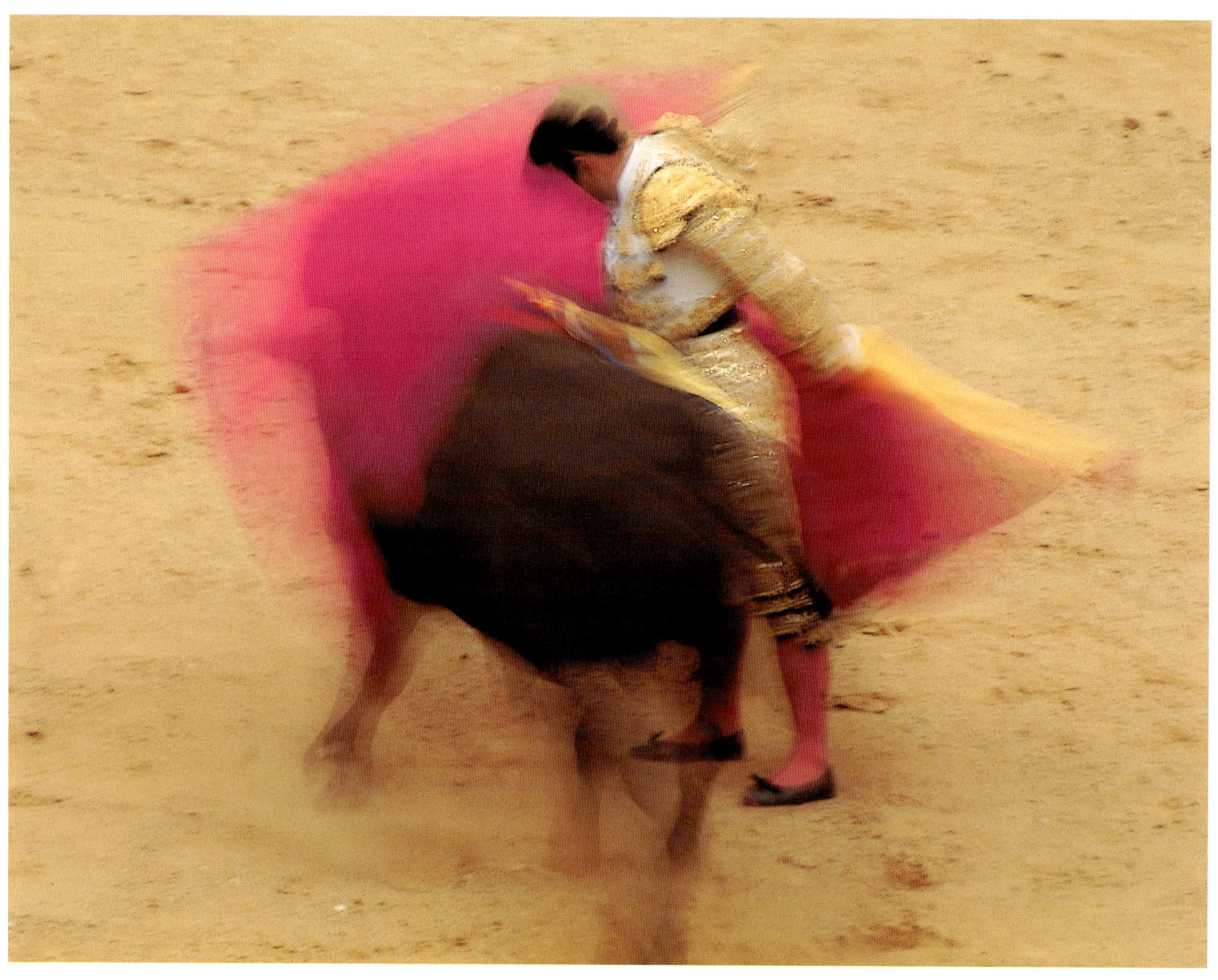

Gaonera
César Rincón; Las Ventas, Madrid; June 11, 1992

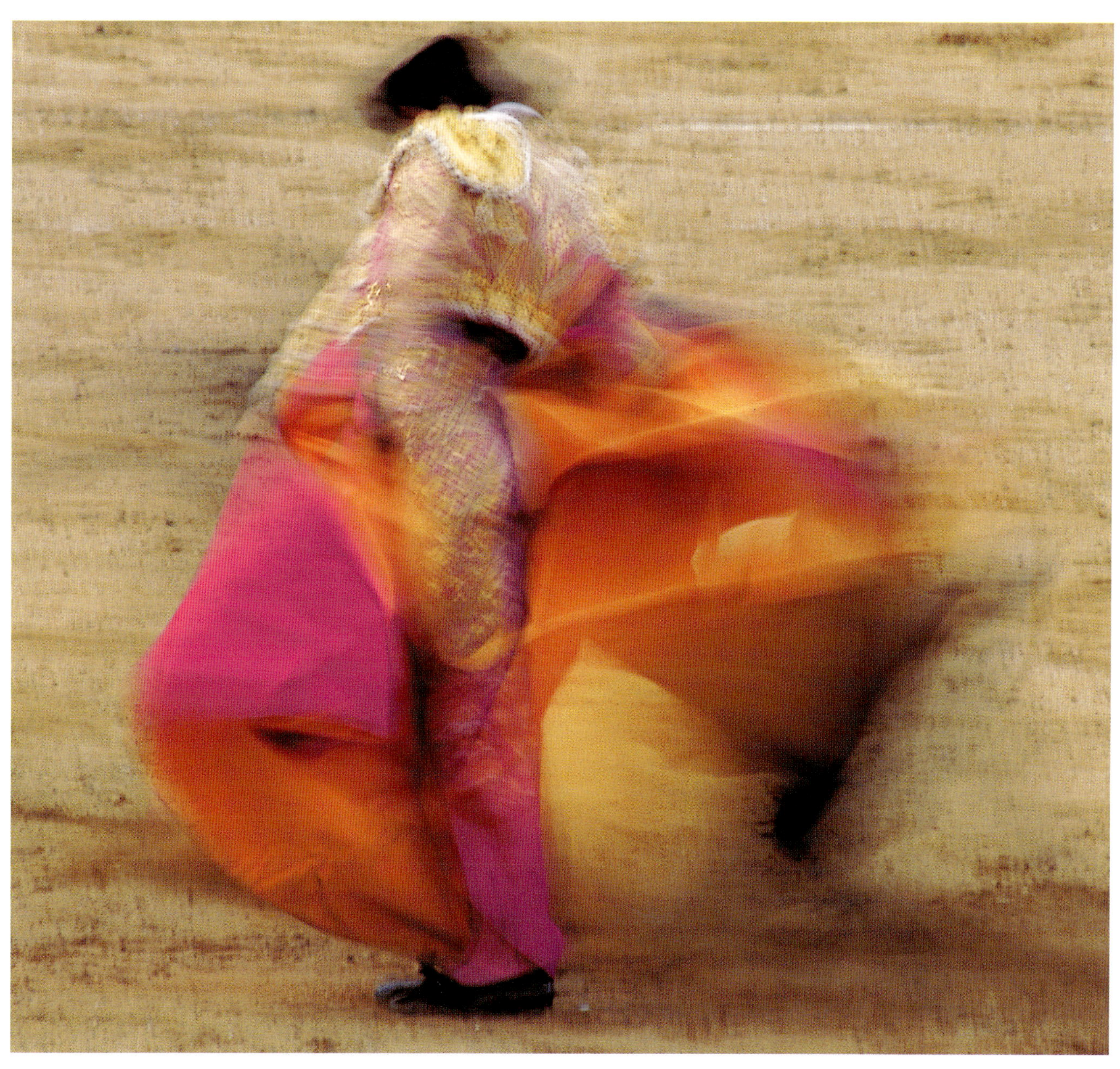

Chicuelina
Joselito; Segovia; June 29, 1992

"Yes, death is present in bullfighting, but as an ally, as an accomplice of life:

death will do as an extra so life may be re-affirmed."

—Fernando Savater, Philosopher, Essayist, Writer

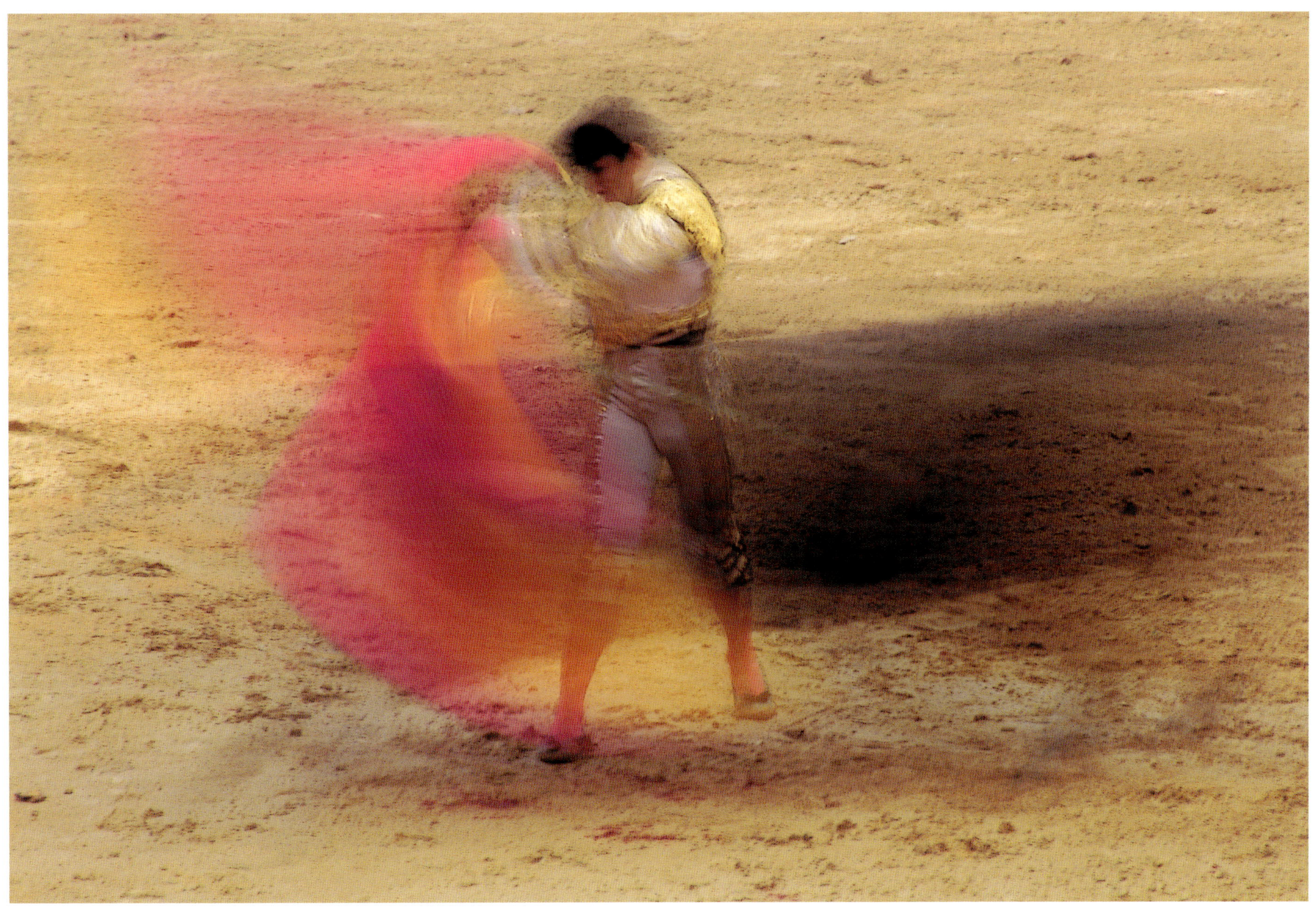

Tafallera
César Rincón; Las Ventas, Madrid; June 1, 1992

"We bullfight with a beat, as we dance and sing--with a rhythm--but also as we live,
or should live, following a compass, a rhythm."

—Rafael de Paula, Toreador

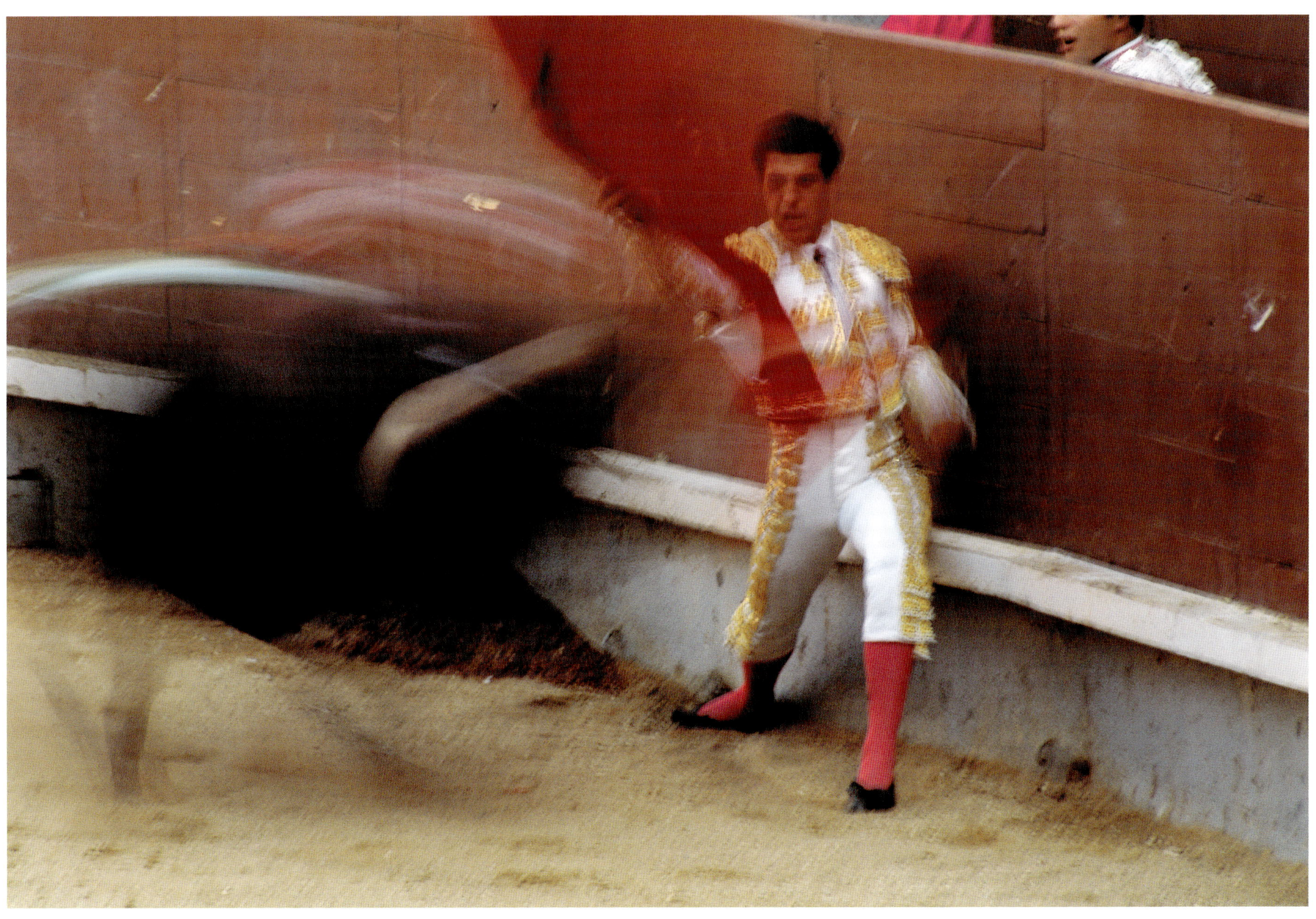

MULETAZO SEATED ON THE BARRERA STEP / *Muletazo sentado en el Estribo*
Javier Vázquez; Las Ventas, Madrid; June 29, 1994

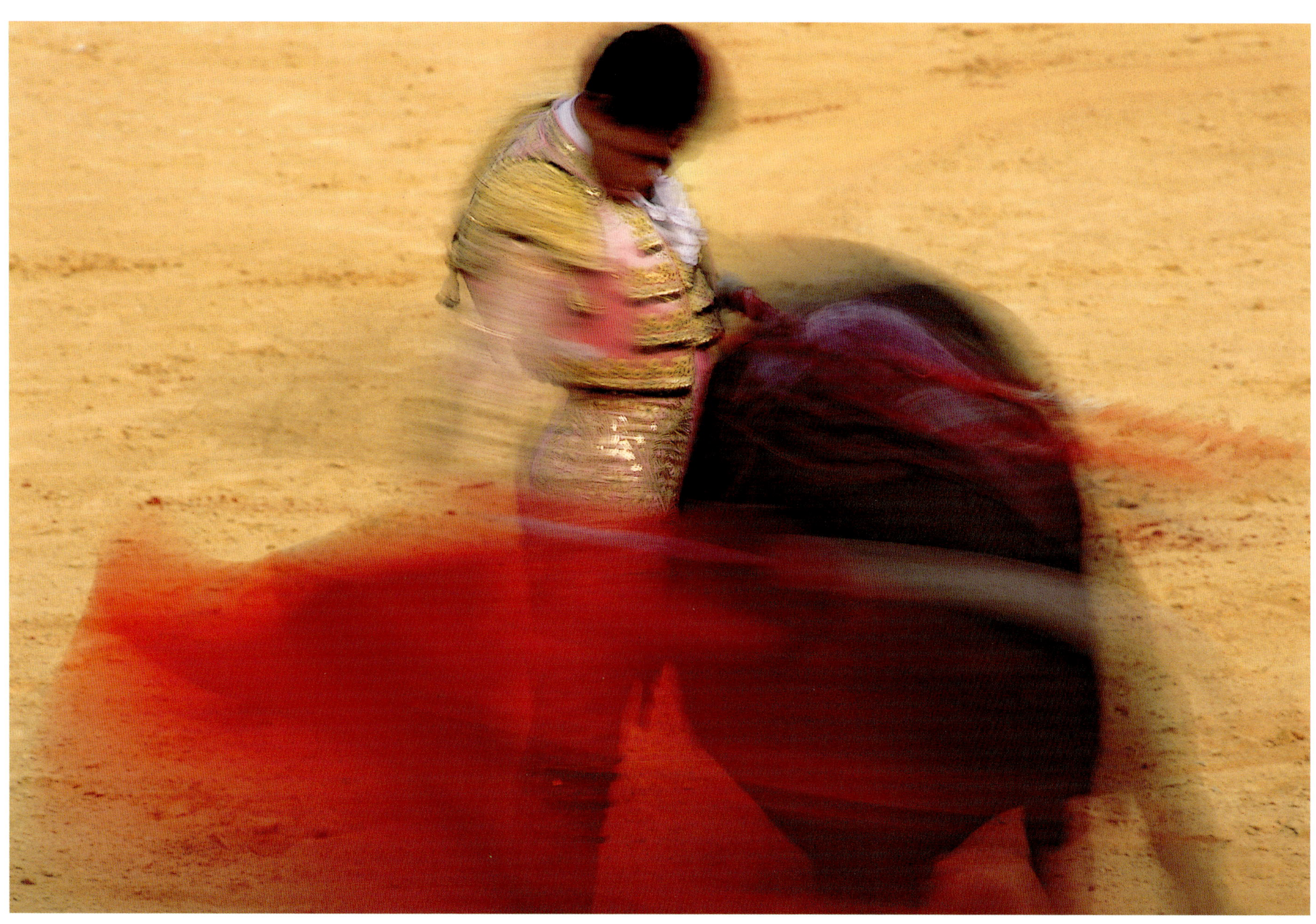

RIGHT-HANDED PASS / *Derechazo*
César Rincón; Esquivias, Toledo; March 7, 1992

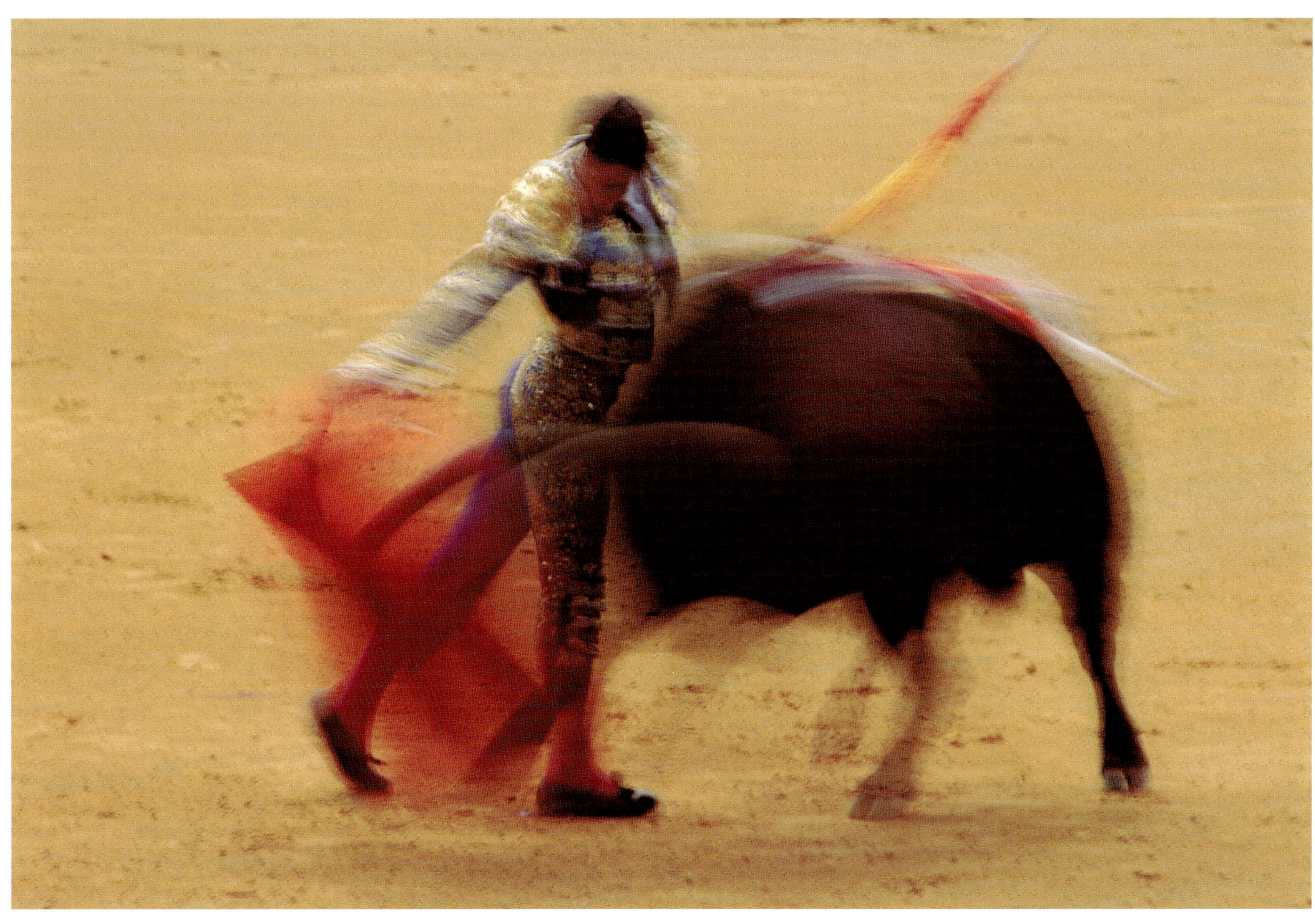

RIGHT-HANDED PASS / *Derechazo*
Joselito; Real Maestranza, Sevilla; May 5, 1993

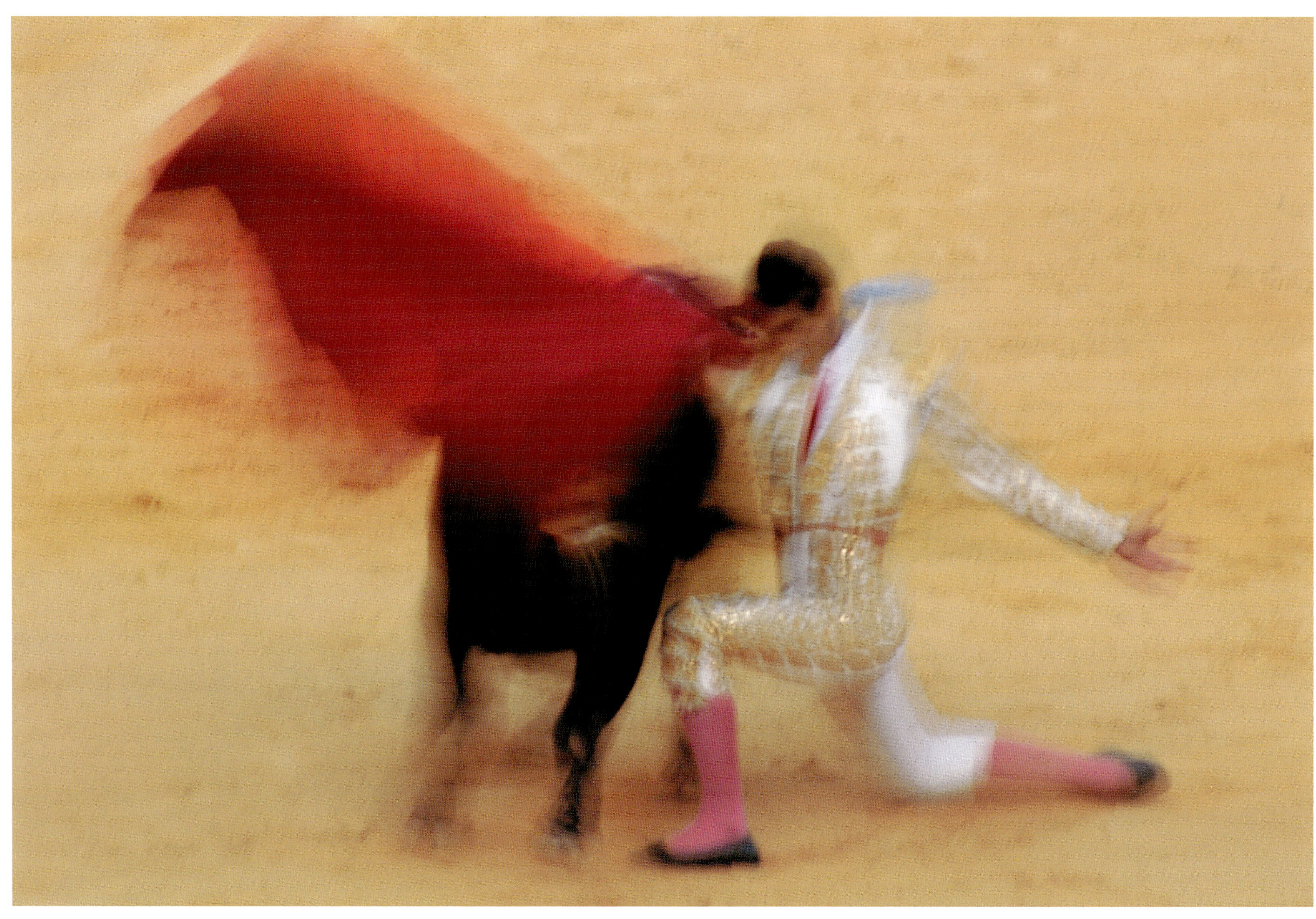

KNEELING CHEST PASS / *Pase de pecho con rodilla en tierra*
Vicente Barrera; Valencia; July 27, 1993

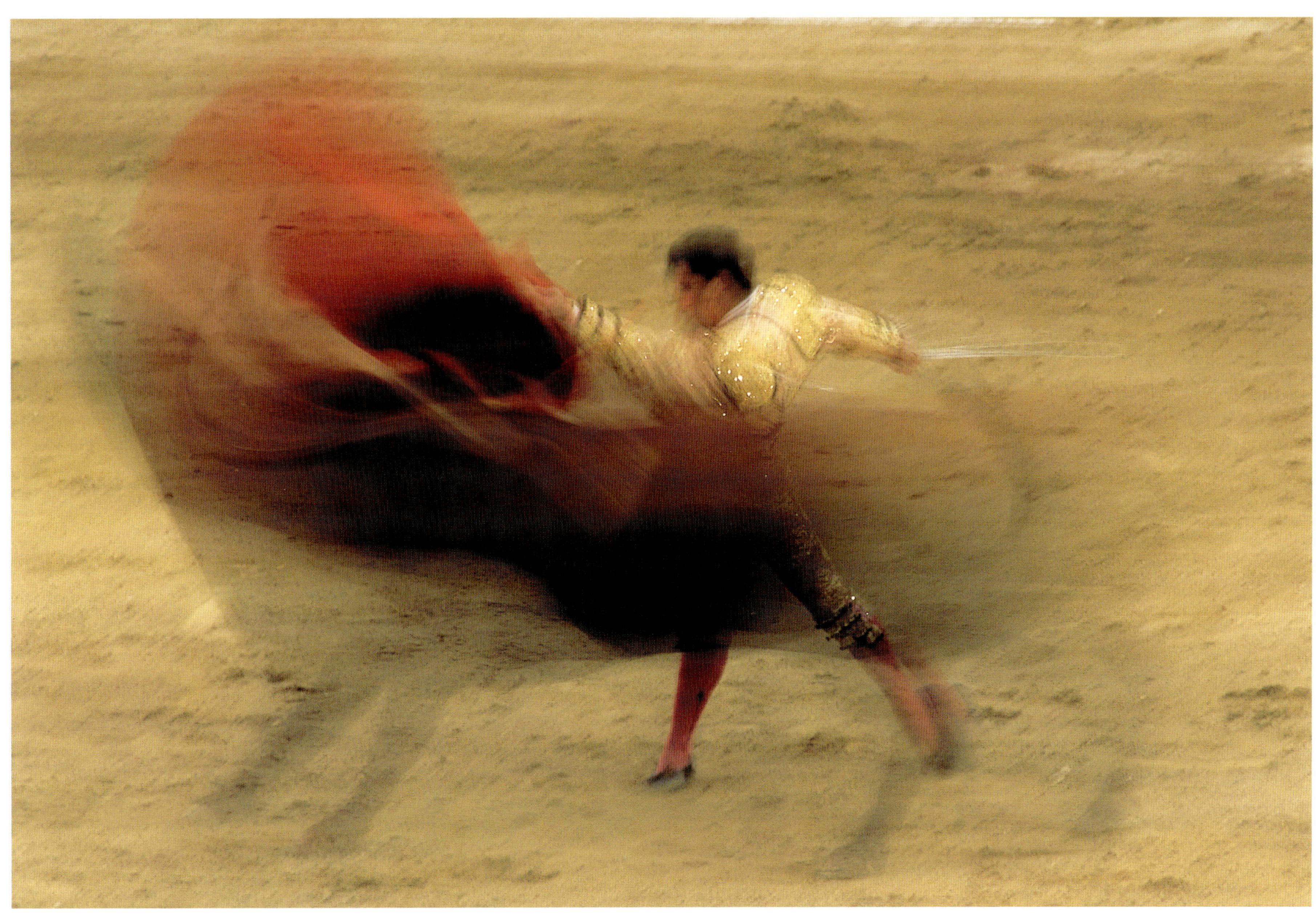

LEFT-HANDED CHEST PASS / *Pase de pecho*
César Rincón; Las Ventas, Madrid; October 10, 1991

"Bullfighting is both a physical and metaphysical exercise of spiritual integration, where what is valued is the significance of what is humanly heroic or purely: in body and soul, apparently immortal."

—José Bergamín, Writer, Essayist, Poet, Playwright

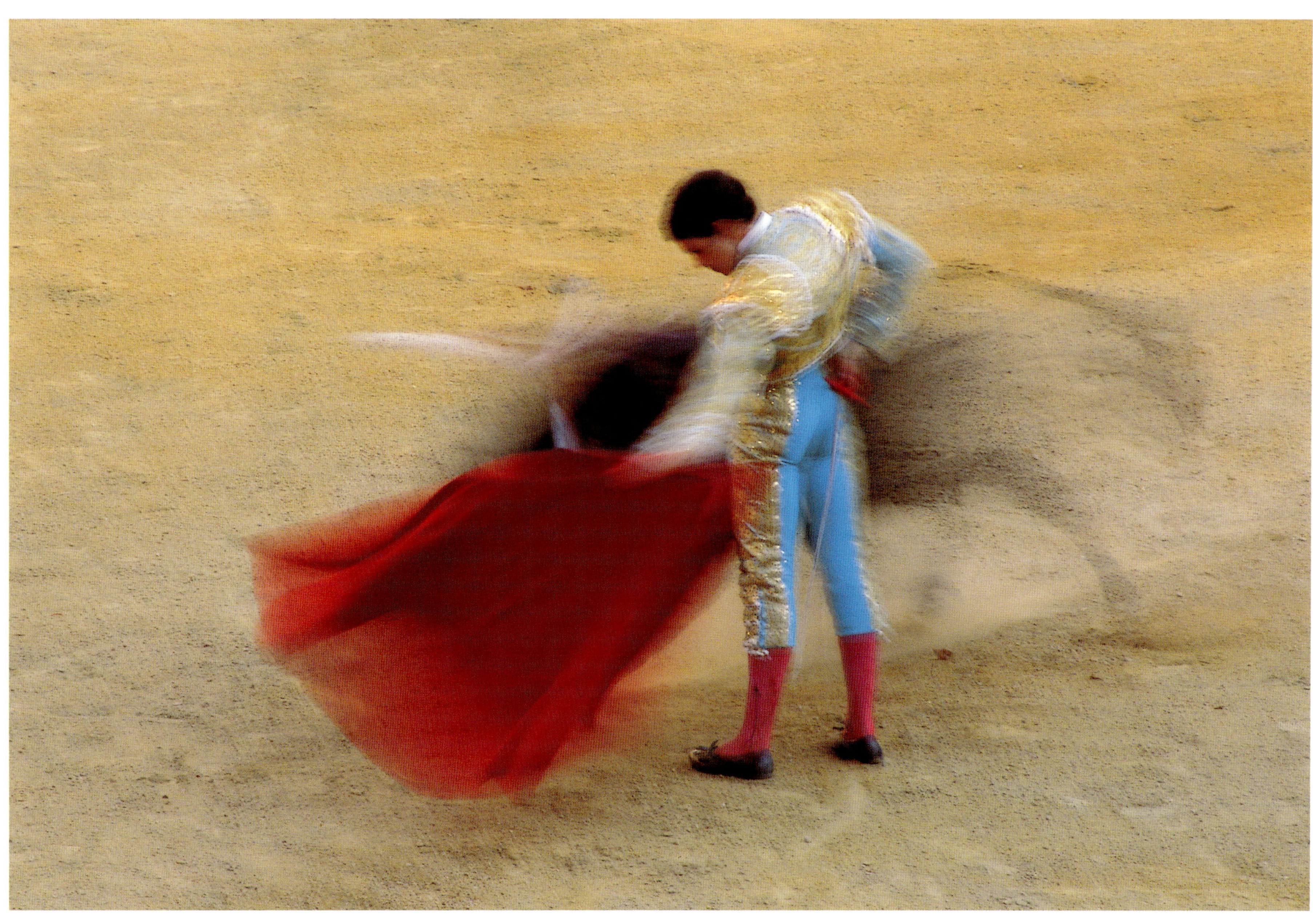

NATURAL PASS / *Natural*
José Tomás; El Parque, León; June 24, 2000

"A man, by the word; and a bull by the horns."

—Anonymous

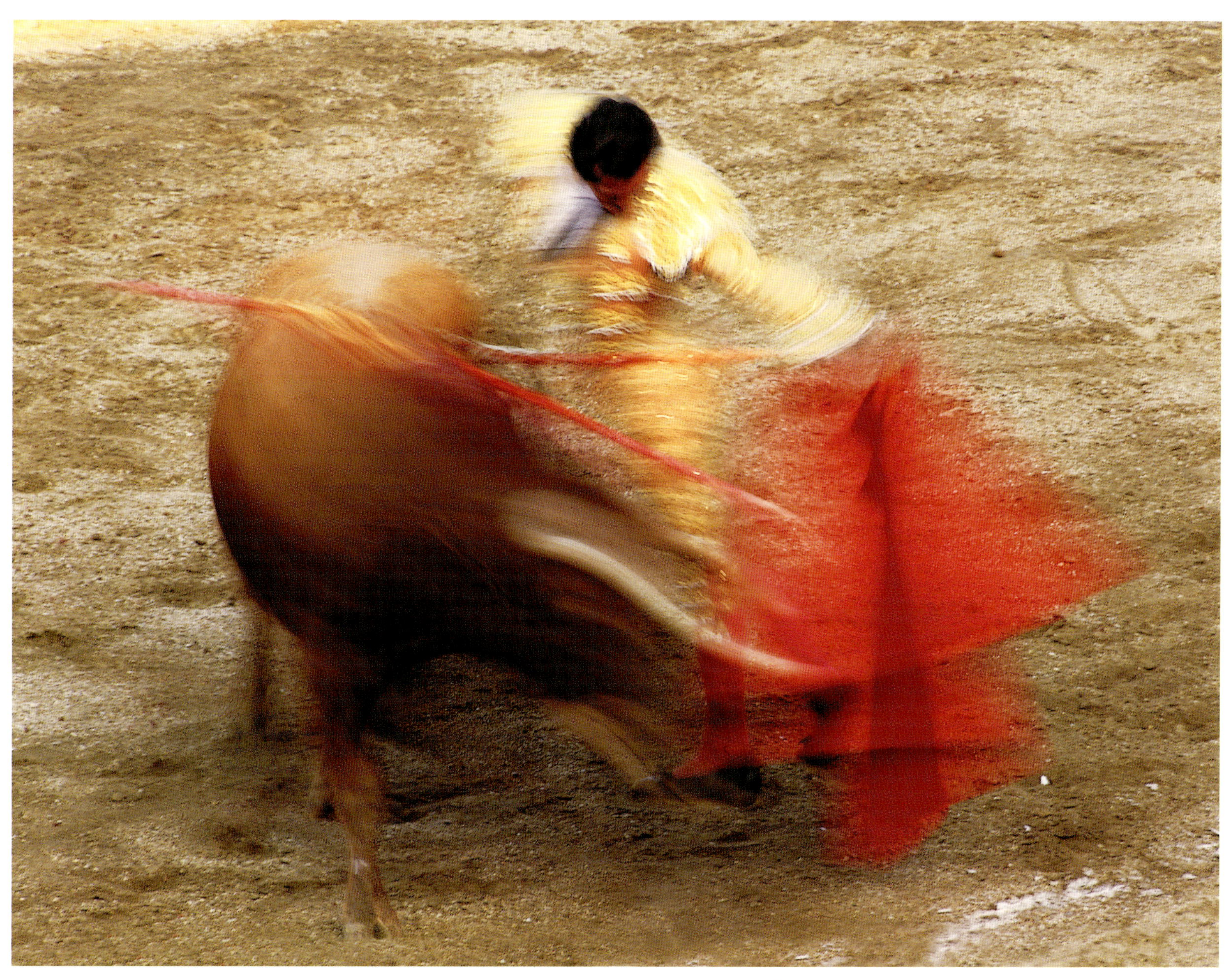

NATURAL PASS / *Natural*
José María; Manzanares, Toledo; April 11, 1992

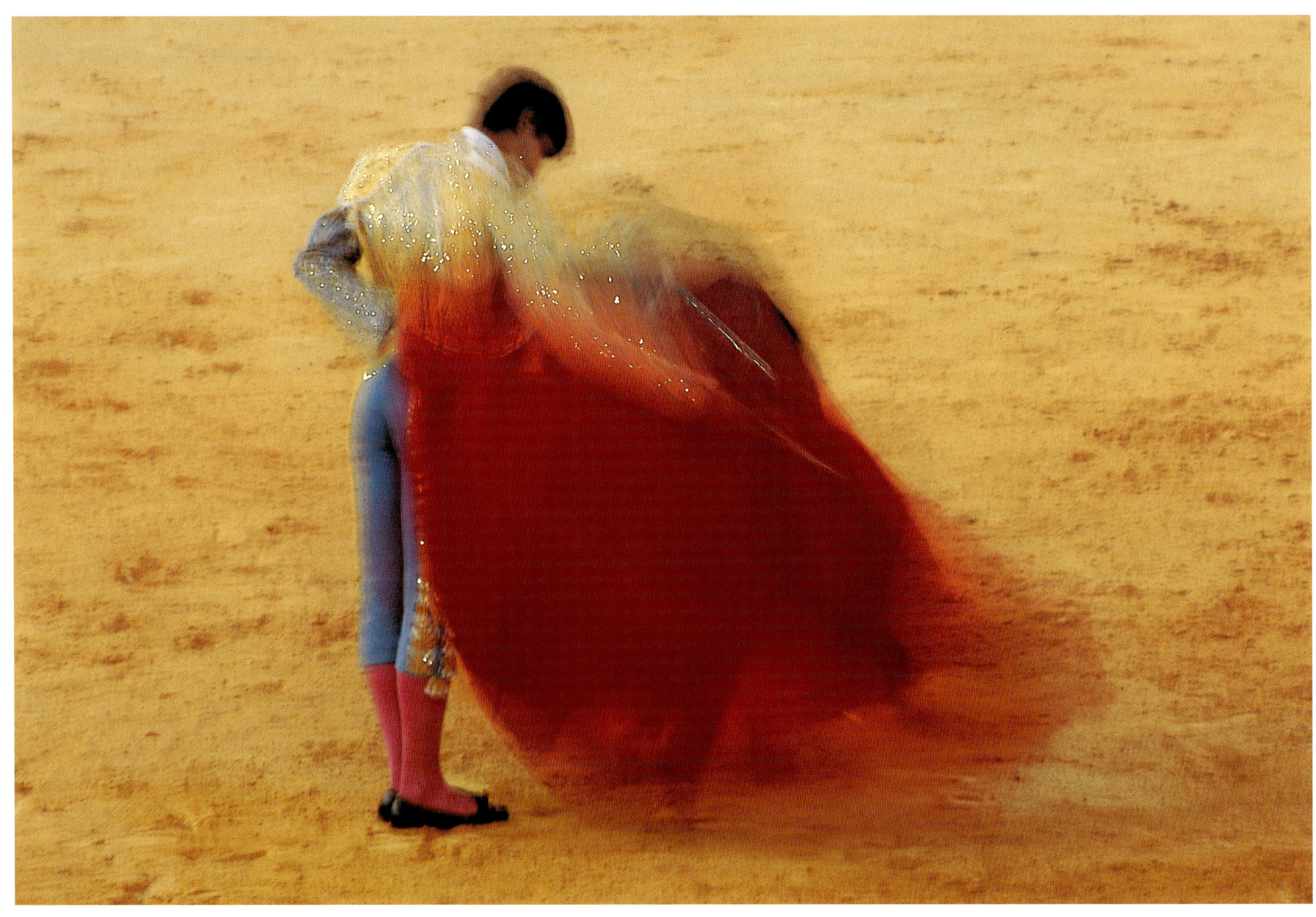

Manoletina
Vicente Barrera; Valencia; July 22, 1993

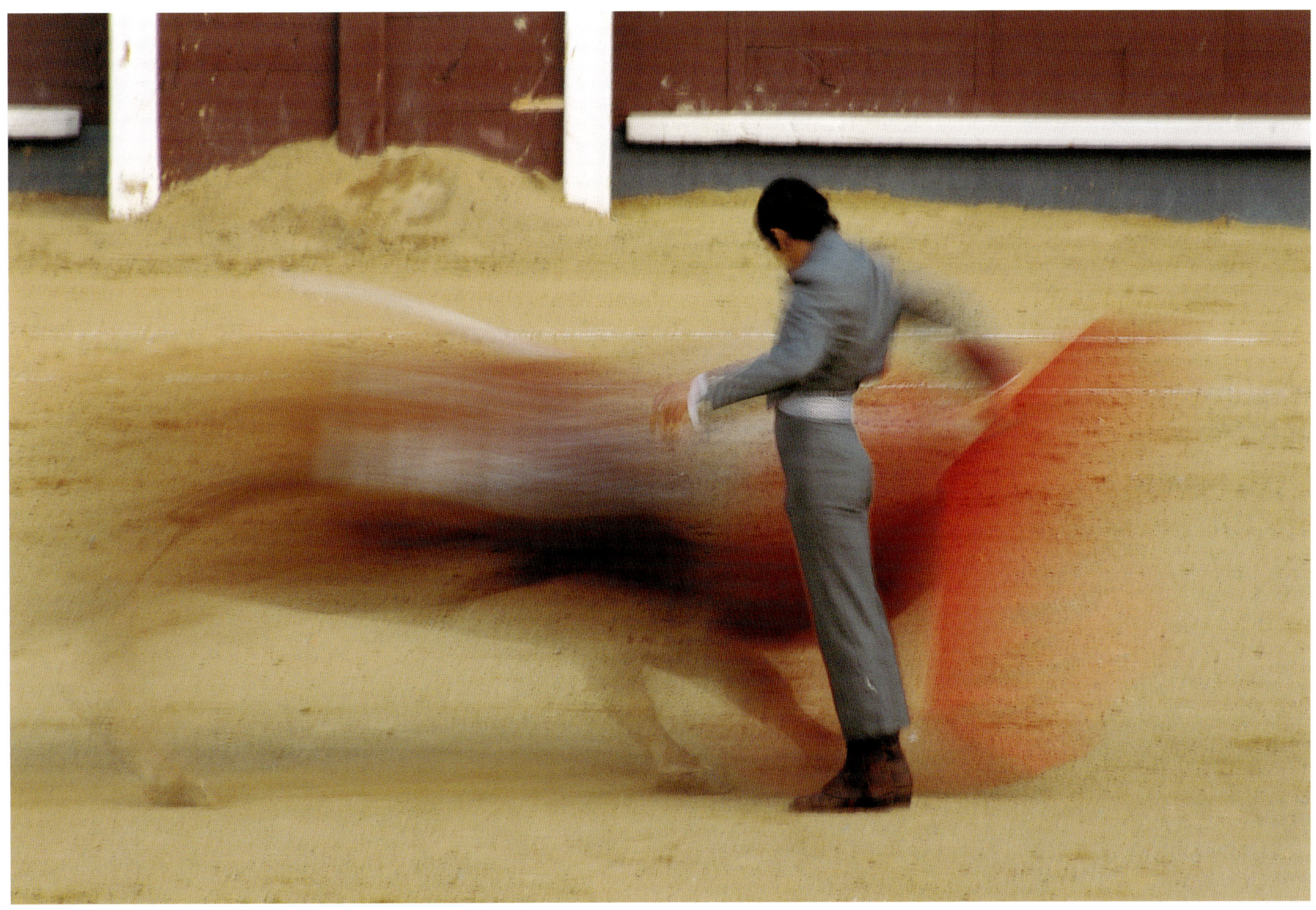

Capeína
Joselito; Las Ventas, Madrid; October 20, 1996

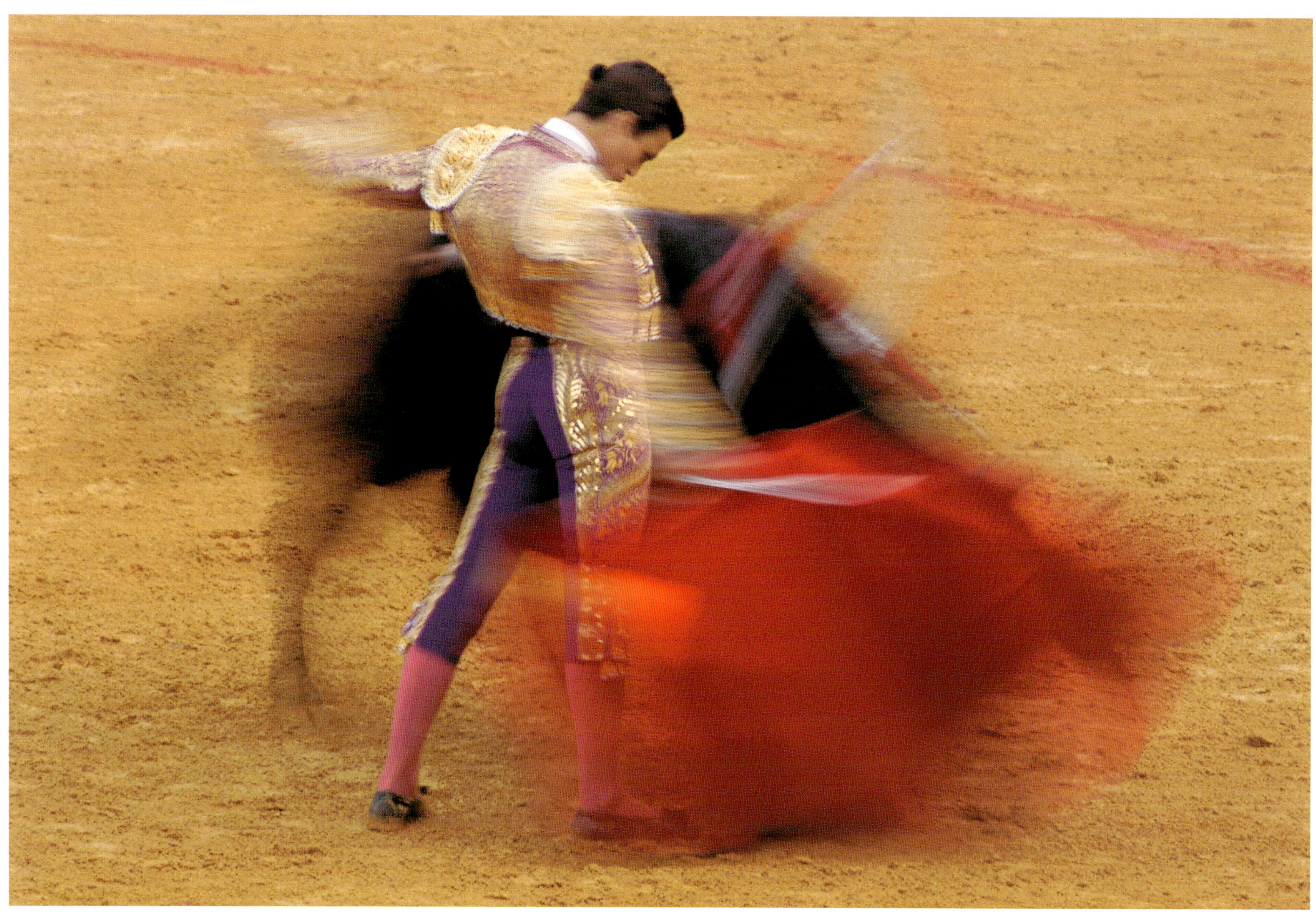

SIGNATURE PASS / *Pase de la firma*
Espartaco; Real Maestranza, Sevilla; April 29, 1993

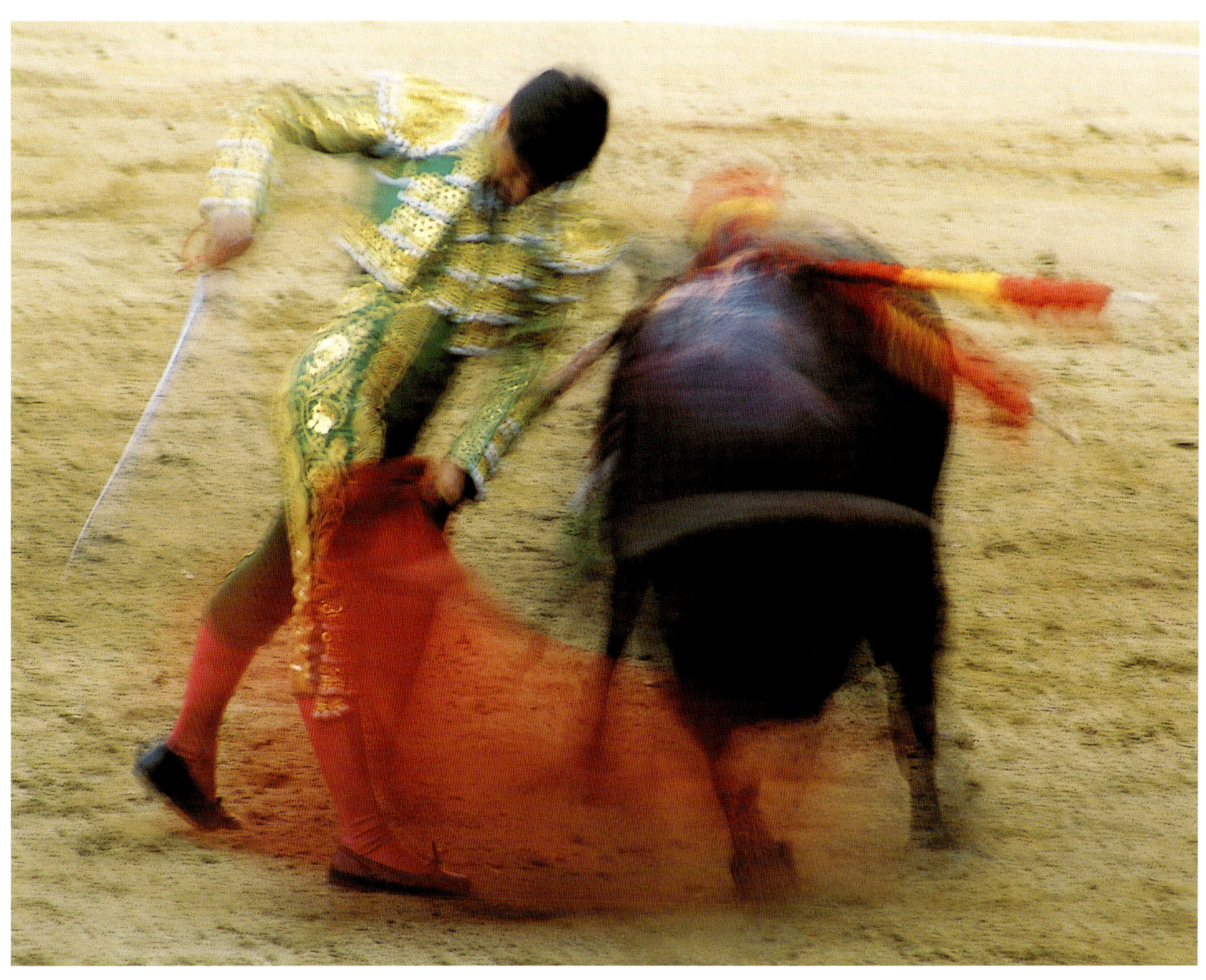

Trincherilla
Morante de la Puebla; Las Ventas, Madrid; May 29, 2000

"Bullfighting is an act of faith: in the art, in the game, in God."

—José Bergamín, Writer, Essayist, Poet, Playwright

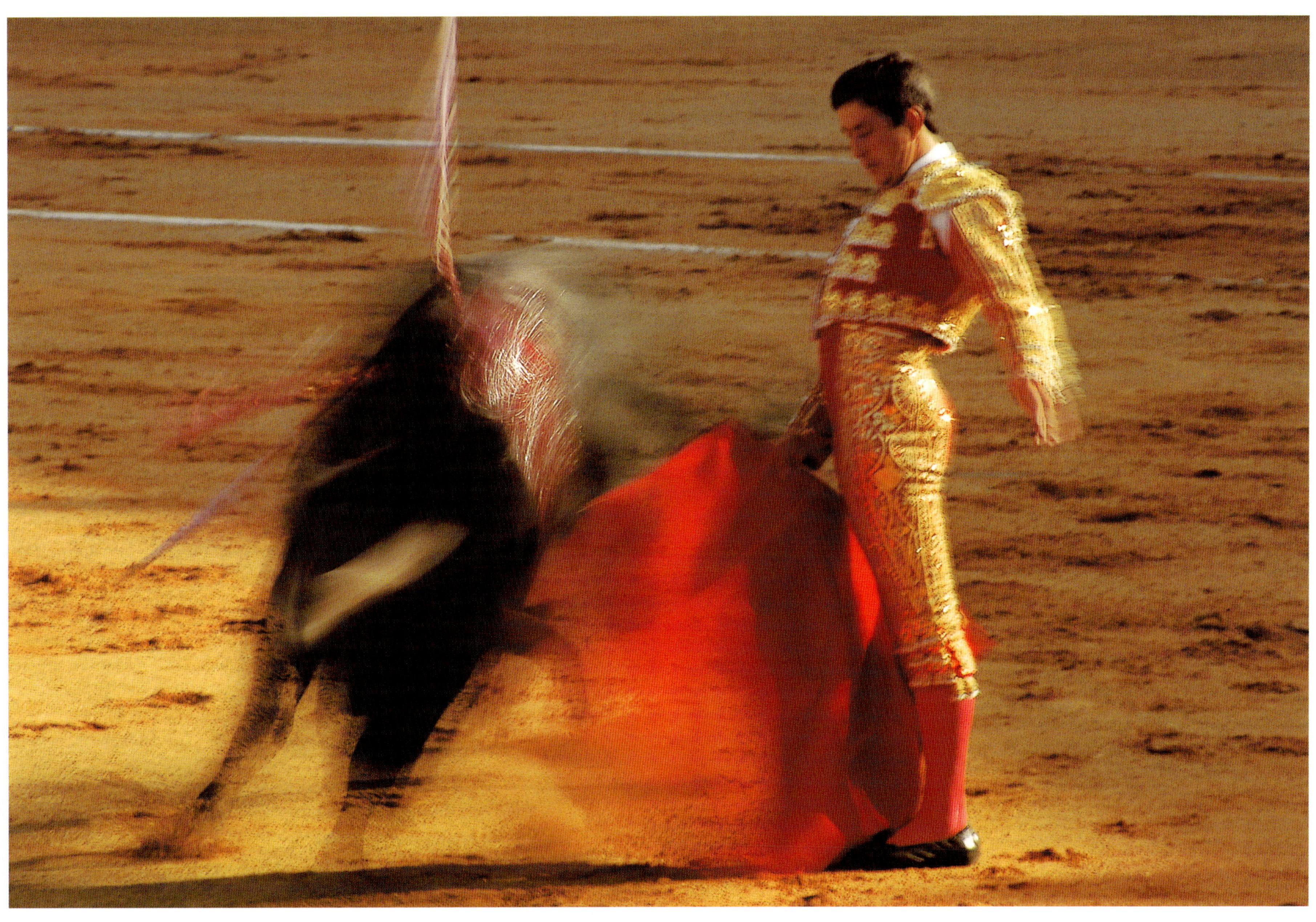

Trincherazo
Niño de la Capea; La Glorieta, Salamanca; September 15, 1992

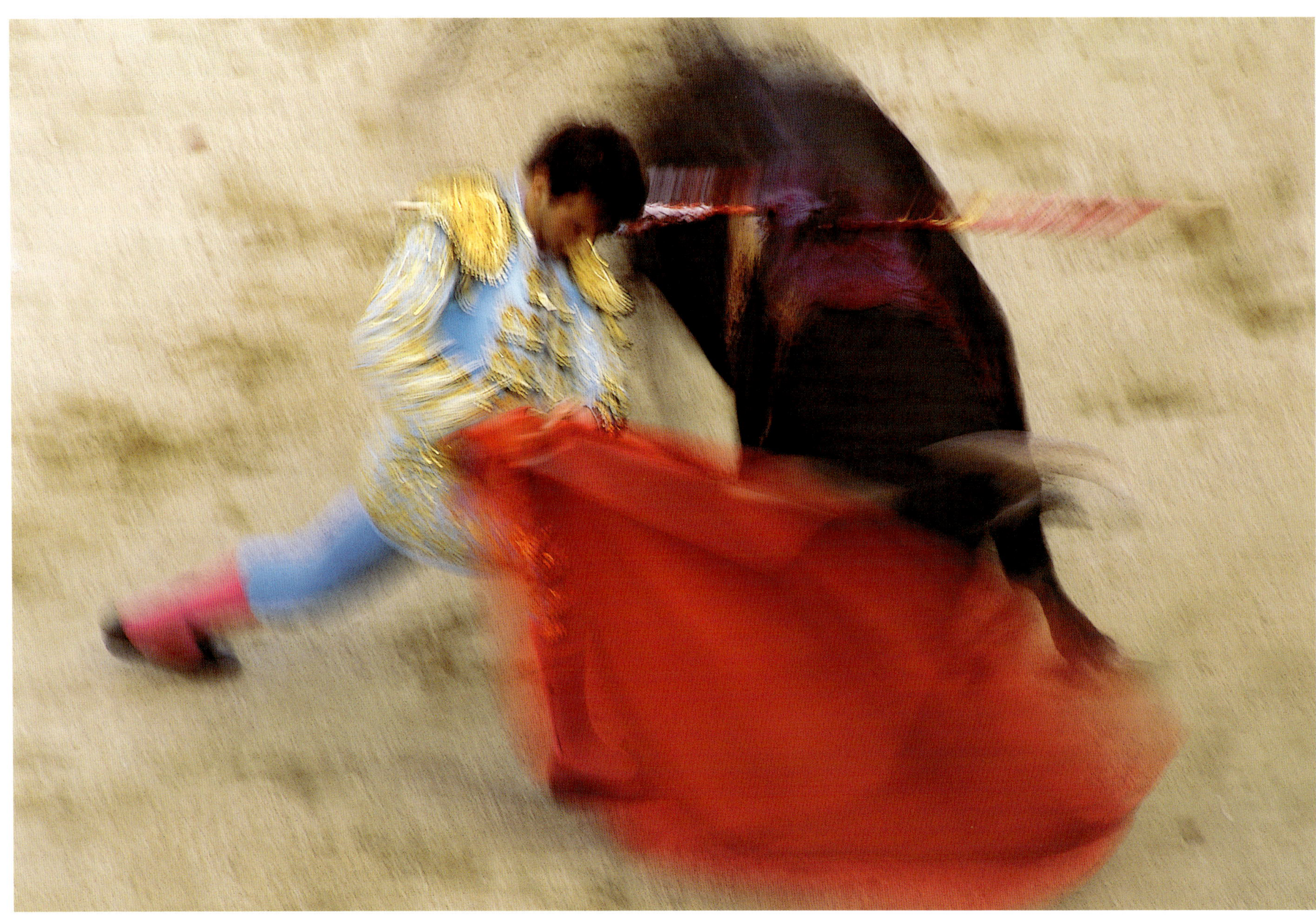

AIDED LOW PASS / *Ayudado por bajo*
Enrique Ponce; Toledo; April 11, 1992

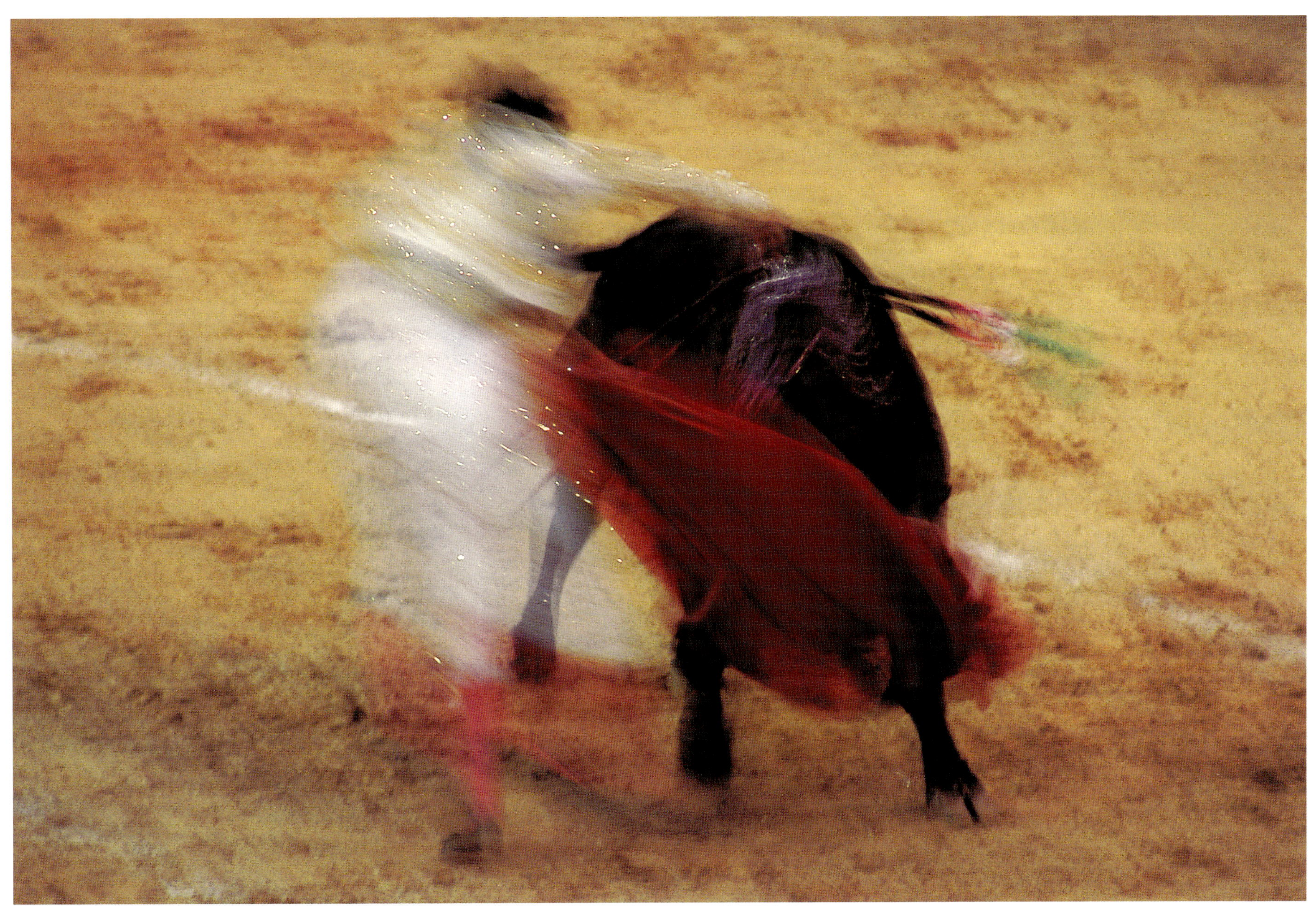

SWORD THRUST / *Estocada* (also known as the *Suerte Suprema*)
Enrique Ponce; Las Ventas, Madrid; May 29, 1992

Sequence Two

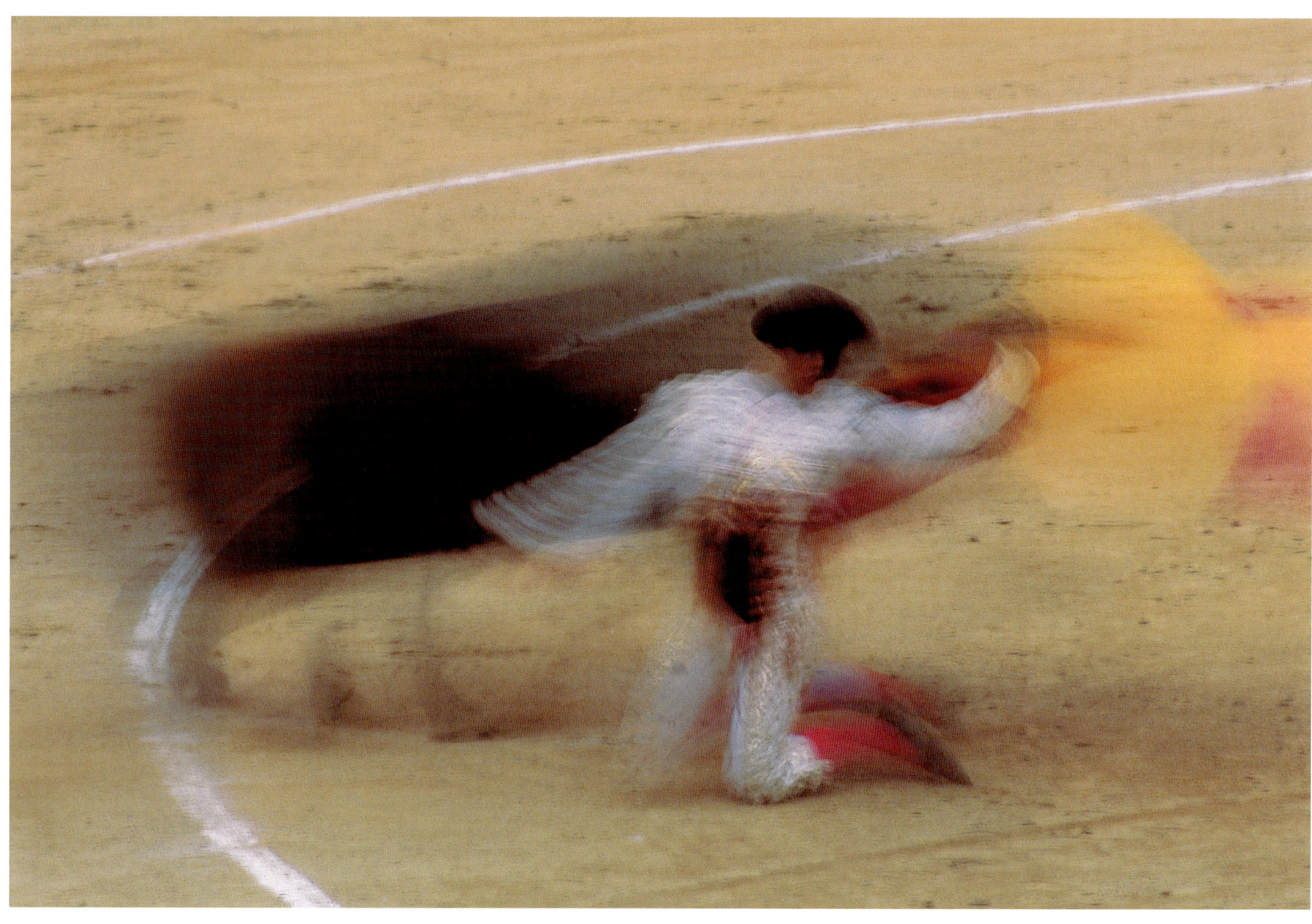

Larga a porta gayola
Miguel Abellán; Las Ventas, Madrid; September 30, 2000

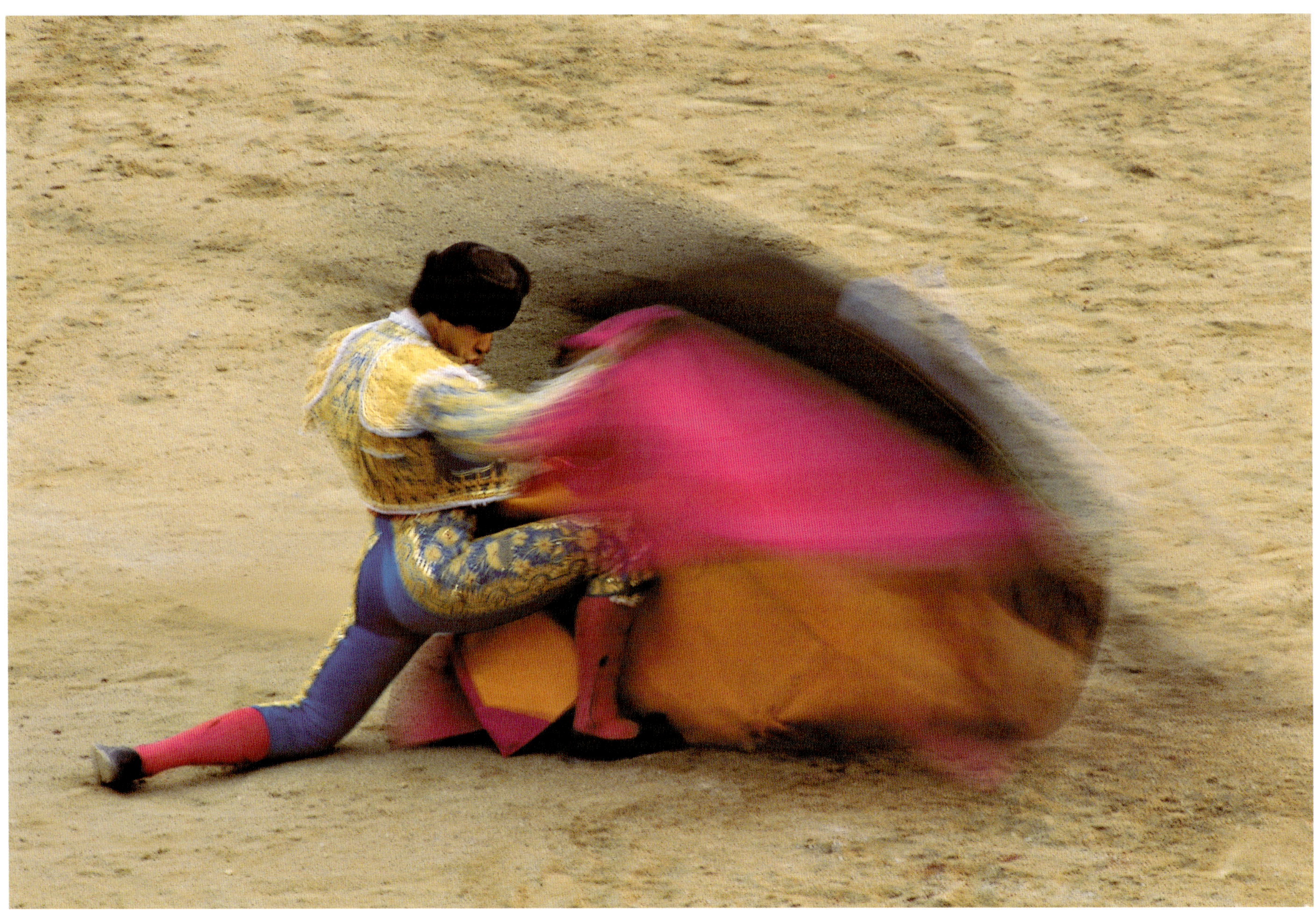

KNEELING VERÓNICA / *Verónica de rodillas*
Víctor Puerto; Las Ventas, Madrid; October 7, 2000

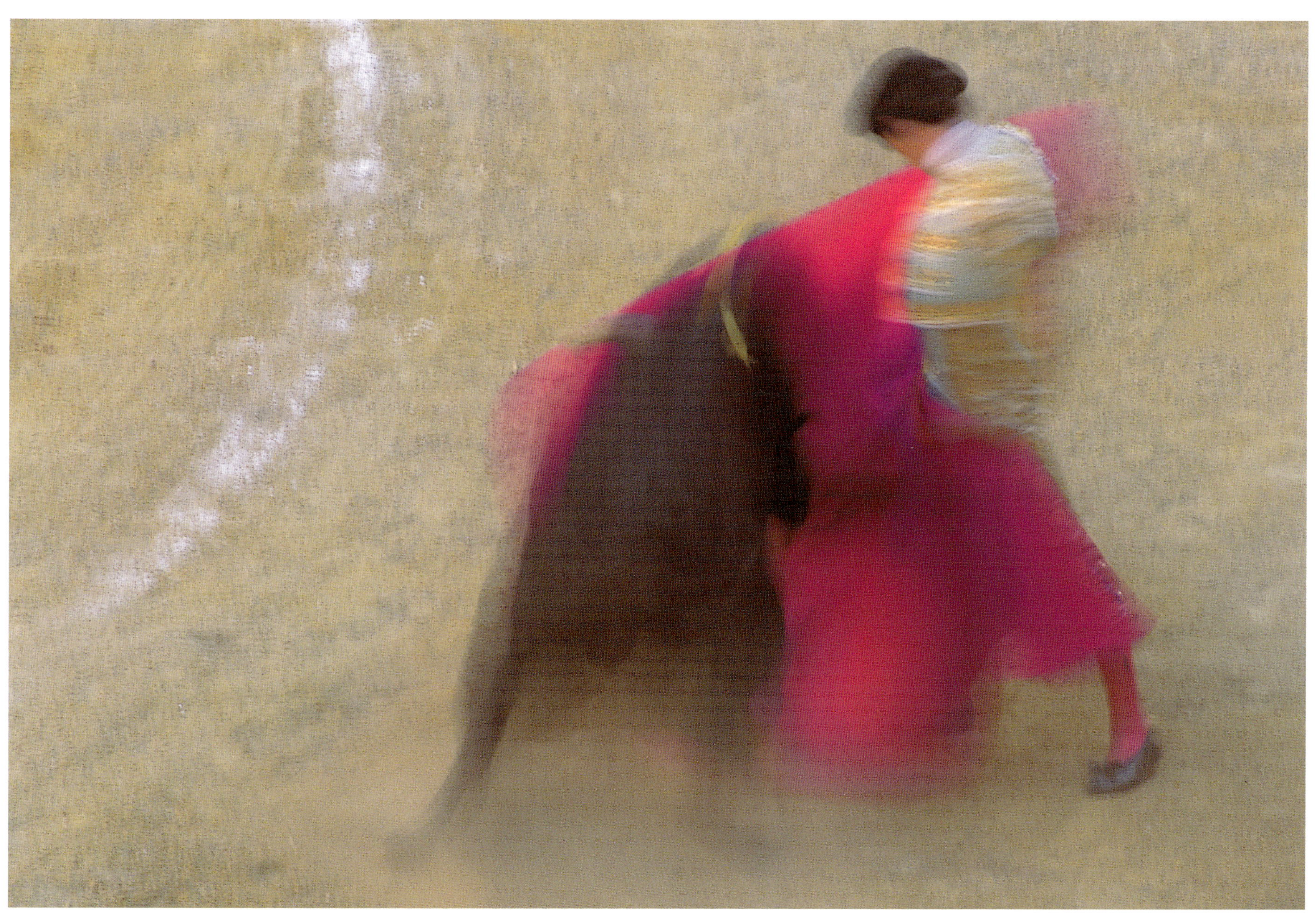

Verónica
José Tomás.; El Parque, León; June 24, 2000

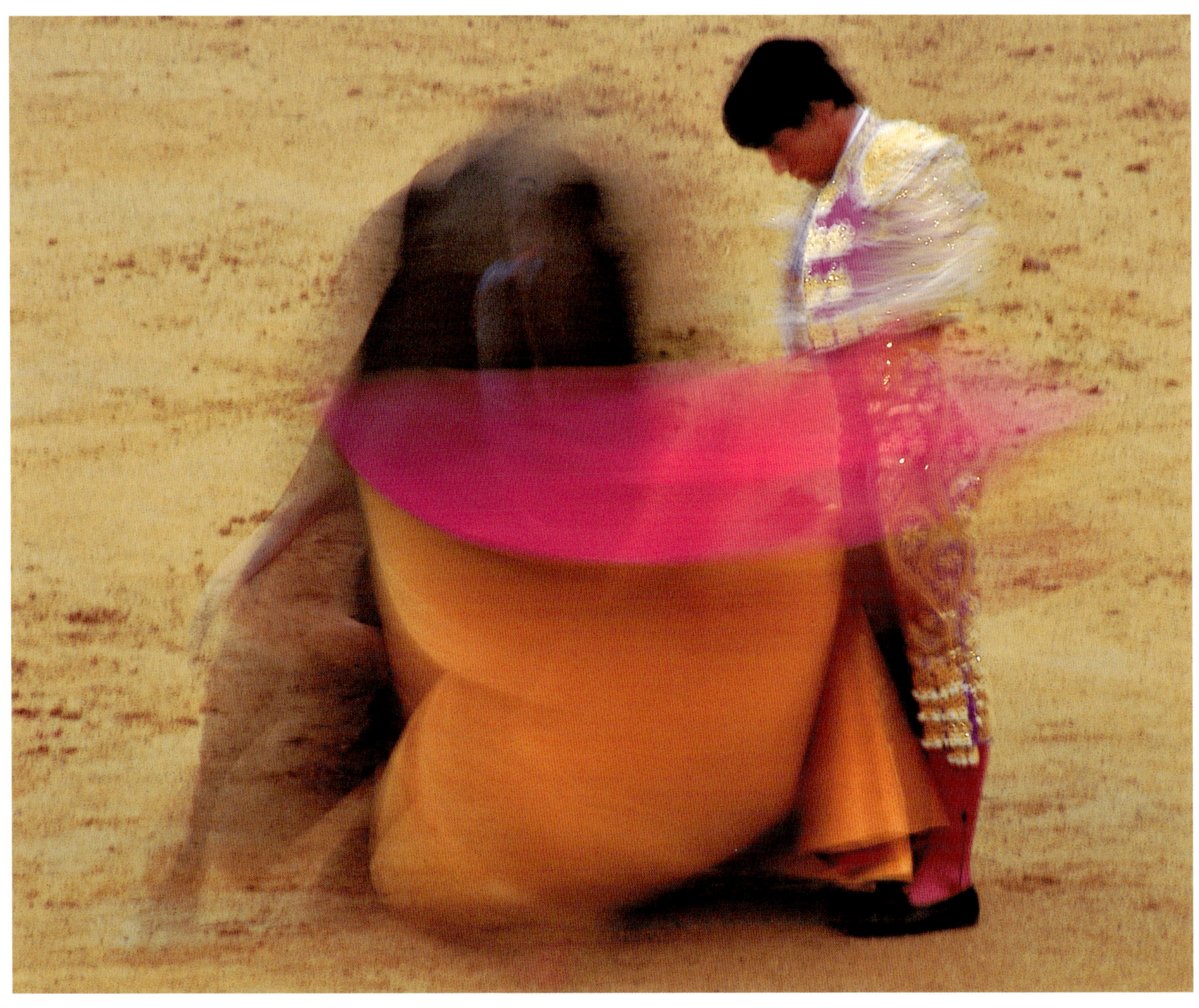

CAPE PASS (OR LANCE) WITH FEET TOGETHER / *Lance*
Joselito; Las Ventas, Madrid; May 28, 1992

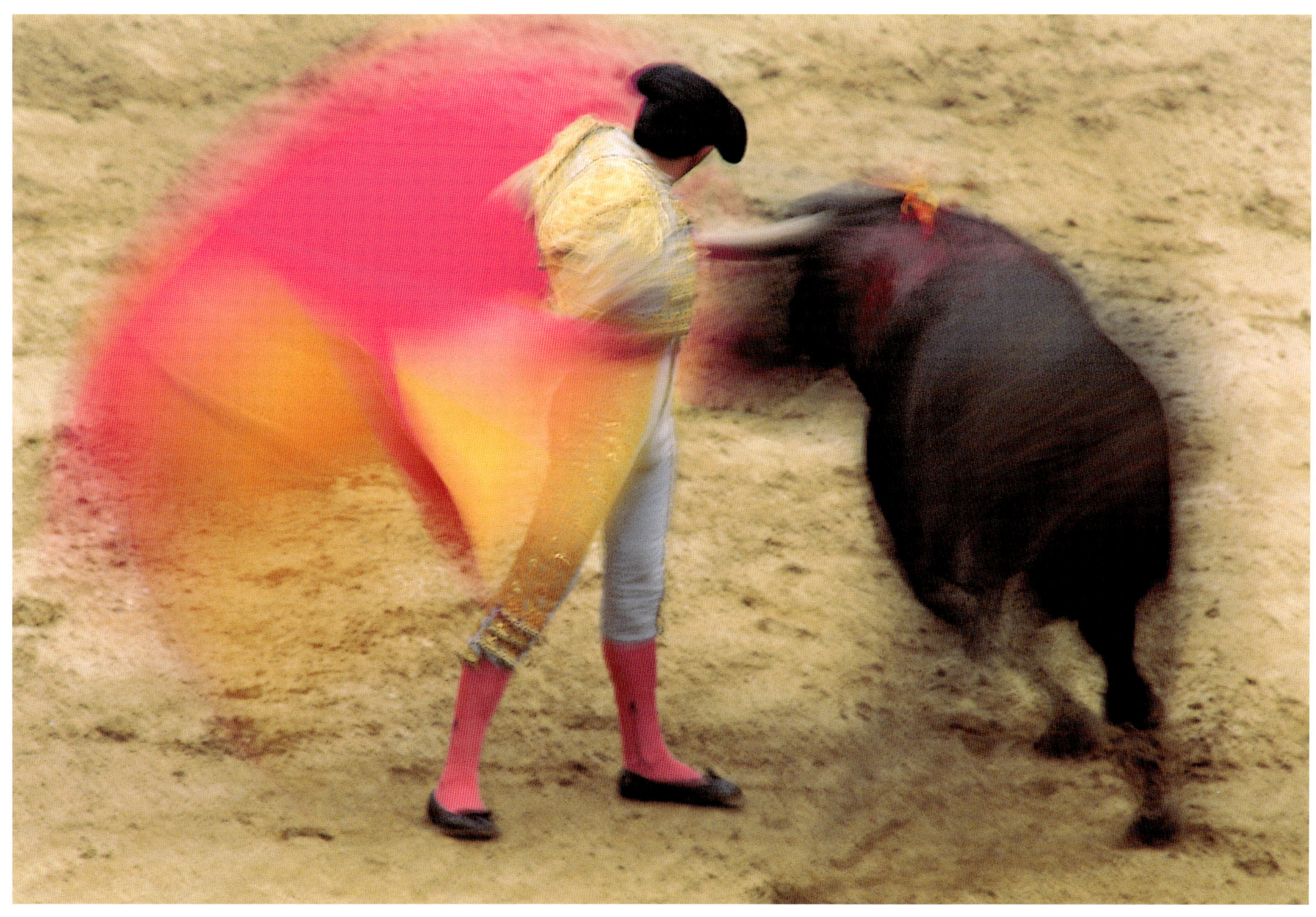

Revolera
Frascuelo; Las Ventas, Madrid; October 12, 1991

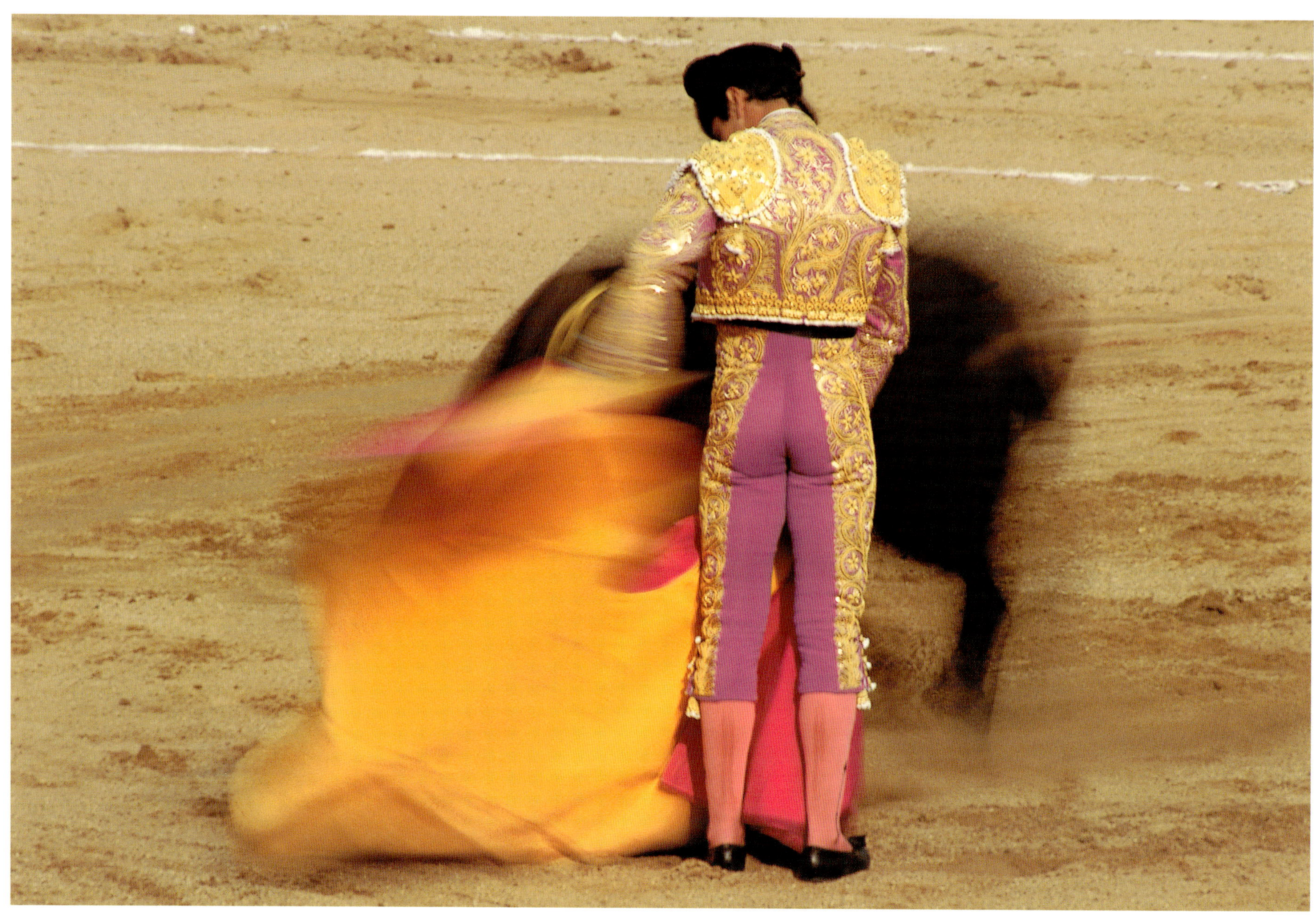

MEDIA VERONICA WITH FEET TOGETHER / *Media Verónica a pies juntos*
Joselito; Toledo; June 21, 1992

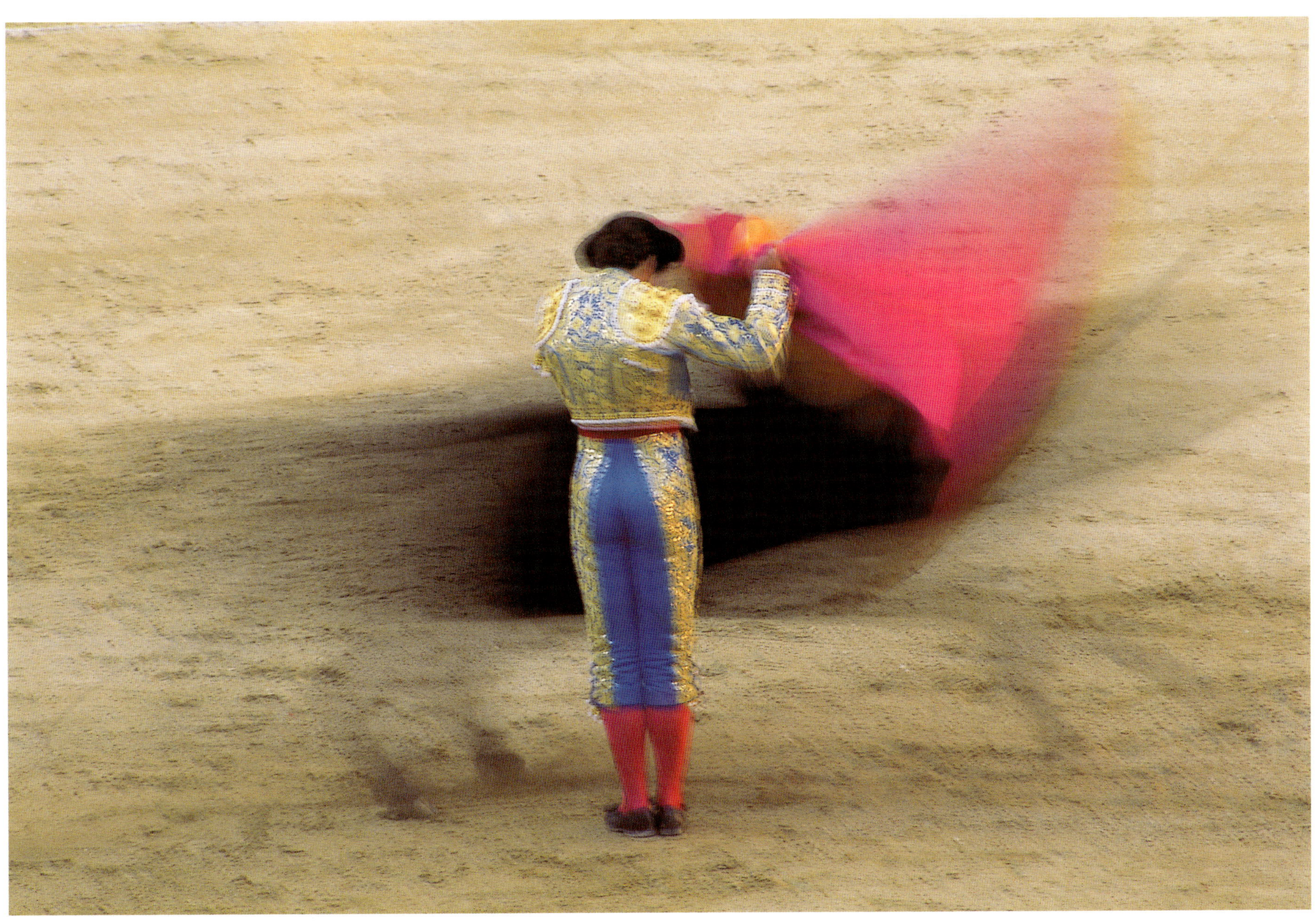

TAFALLERA WITH FEET TOGETHER / *Tafallera*
Víctor Puerto; Las Ventas, Madrid; October 7, 2000

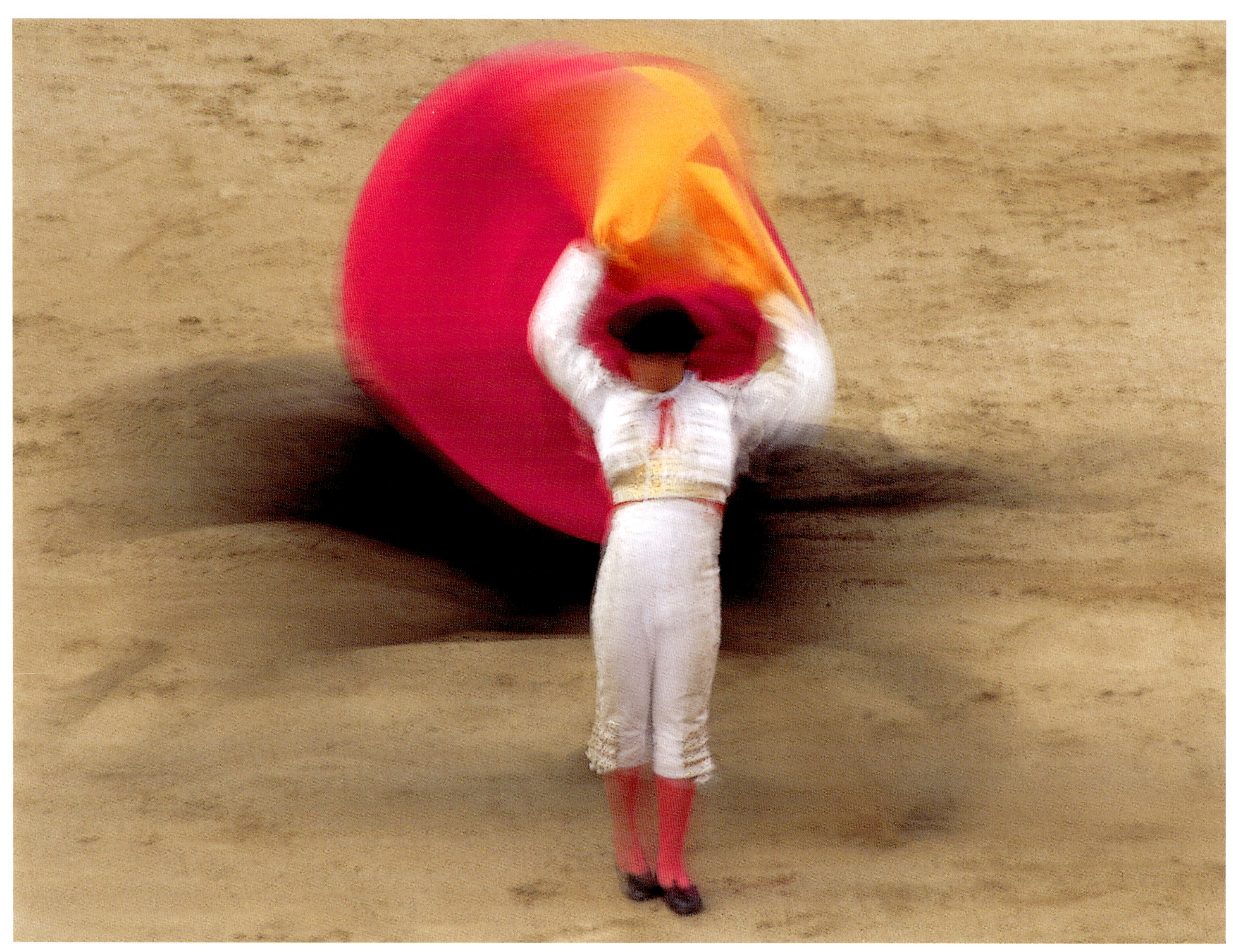

INVERTED FAROL / *Farol invertida*
El Juli; Las Ventas, Madrid; June 15, 2000

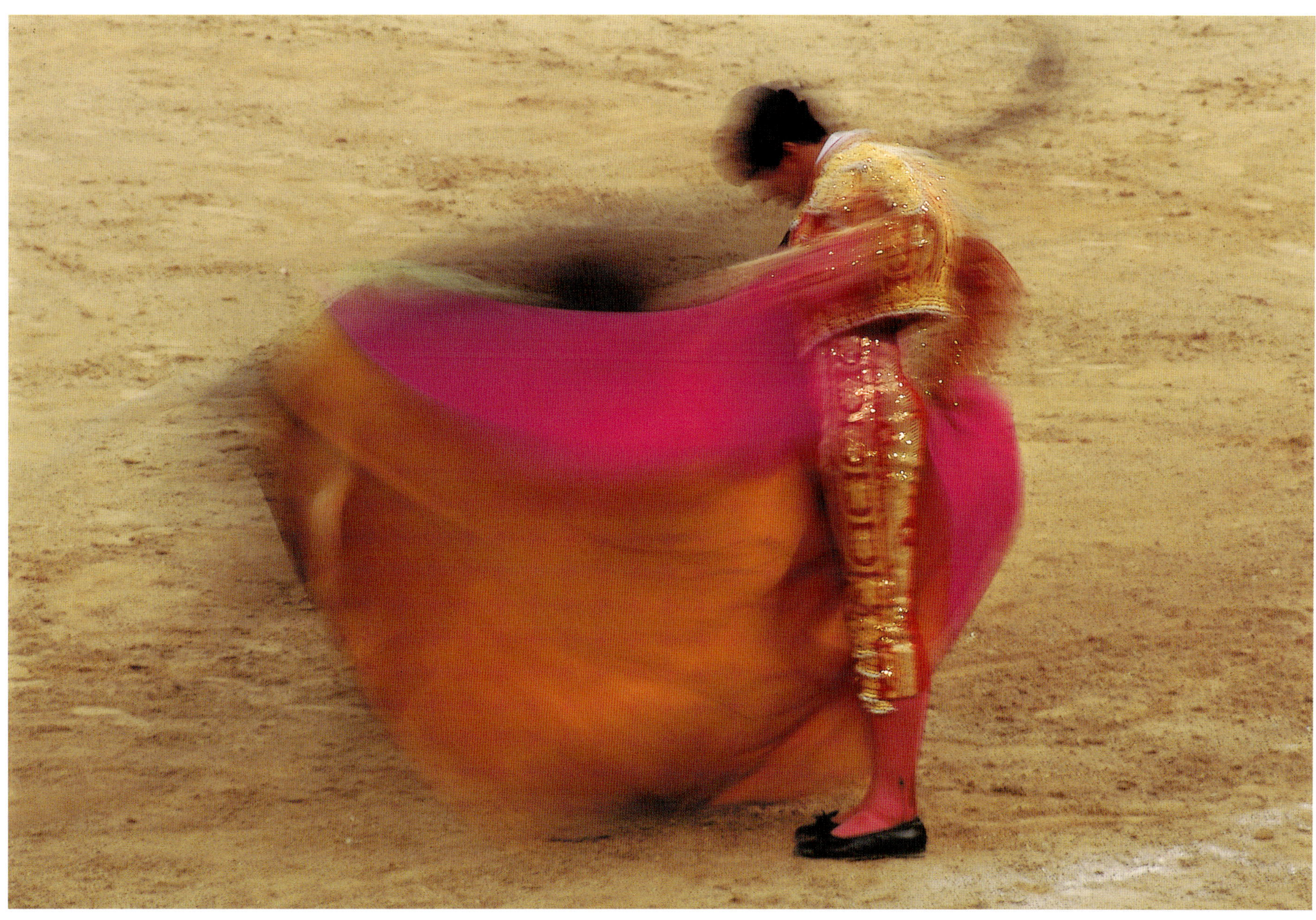

APRON PASS / *Delantal*
Javier Vázquez; Las Ventas, Madrid; September 30, 1993

"When a man has compassion for all the living creatures, only then will he be noble."

—Buddha

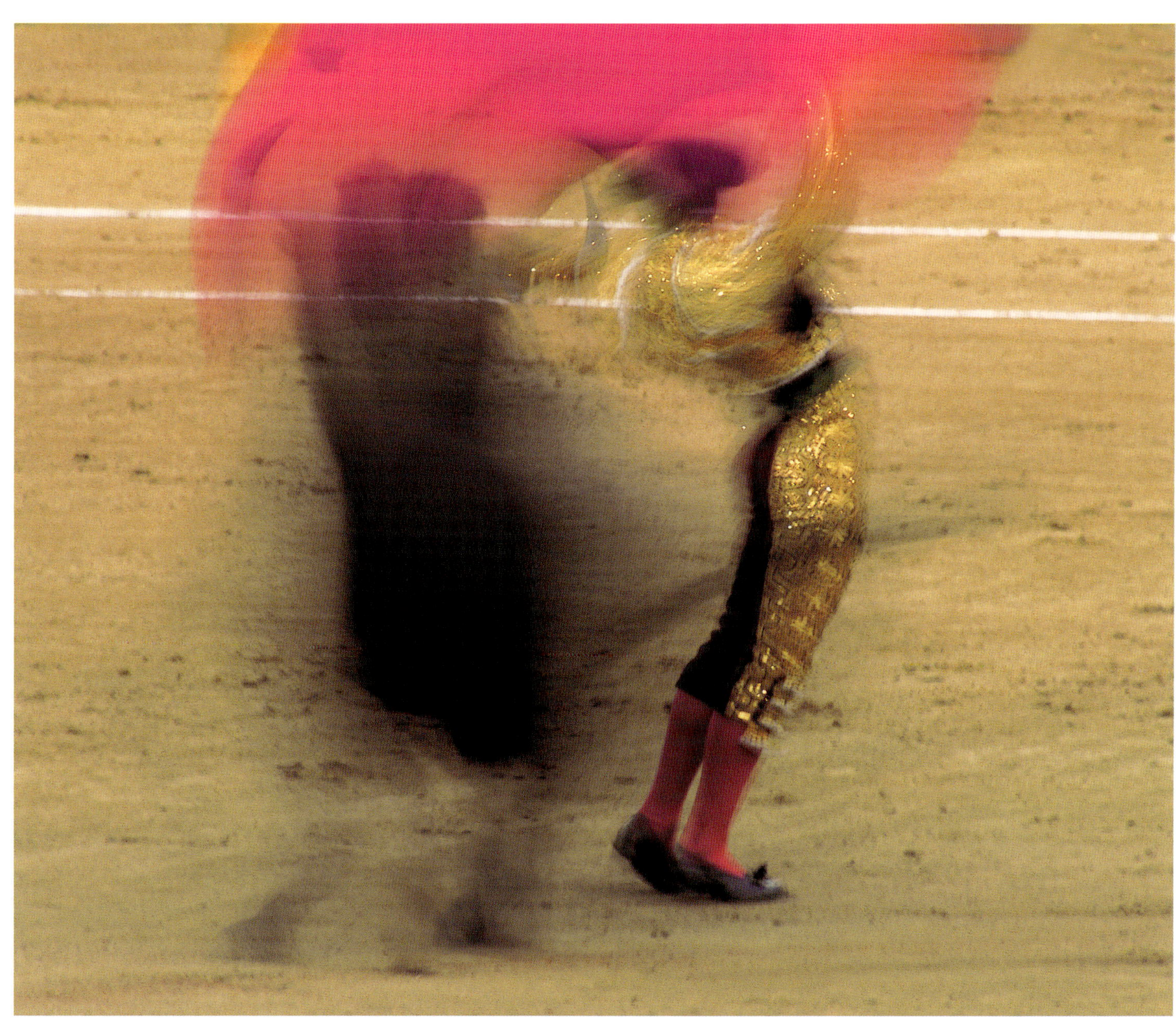

INVERTED FAROL / *Farol invertida*
El Juli; Las Ventas, Madrid; May 17, 2000

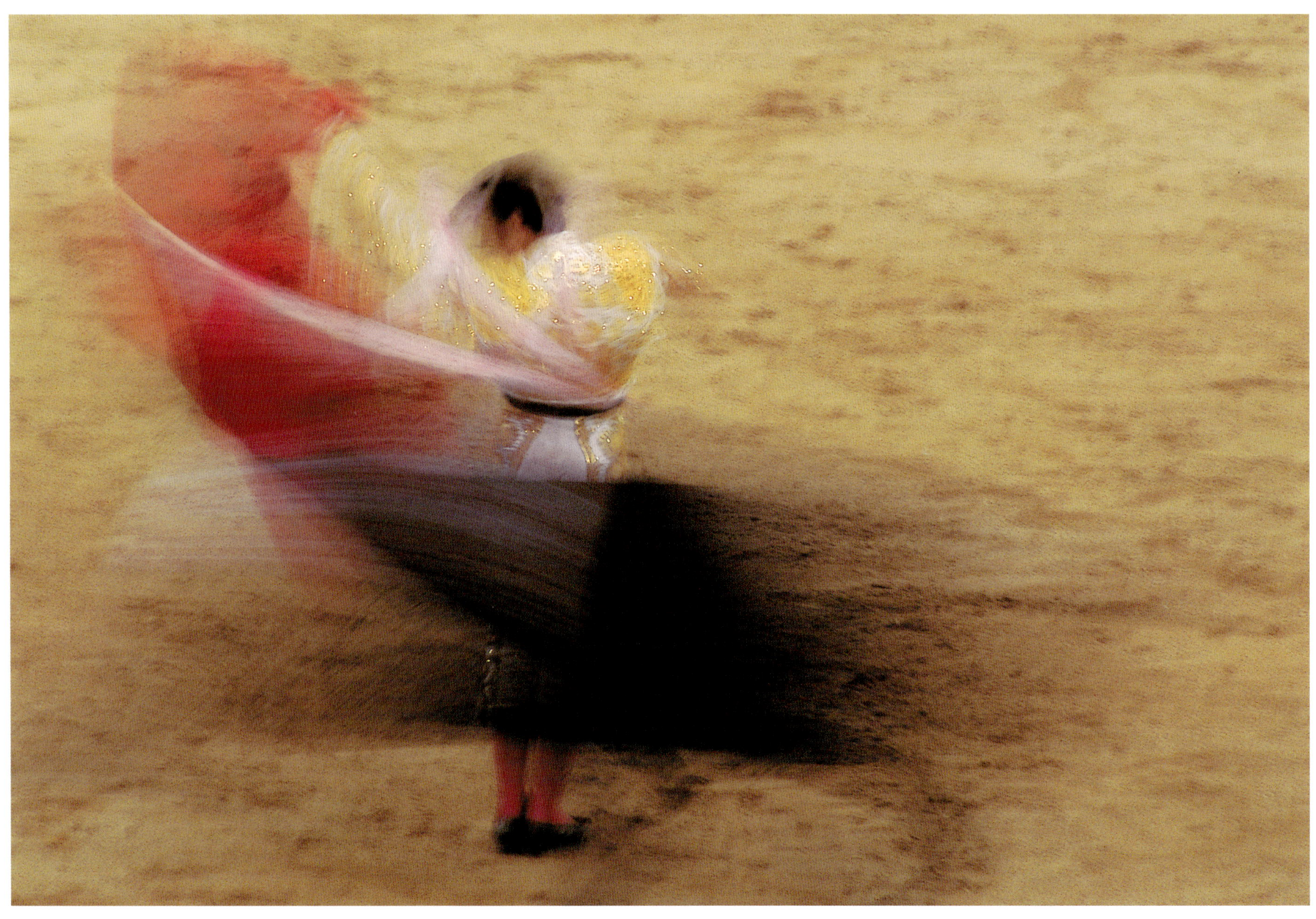

Pedresina
Javier Vázquez; Las Ventas, Madrid; May 31, 1993

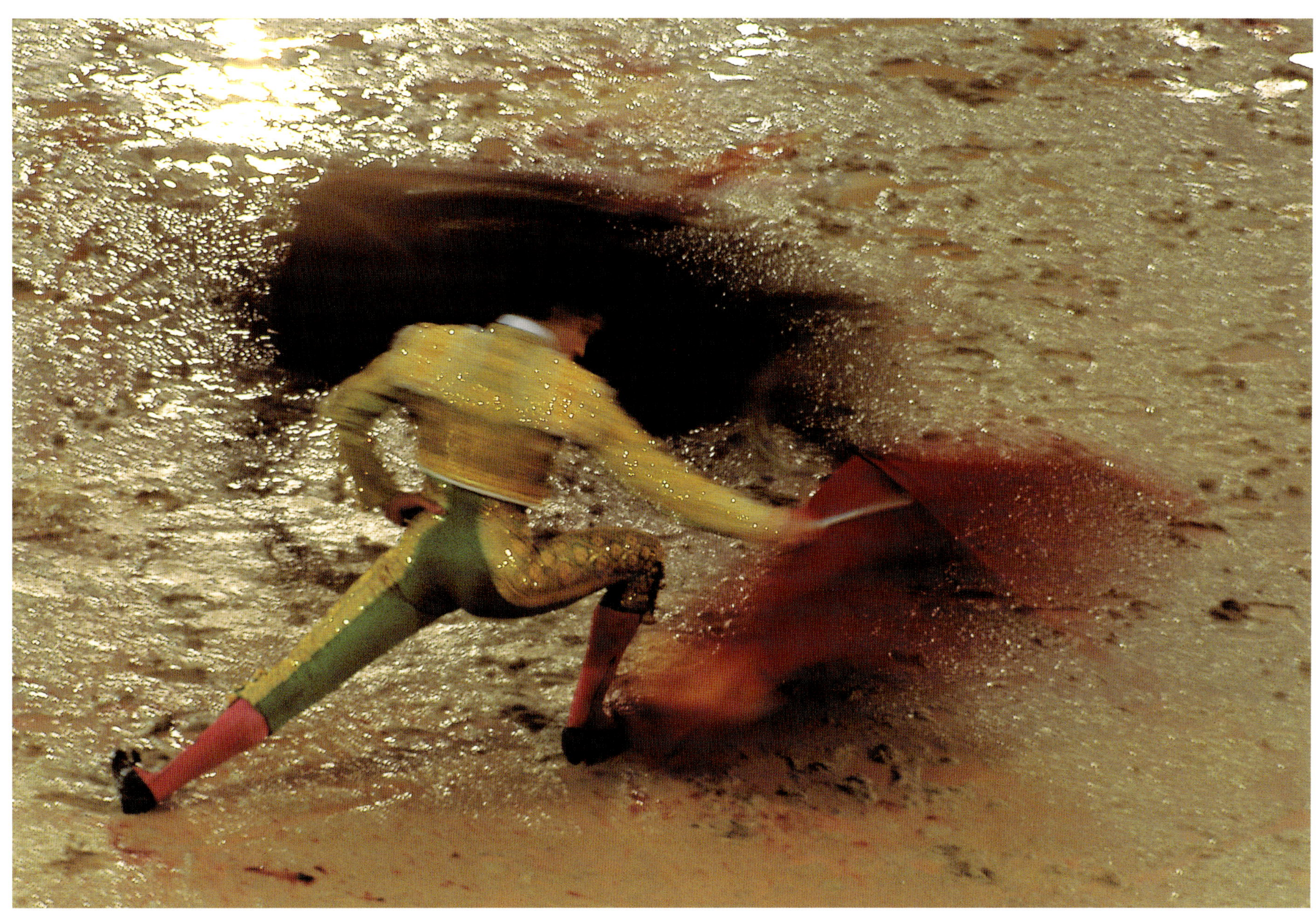

DOUBLING PASS WITH ONE KNEE ON THE GROUND / *Doblón*
José Tomás; Las Ventas, Madrid; May 15, 1998

Bullfight critics ranked in rows

Crowd the enormous Plaza de Toros

But only one is there who knows—

And he's the one who fights the bull.

—Bullfighter Domingo Ortega from his poem,
"Bullfight Critics," translated by Robert Graves

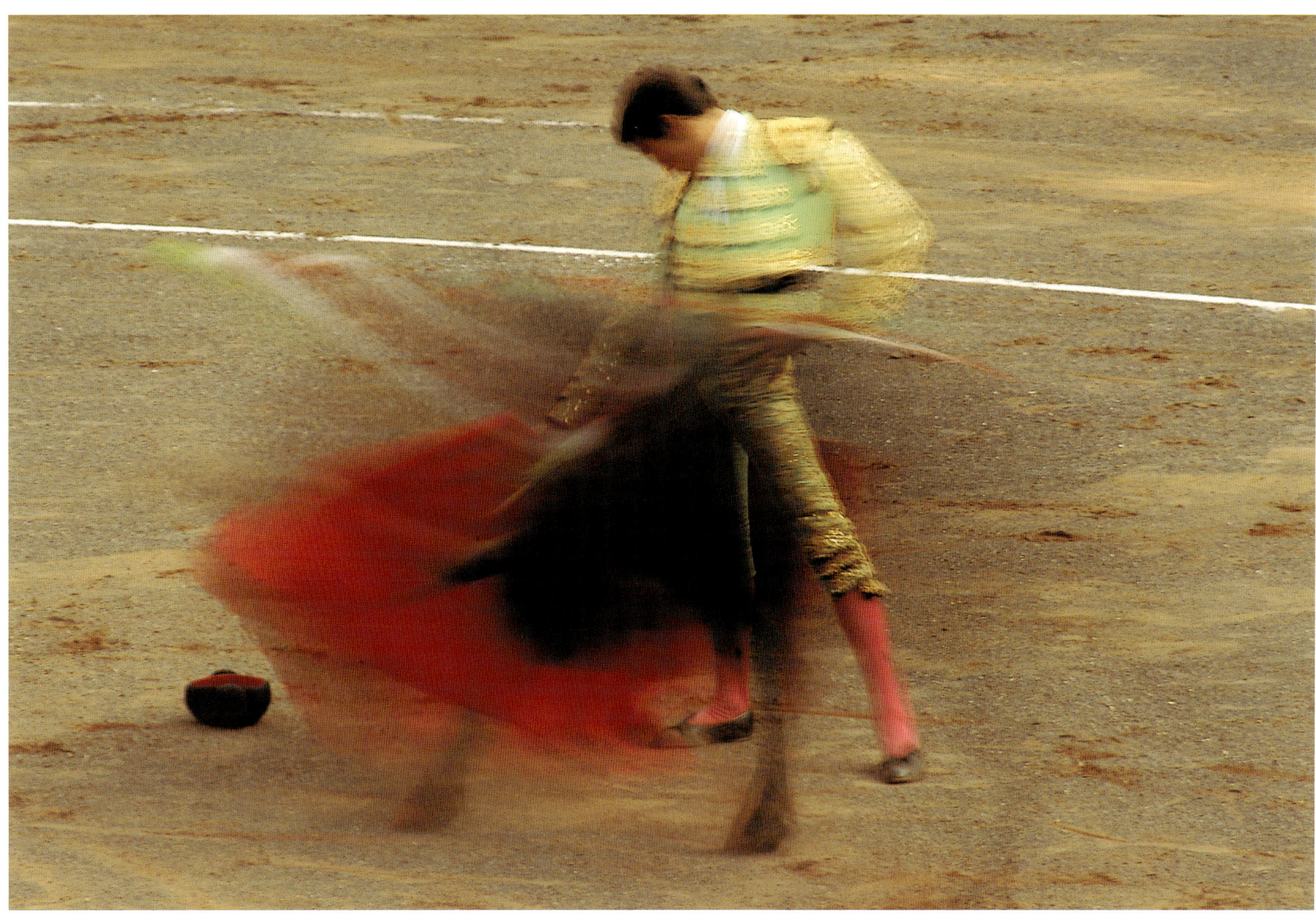

RIGHT-HANDED PASS / *Derechazo*
Enrique Ponce; Vista Alegre, Bilbao; June 7, 1992

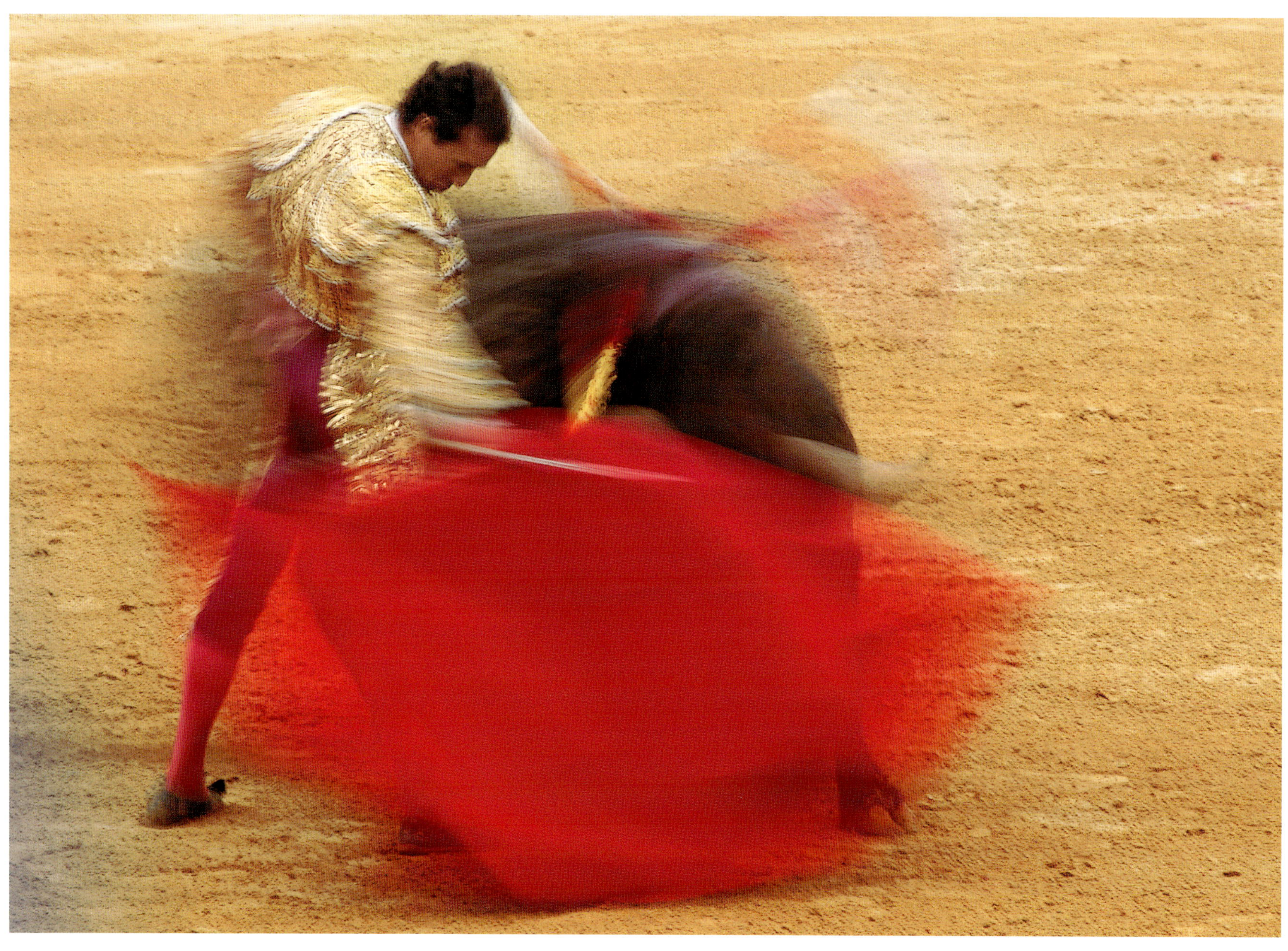

RIGHT-HANDED PASS / *Derechazo*
José María Manzanares; Real Maestranza, Sevilla; April 29, 1993

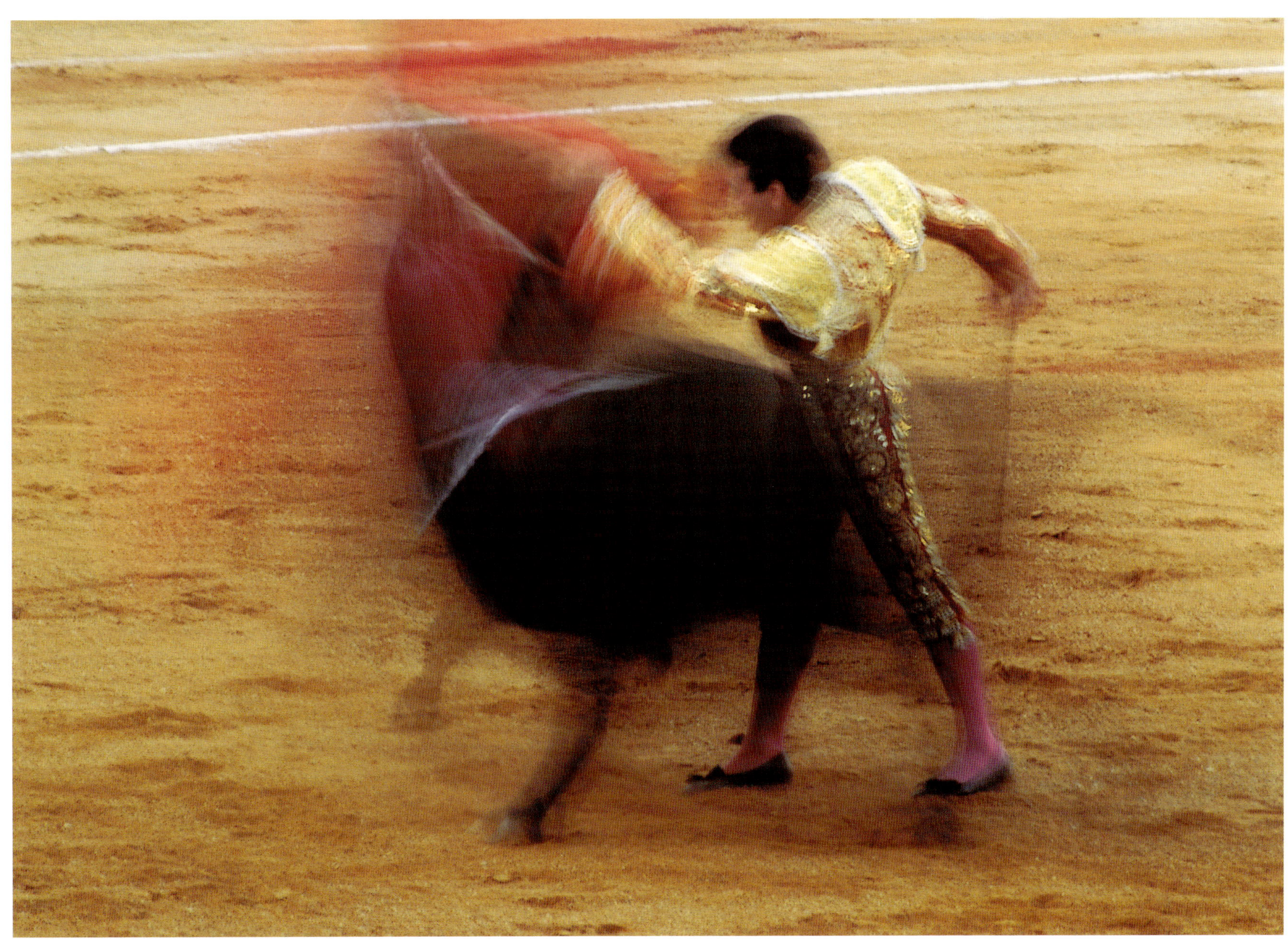

CHEST PASS ON THE LEFT / *Pase de pecho*
Ortega Cano; La Glorieta, Salamanca; September 14, 1992

"Bullfighting is a drama which follows a detailed choreography. This drama has three acts, the 'Tercios.' First, the bull is provoked and wounded, but everything rests on the last act: at the end the torero gives the deadly thrust with a sword. Utmost concentration is needed to know when the right moment has come. You are an artist, but unlike a painter or a writer, you only have one chance. The sole aim of a bullfighter is the death of the bull: for that every torero puts his life in danger."

—Luis Dávila Miura, Bullfighter

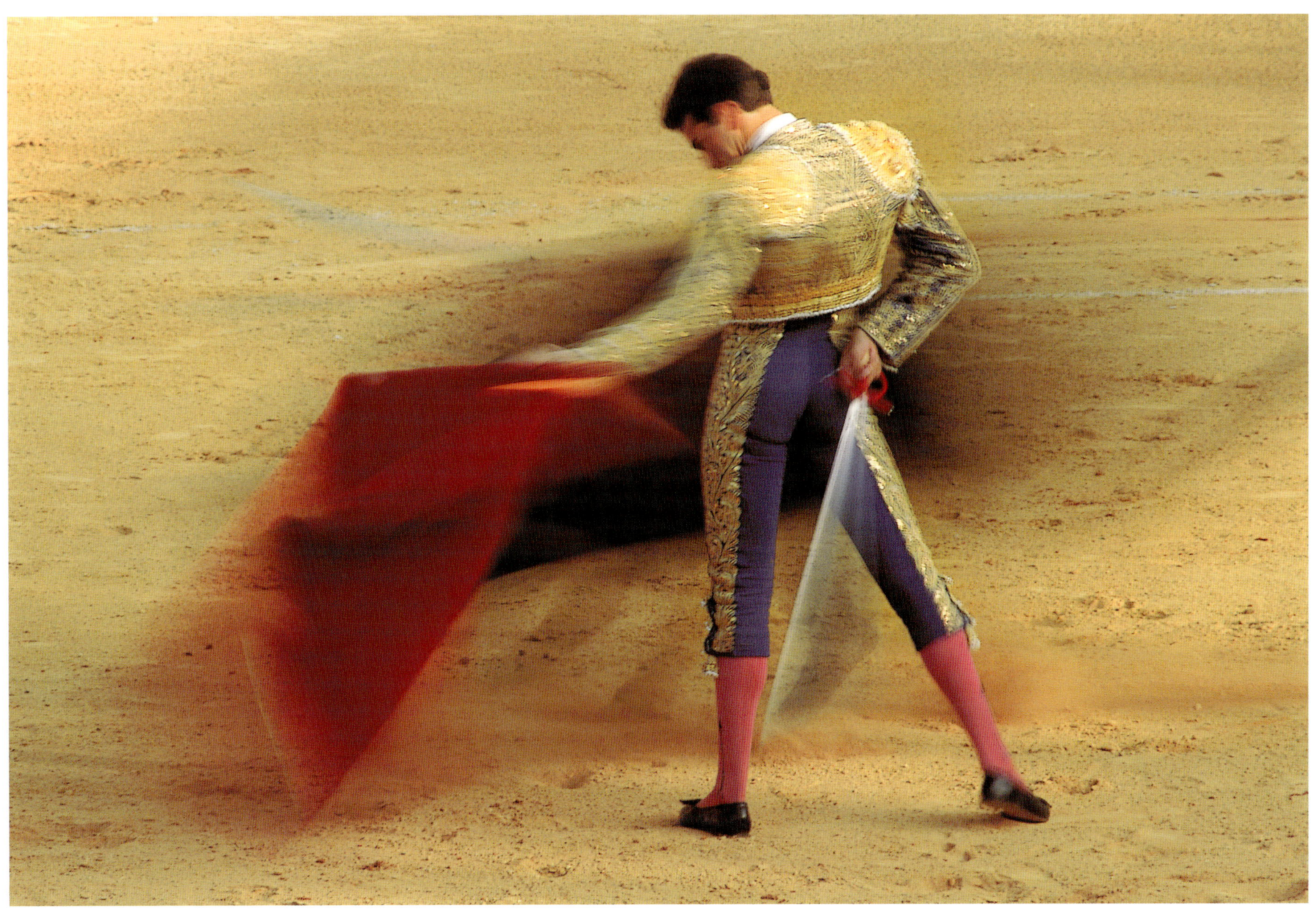

NATURAL PASS / *Natural*
Enrique Ponce; Esquivias, Toledo; March 6, 1993

The eye of the Bull

The curtain

The painter

The bunch of flowers

The light falling

The iron door

Constantly adjusting skirt

Wounding and stabbing

Flying darts

Wings

Insults

Female bullfighter

Hiding shame under tablecloth

Bandaged eyes

The painter's long hair

Two halves, (the half that smiles, the half that sighs).

—Pablo Picasso, Painter, from his 1935 poem translated in 1992

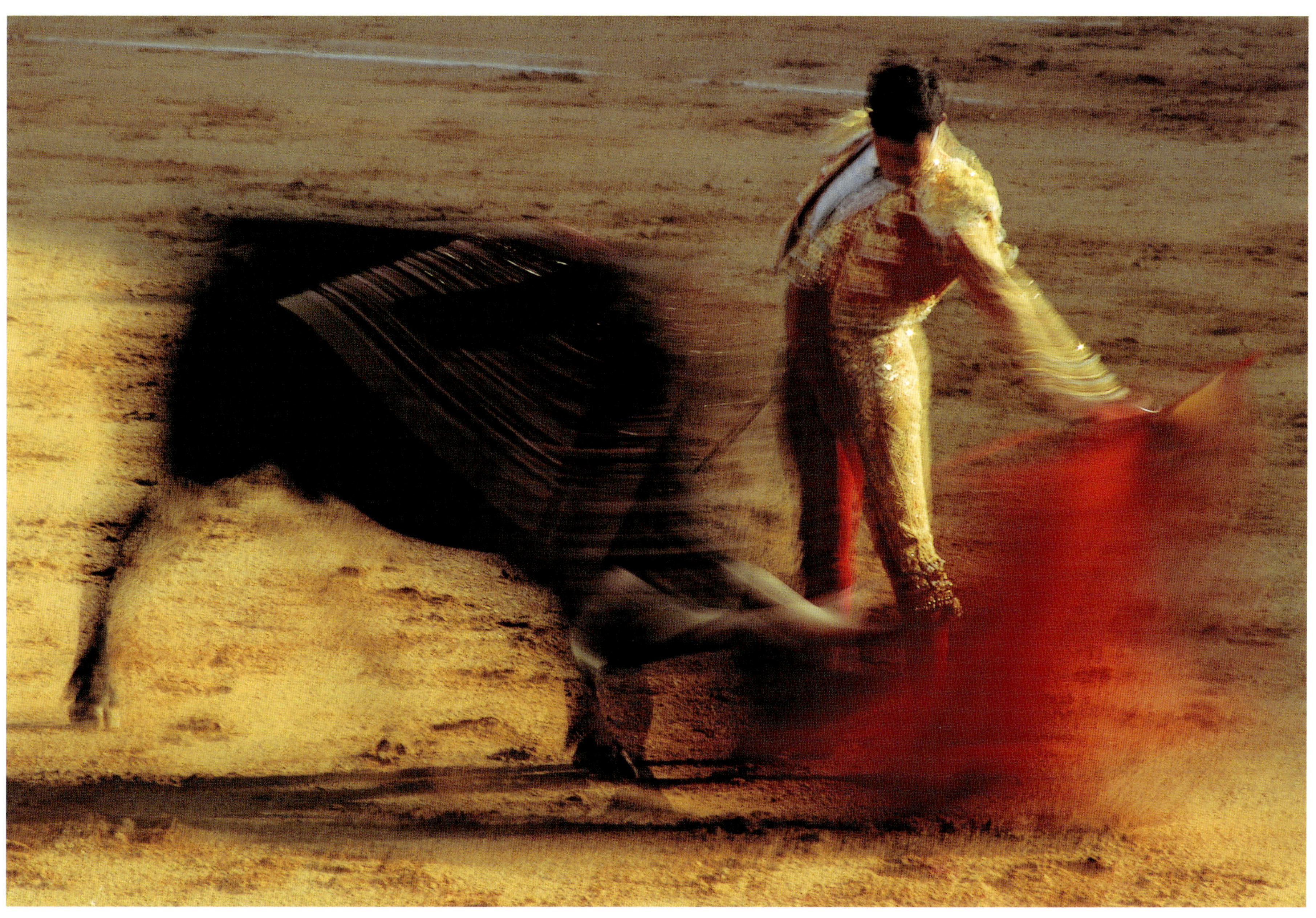

NATURAL PASS / *Natural*
Niño de la Capea; La Glorieta, Salamanca; September 15, 1992

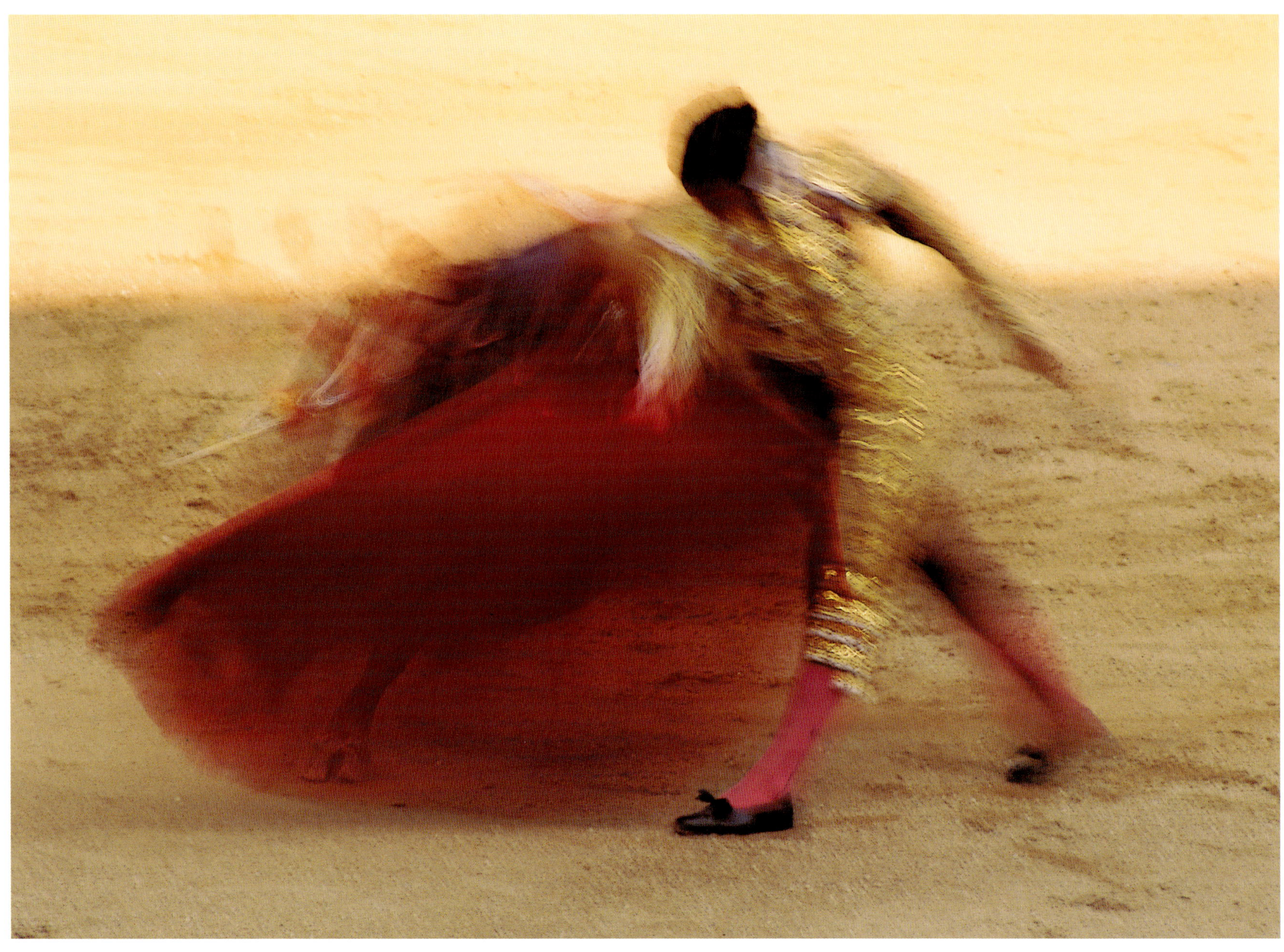

CHEST PASS ON THE RIGHT / *Pase de pecho*
Joselito.;Madrid; June 17, 1993

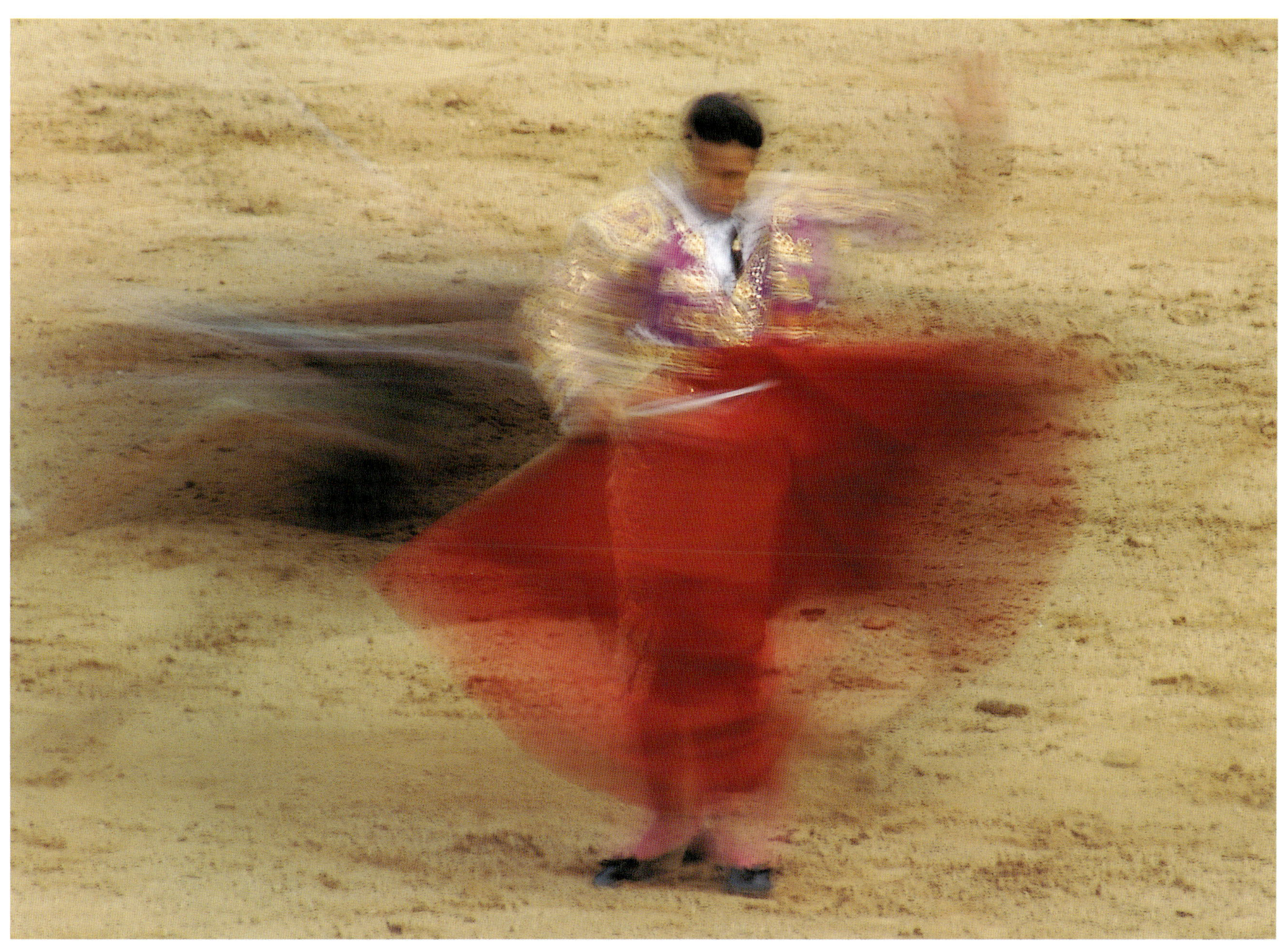

WINDMILL PASS WITH THE RIGHT HAND / *Molinete*
Paco Ojeda; Las Ventas, Madrid; May 18, 1992

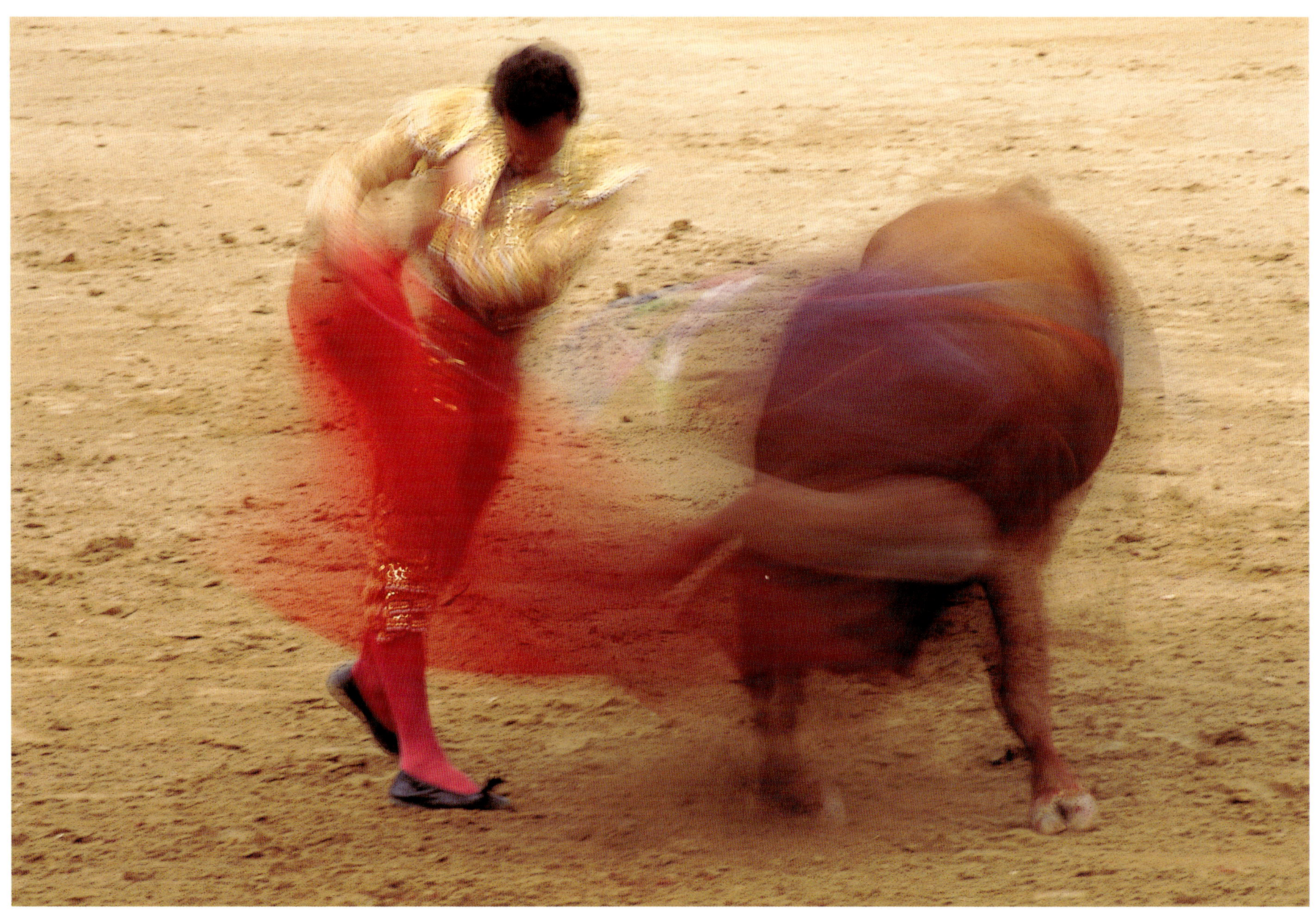

AIDED HIGH PASS / *Ayudado por alto*
José María Manzanares; Las Ventas, Madrid; May 12, 1993

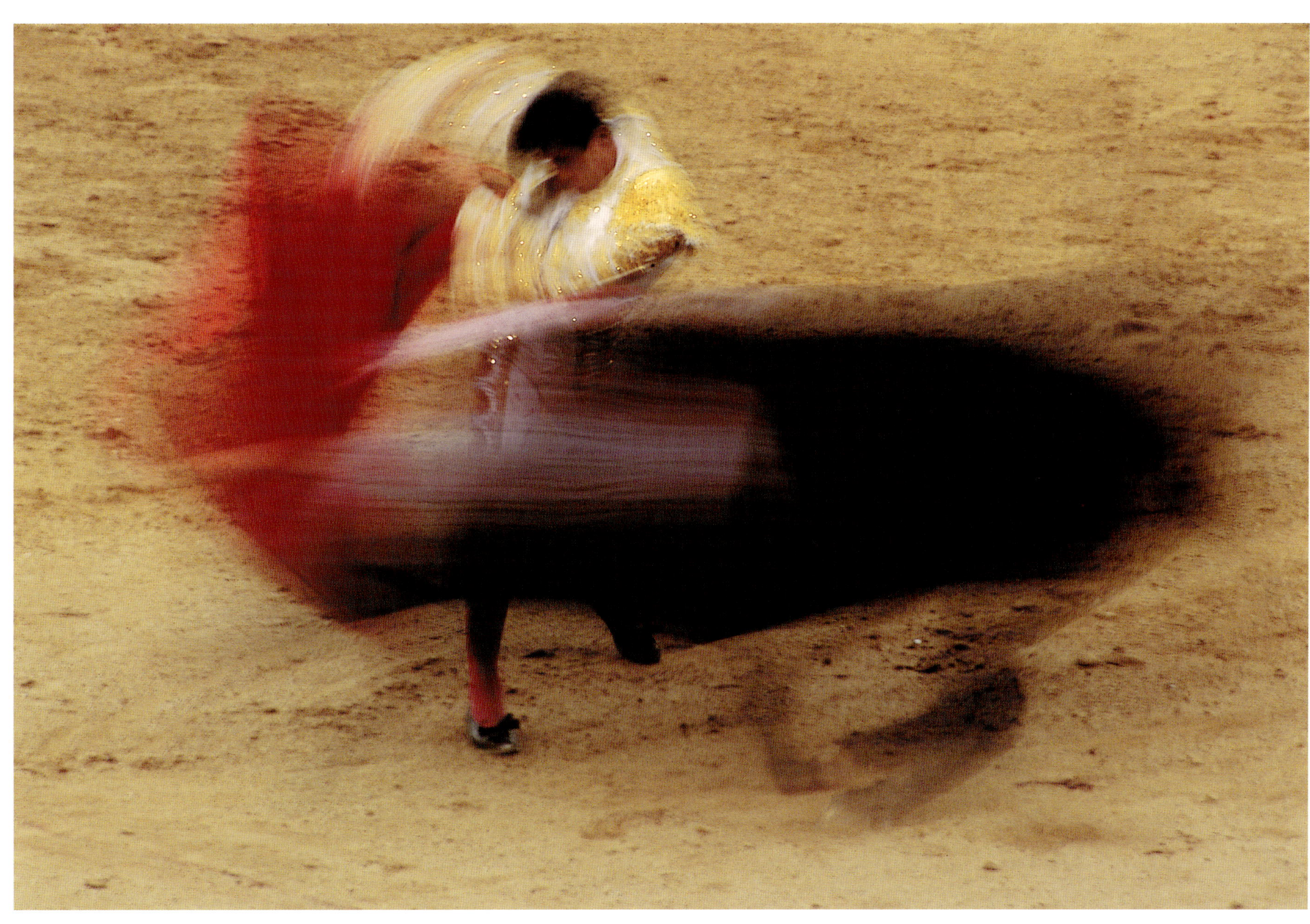

AIDED HIGH PASS / *Ayudado por alto*
Javier Vázquez; Las Ventas, Madrid; May 31, 1993

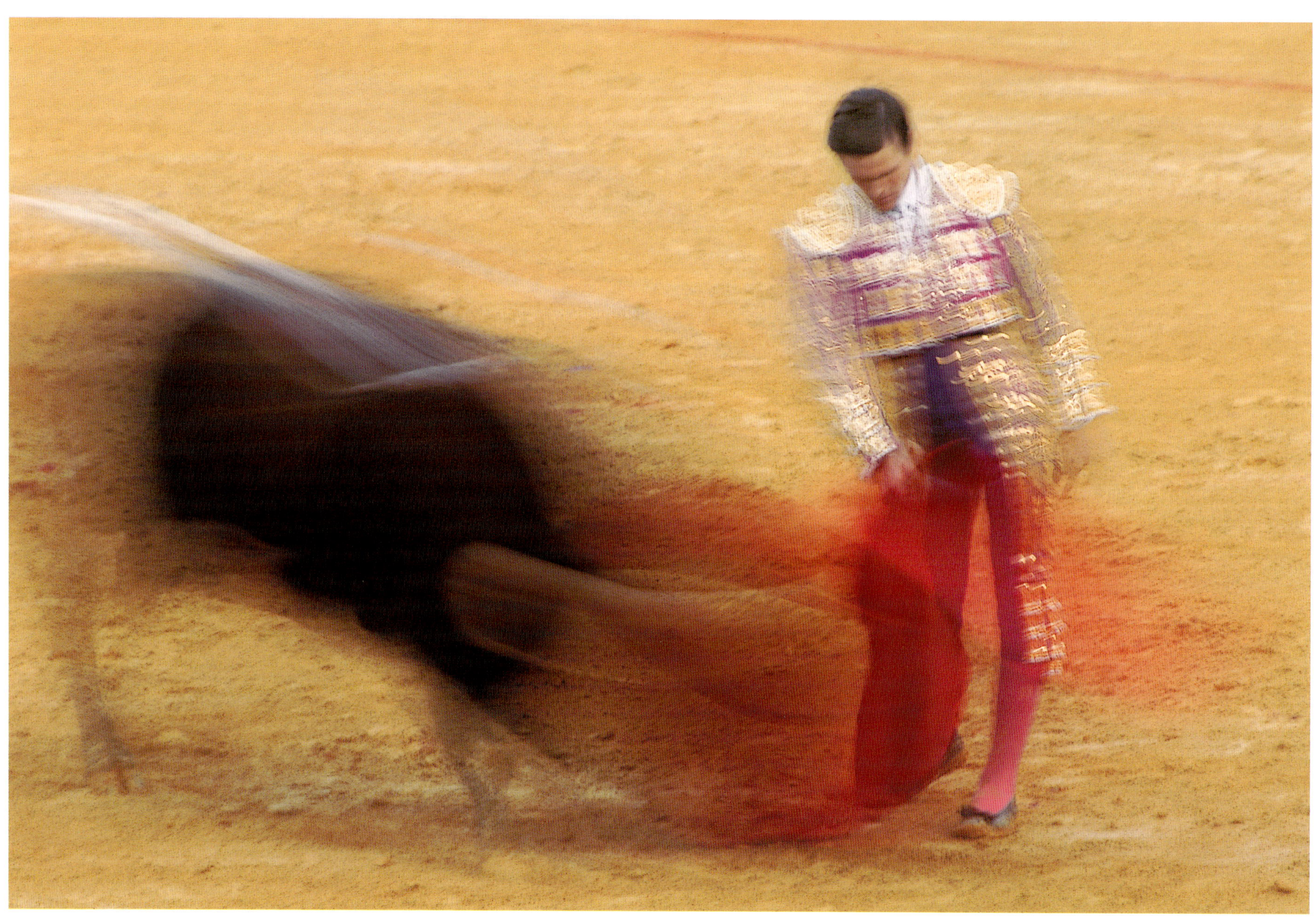

Trincherazo
Espartaco; Real Maestranza, Sevilla; April 29, 1993

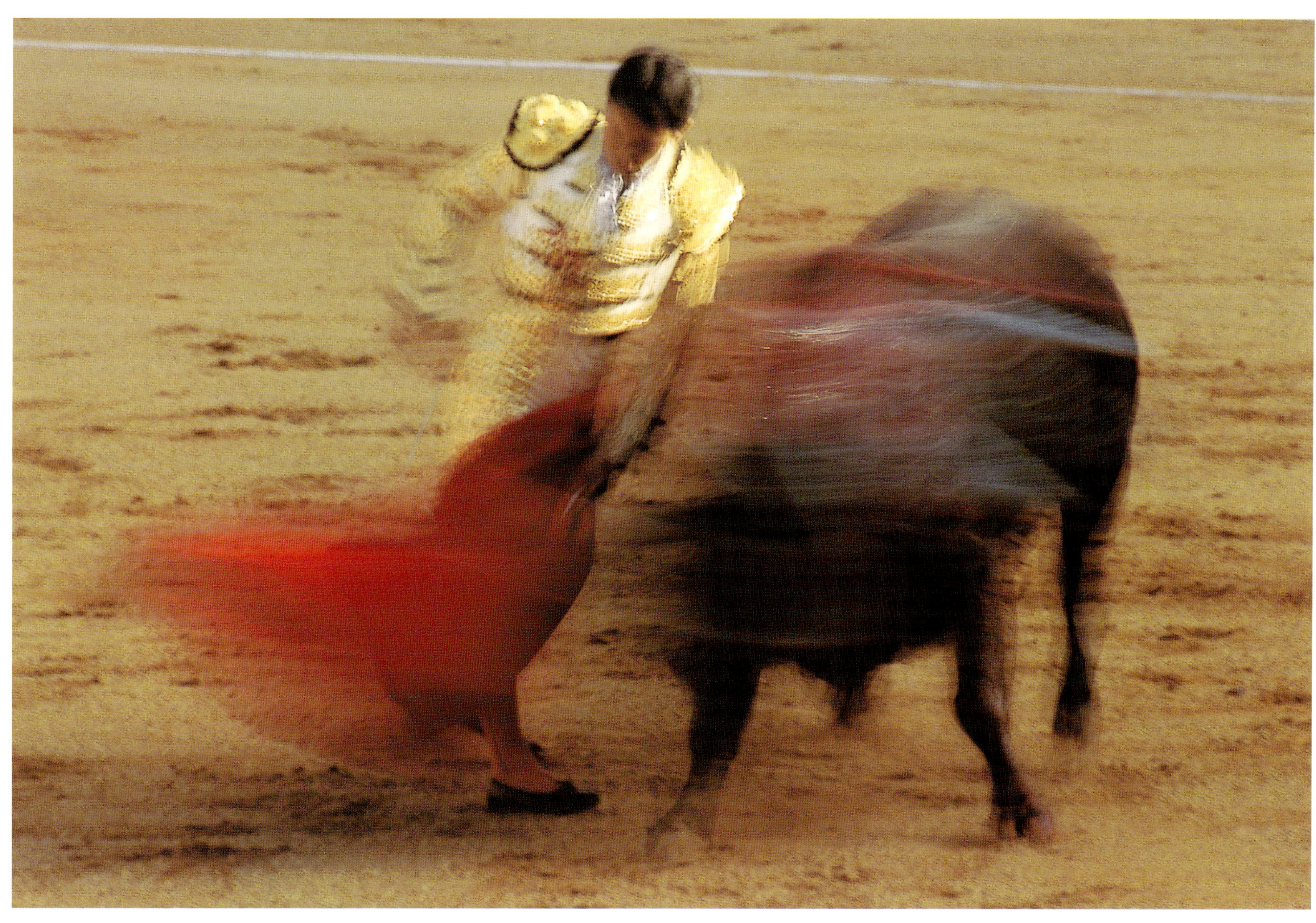

Trincherilla
César Rincón; La Glorieta, Salamanca; September 15, 1992

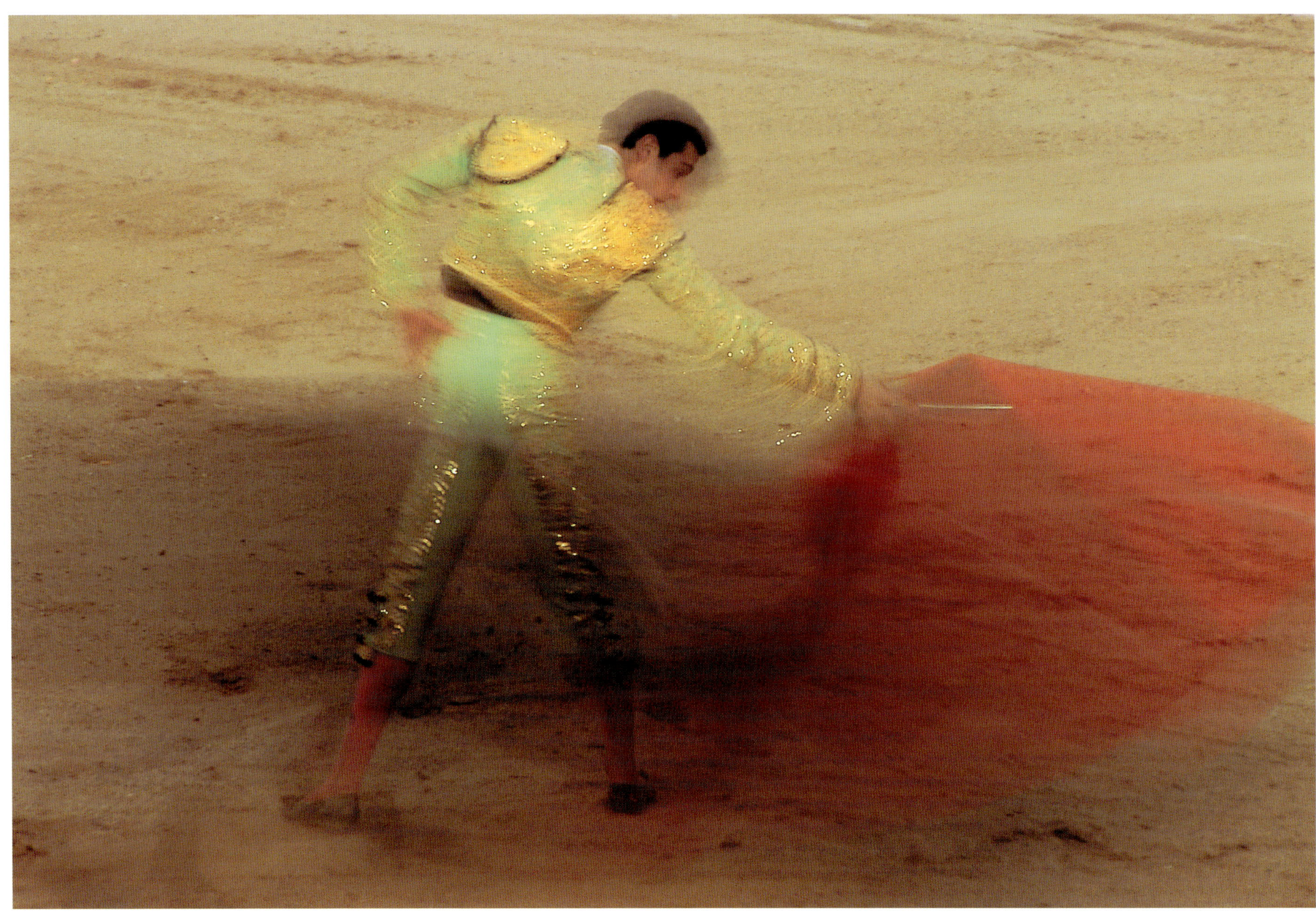

INVERTED CIRCULAR PASS / *Circular invertido*
Enrique Ponce; Guadalajara; September 20, 1992

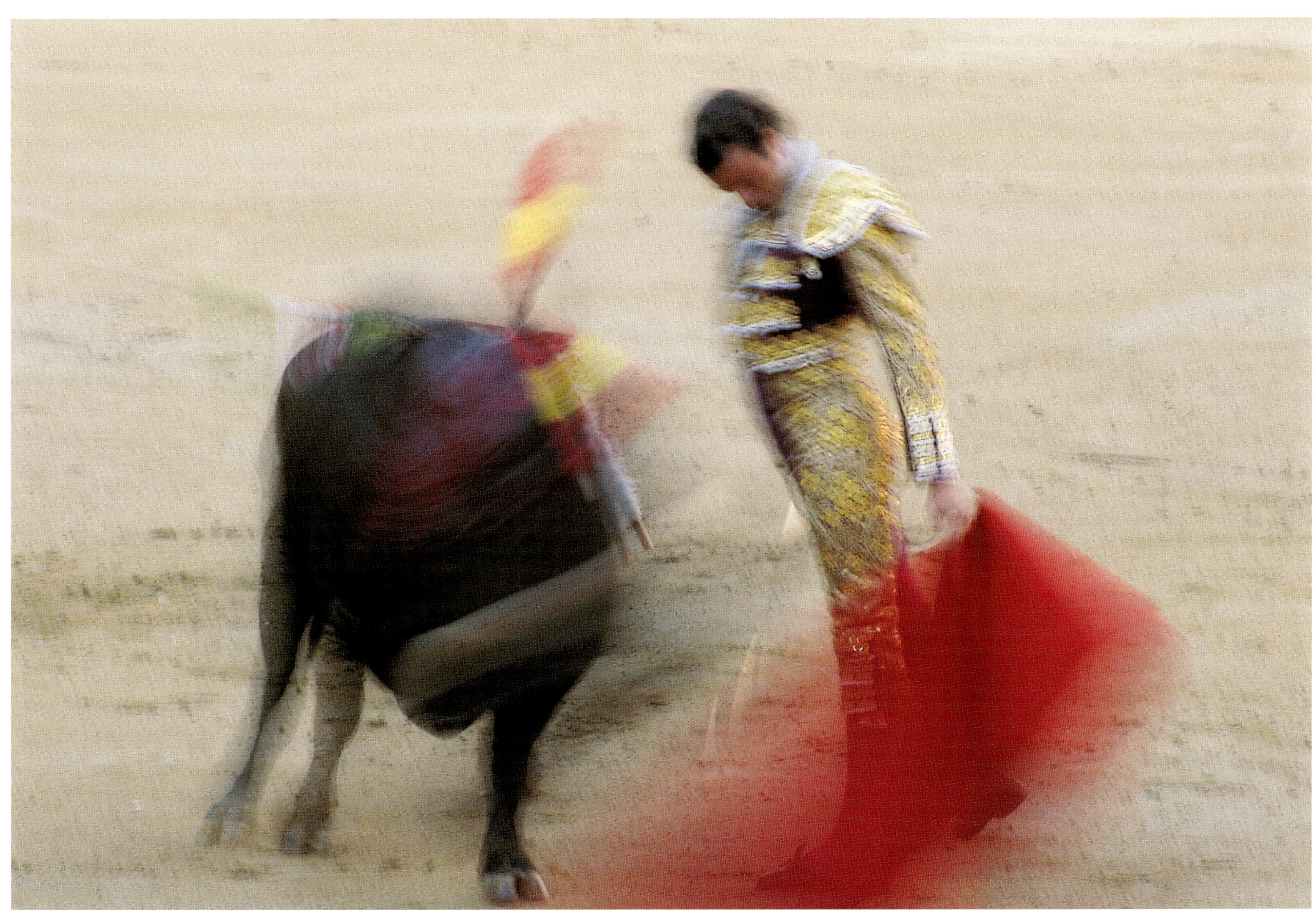

SIGNATURE PASS ON THE LEFT / *Pase de la firma*
Finito de Córdoba; Las Ventas, Madrid; May 29, 2000

It's not the same to talk of bulls as to be in the bullring.

—Spanish proverb

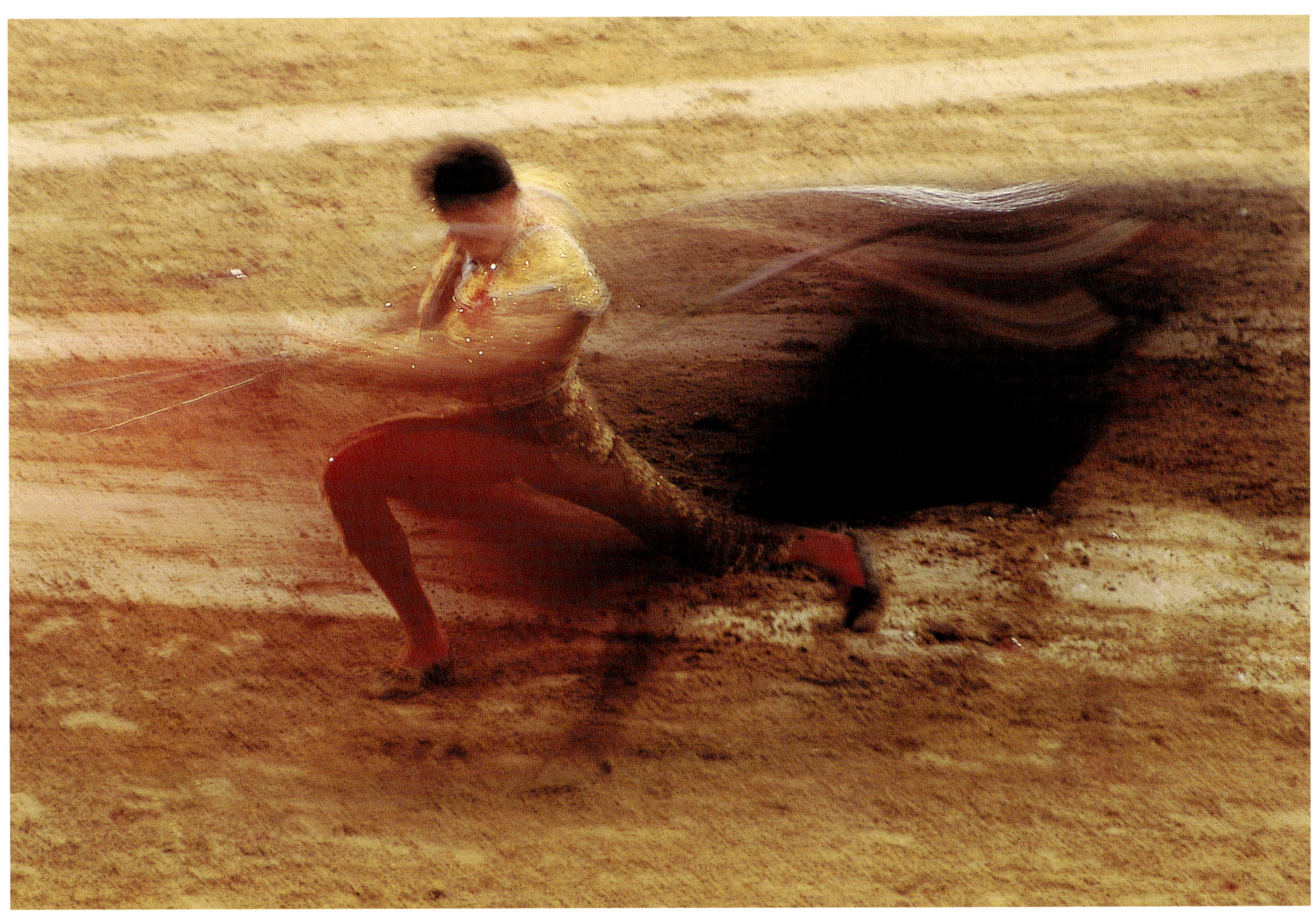

AIDED LOW PASS / *Ayudado por bajo*
Enrique Ponce; Las Ventas, Madrid; May 24, 1993

"They say that the torero goes to the ring to earn money, prestige, glory, applause…but this is not true. He goes to the ring to be alone with the bull, an animal he both fears and adores, and to whom he has much to say."

—Federico Garcia Lorca, Spanish poet, on his "Poem of the Bull"

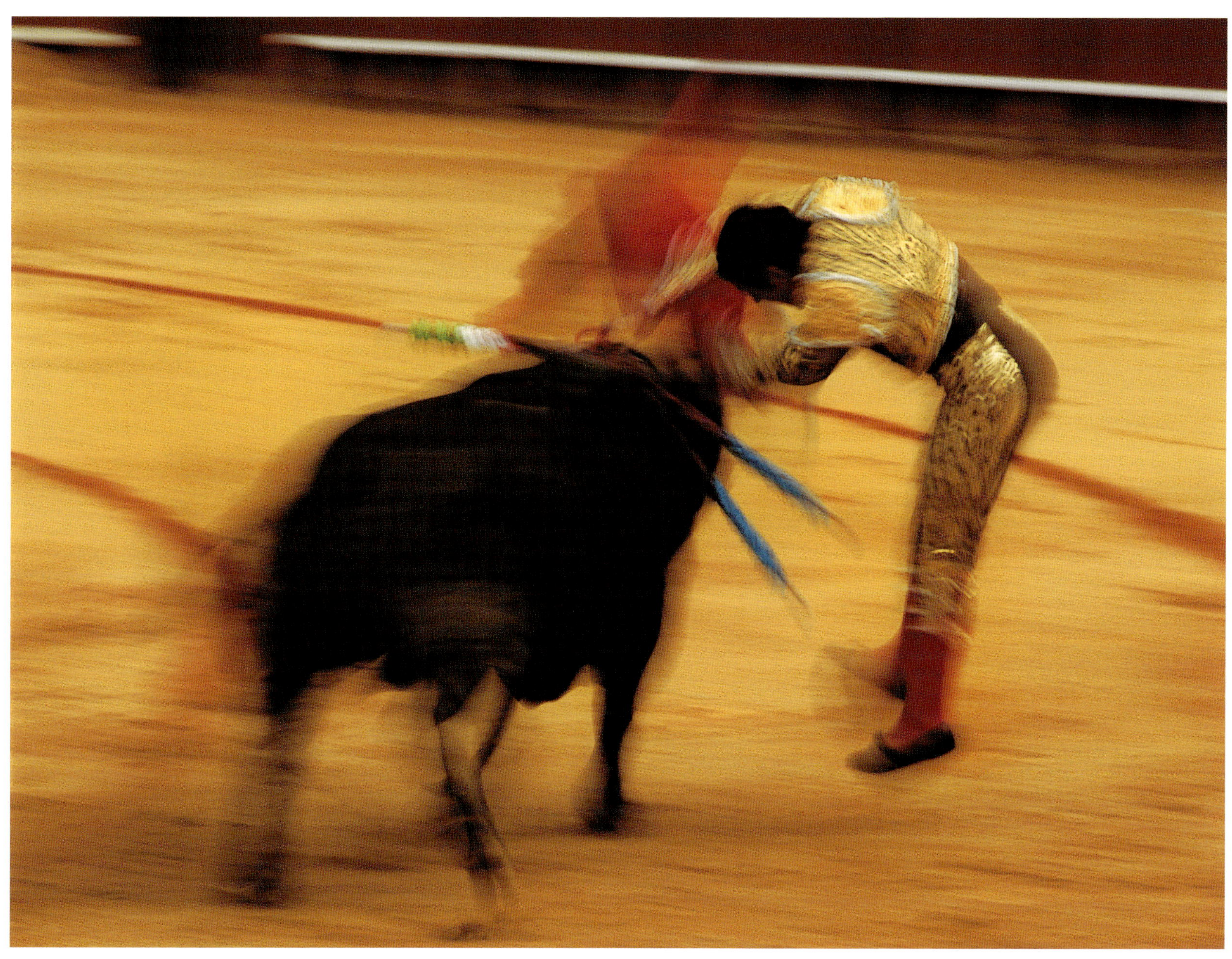

SWORD THRUST / *Estocada al volapie*
Joselito; Real Maestranza, Sevilla; April 30, 1993

Sequence Three

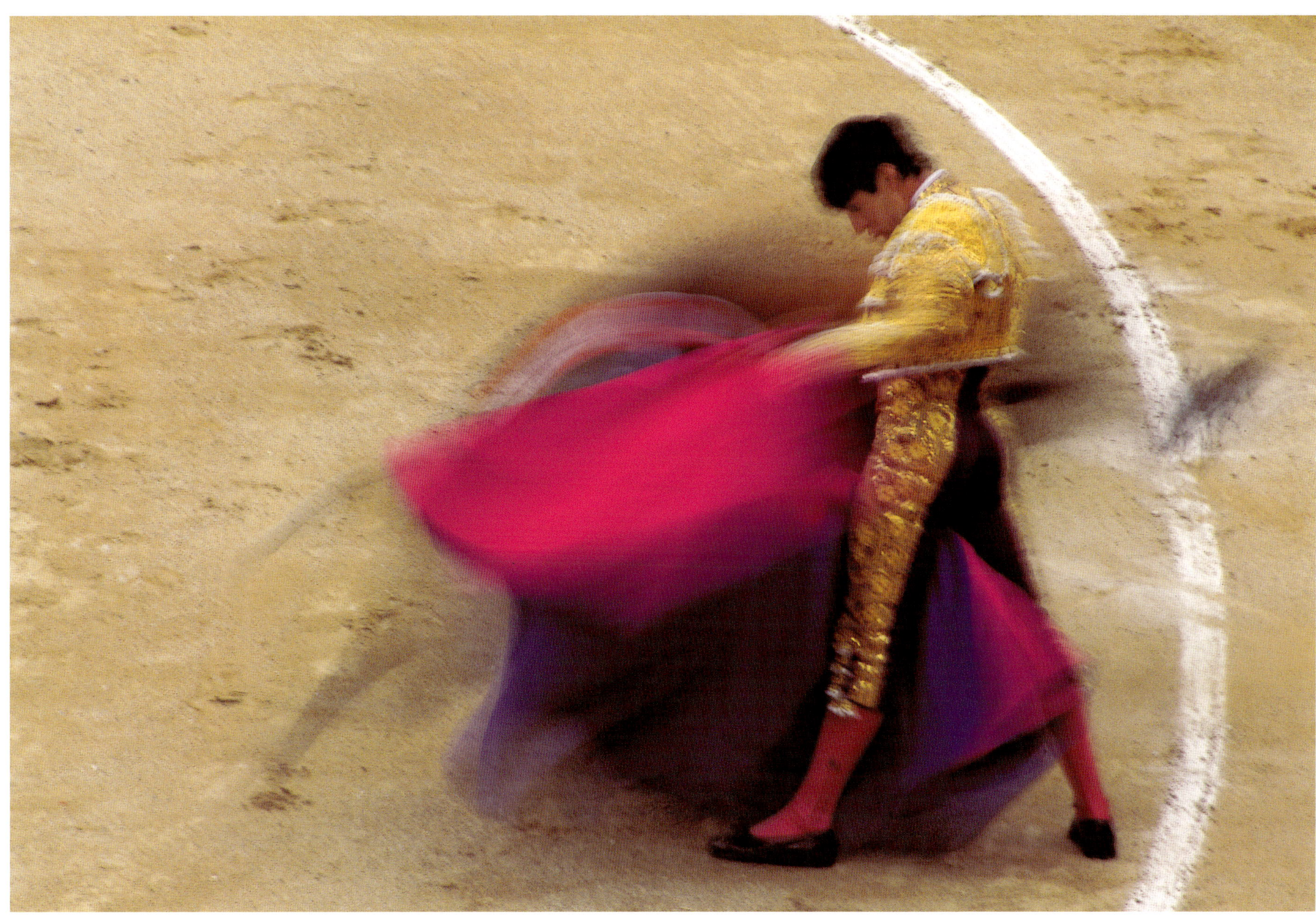

Verónica
Joselito; Las Ventas, Madrid; June 19. 1997

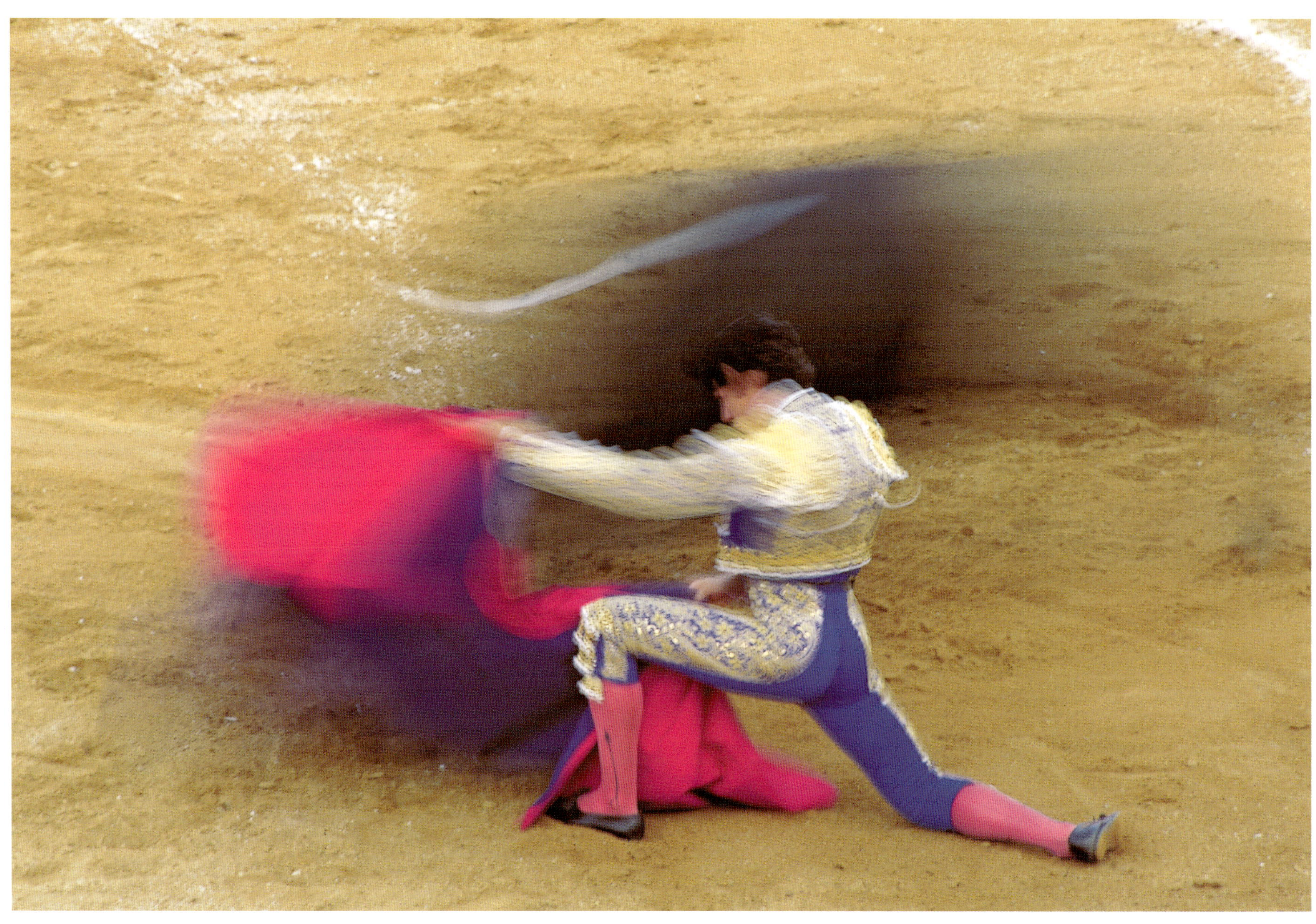

KNEELING VERONICA / *Verónica de rodillas*
Joselito; La Tercera, San Sebastián de los Reyes, Madrid; September 2, 1994

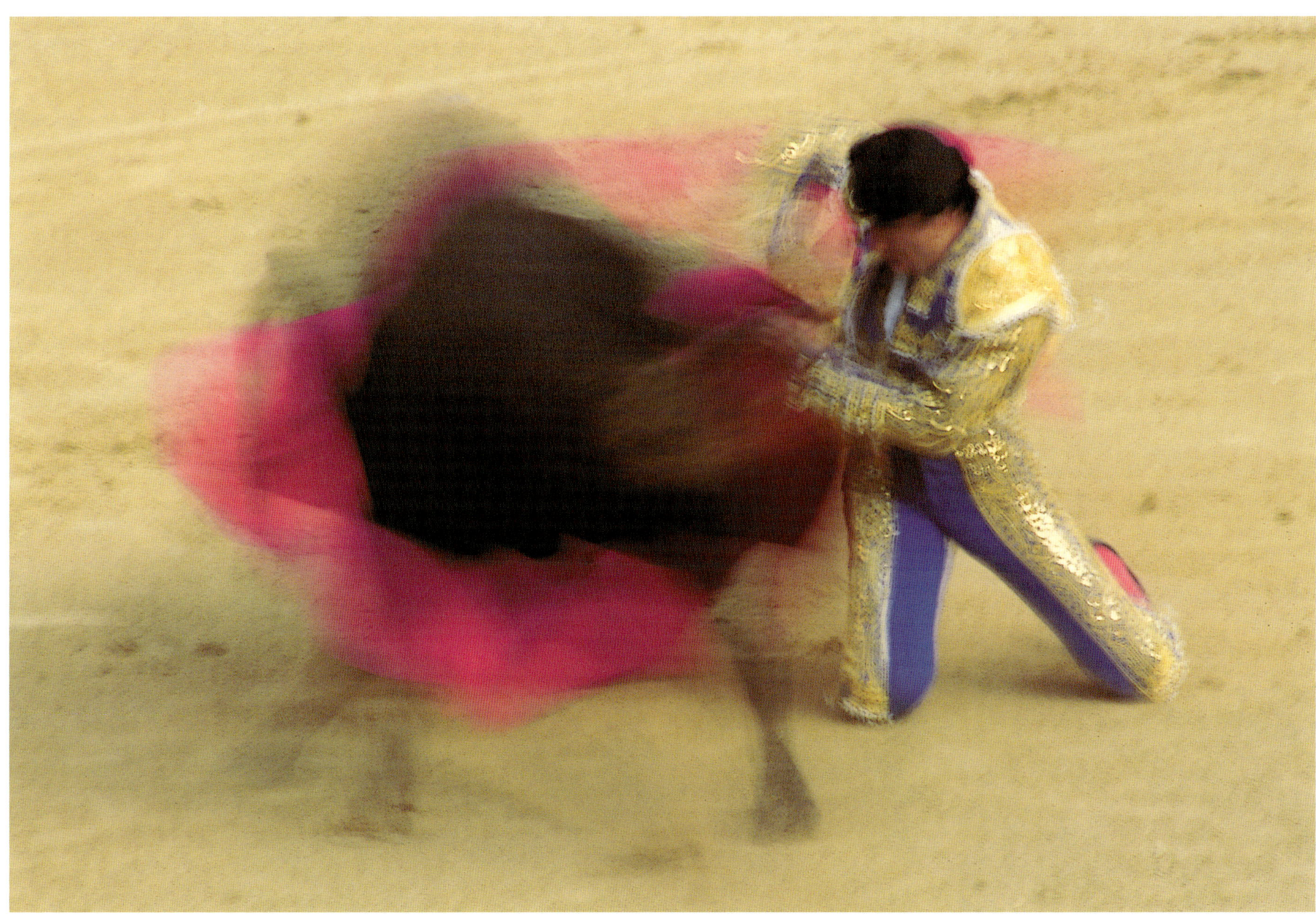

KNEELING HALF VERONICA / *Media Verónica de rodillas*
Ortega Cano; Las Ventas, Madrid; May 25, 1992

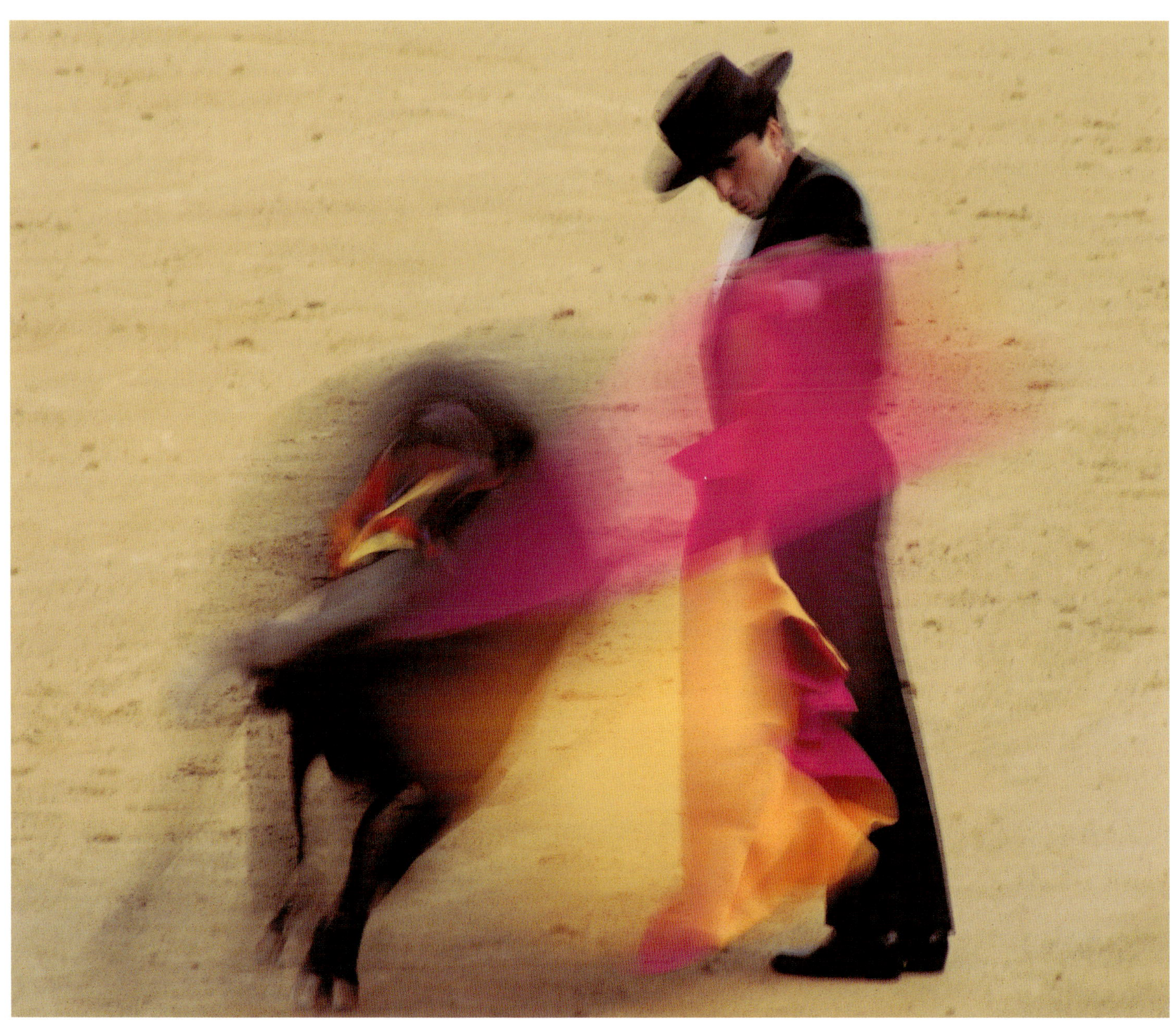

CAPE LANCE WITH FEET TOGETHER / *Lance*
Ortega Cano; Las Ventas, Madrid; October 2, 1992

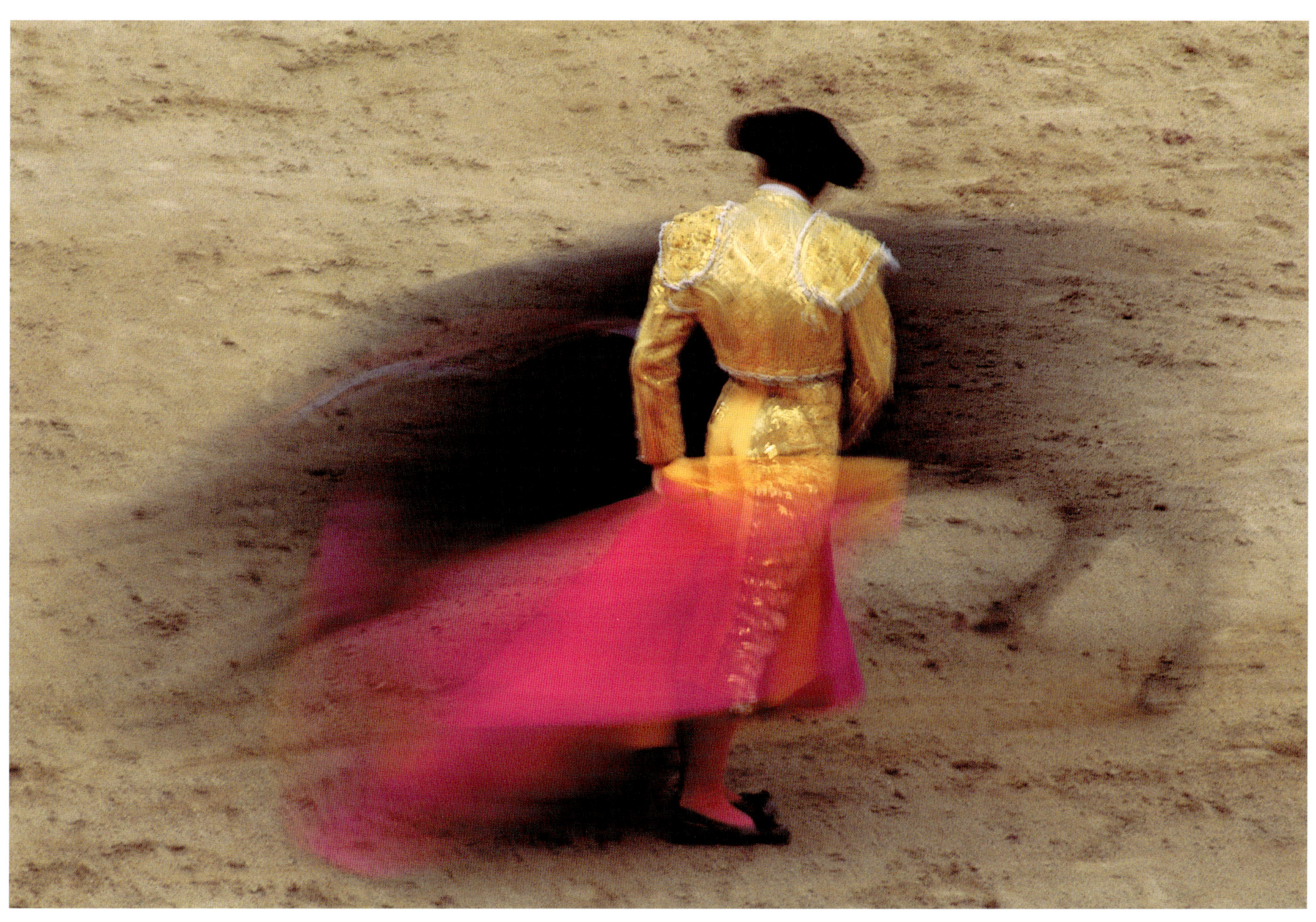

MEDIA VERONICA WITH FEET TOGETHER / *Media Verónica a pies juntos*
Juan Mora; Las Ventas, Madrid; May 18, 2000

"Bullfighting is the art which best expresses life, death, astuteness, fear, terror, agony, intelligence, and good taste. There is not a ritual in the world as didactic, tragic, and beautiful as are the bulls."

—Albert Boadella, Theater director, Playwright

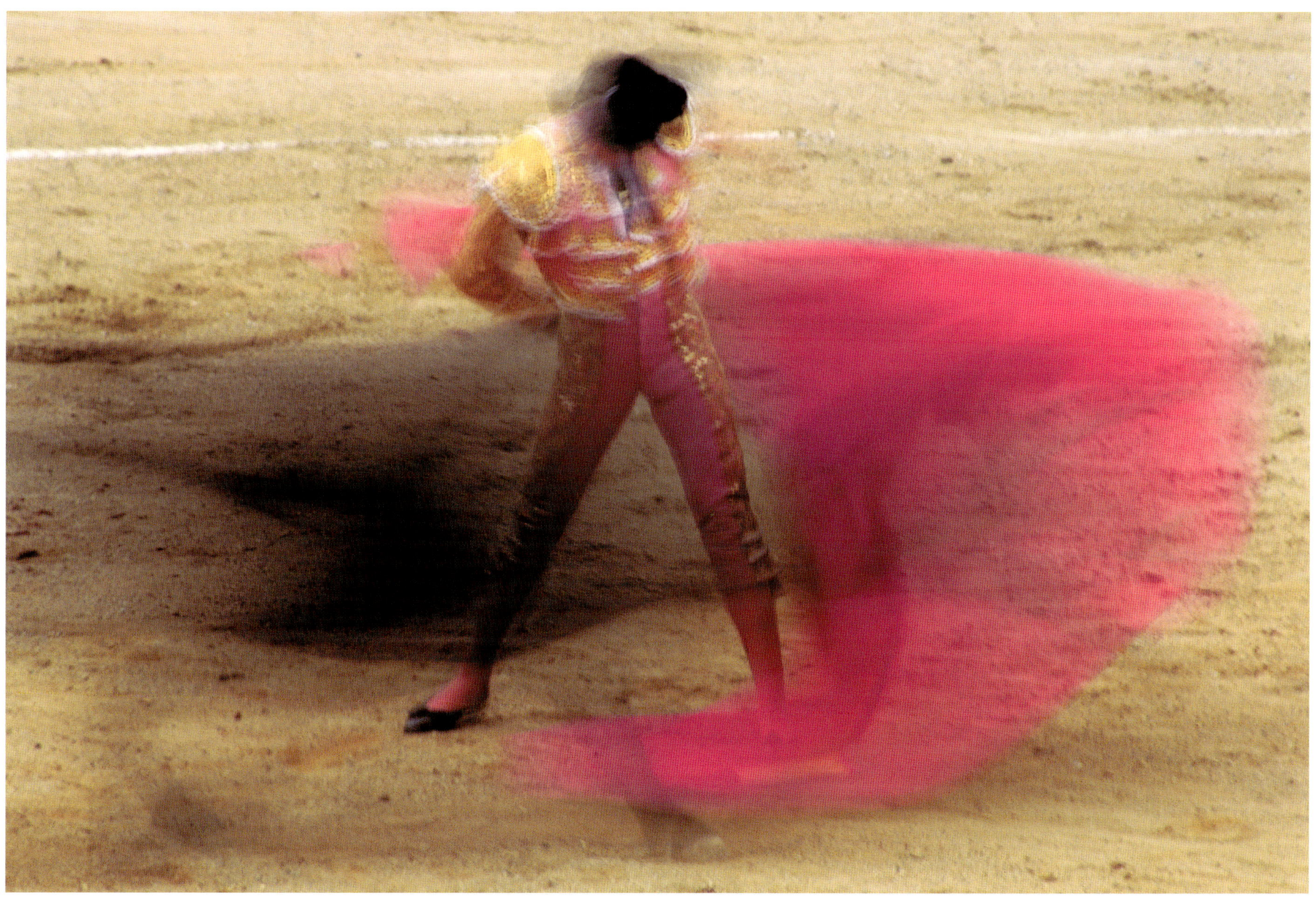

Revolera
Enrique Ponce; Segovia; June 30, 1993

"An actor and a torero (bullfighter) meet. The actor says to the torero, 'actually our jobs are really similar. We both appear before audiences and we could both lose our lives.' The torero answers 'that's true. Only you can die several times—but not I."

—Anonymous

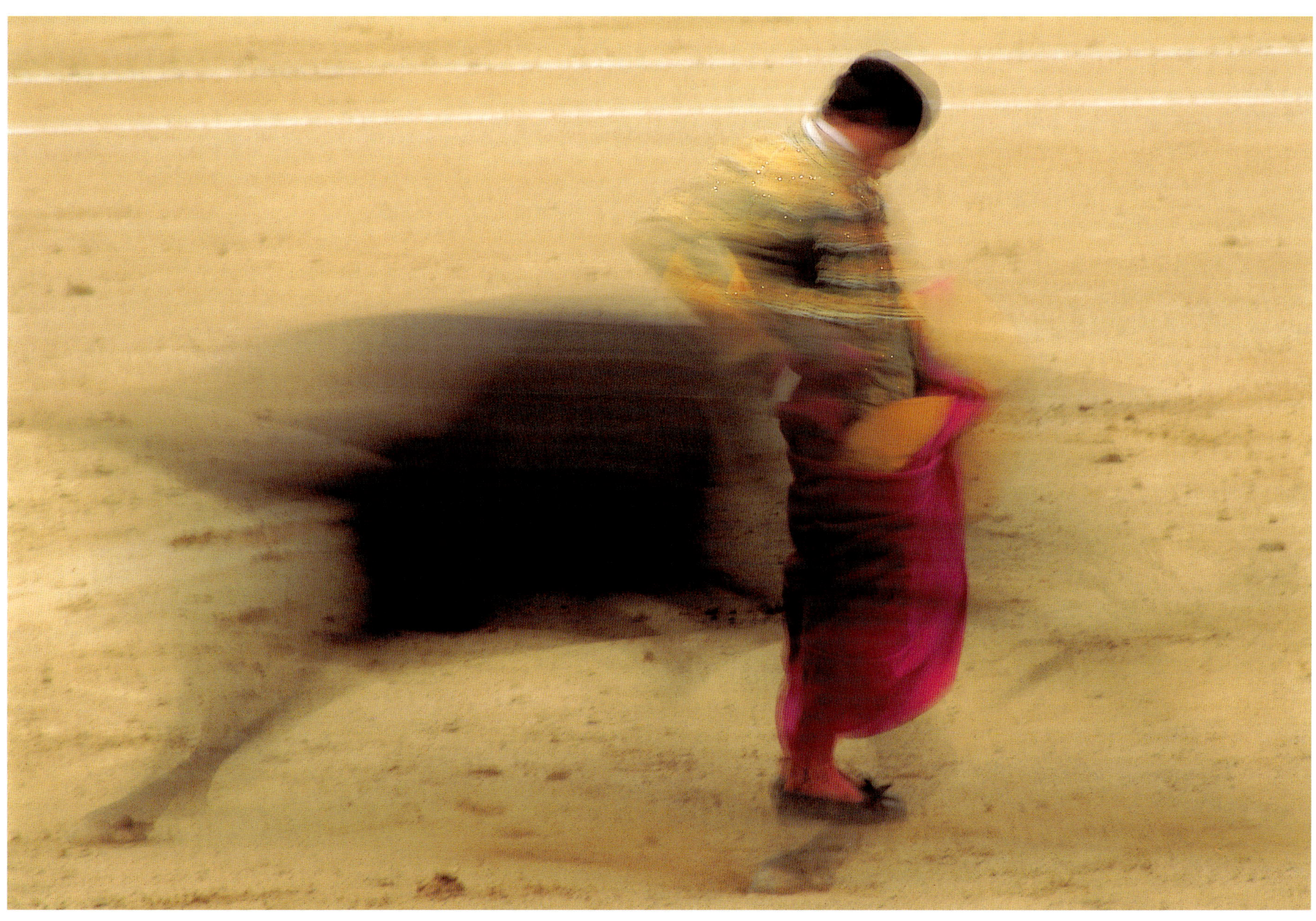

Chicuelina
Morante de la Puebla; Las Ventas, Madrid; May 29, 2000

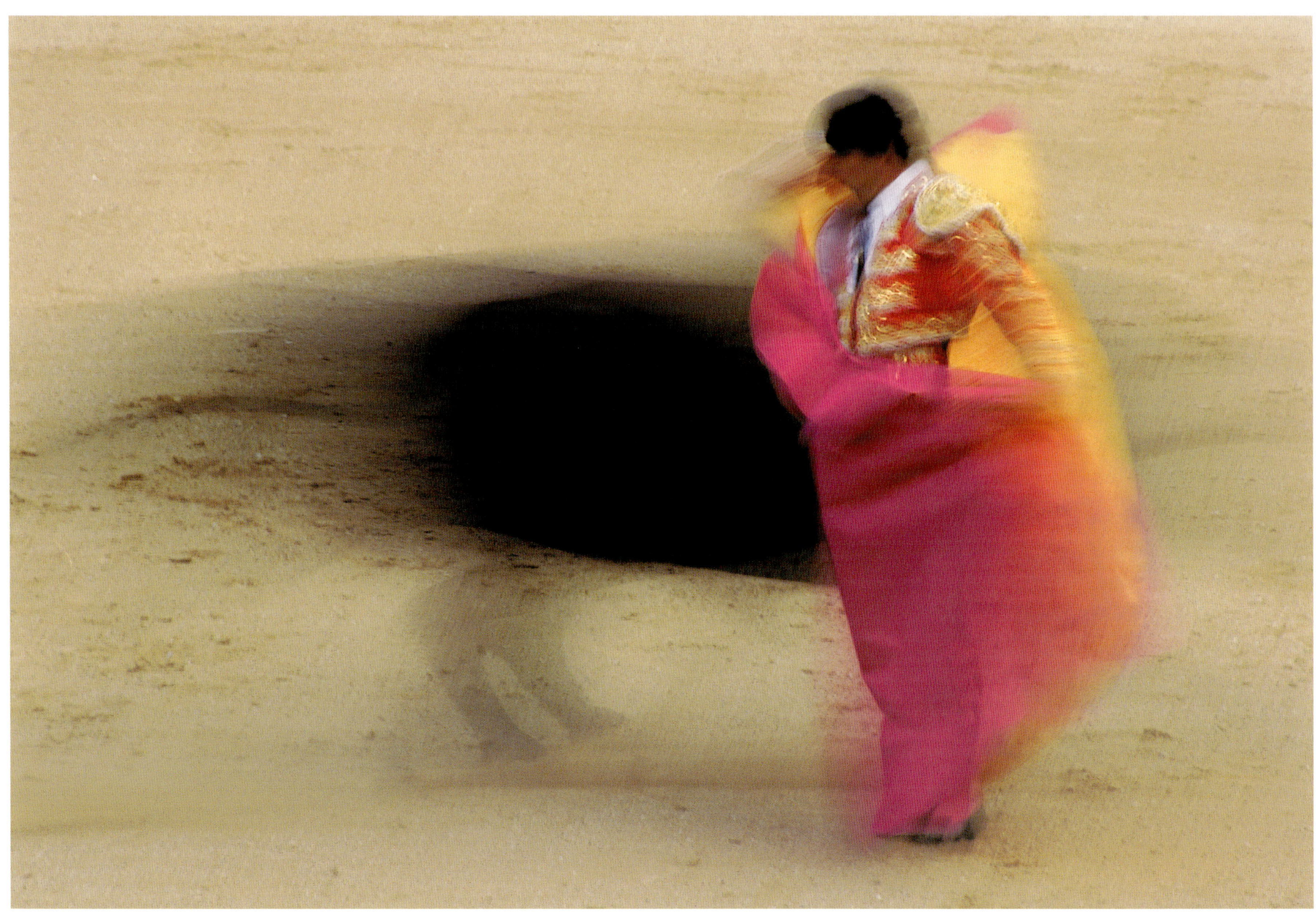

Chicuelina
Niño de la Taurina; Las Ventas, Madrid; April 3, 1994

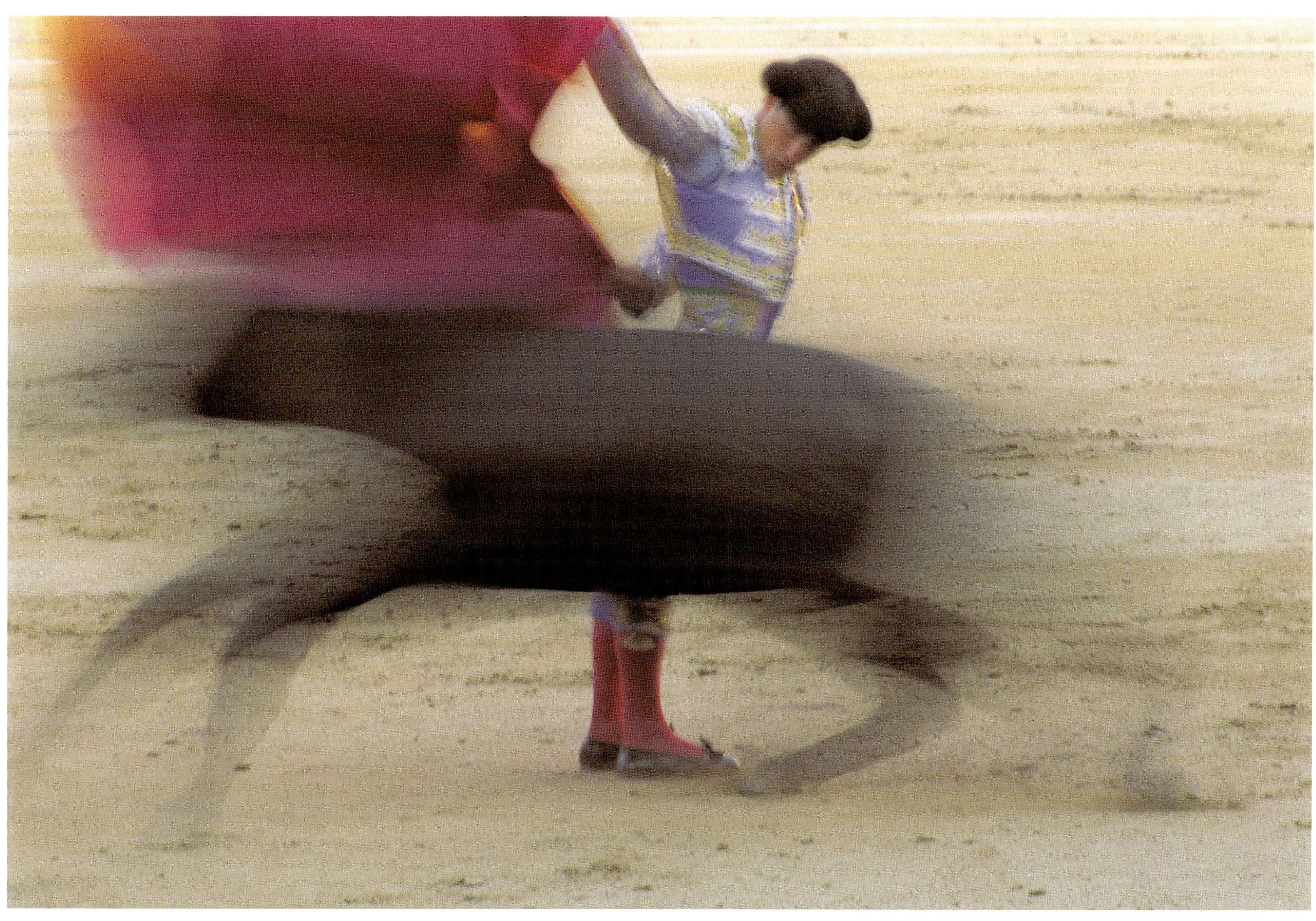

Saltillera
Miguel Abellán; Las Ventas, Madrid; May 29, 2000

"Bullfighting is the only art in which the artist is in danger of death and in which
the degree of brilliance in the performance is left to the fighters honor."

—Ernest Hemingway, Writer

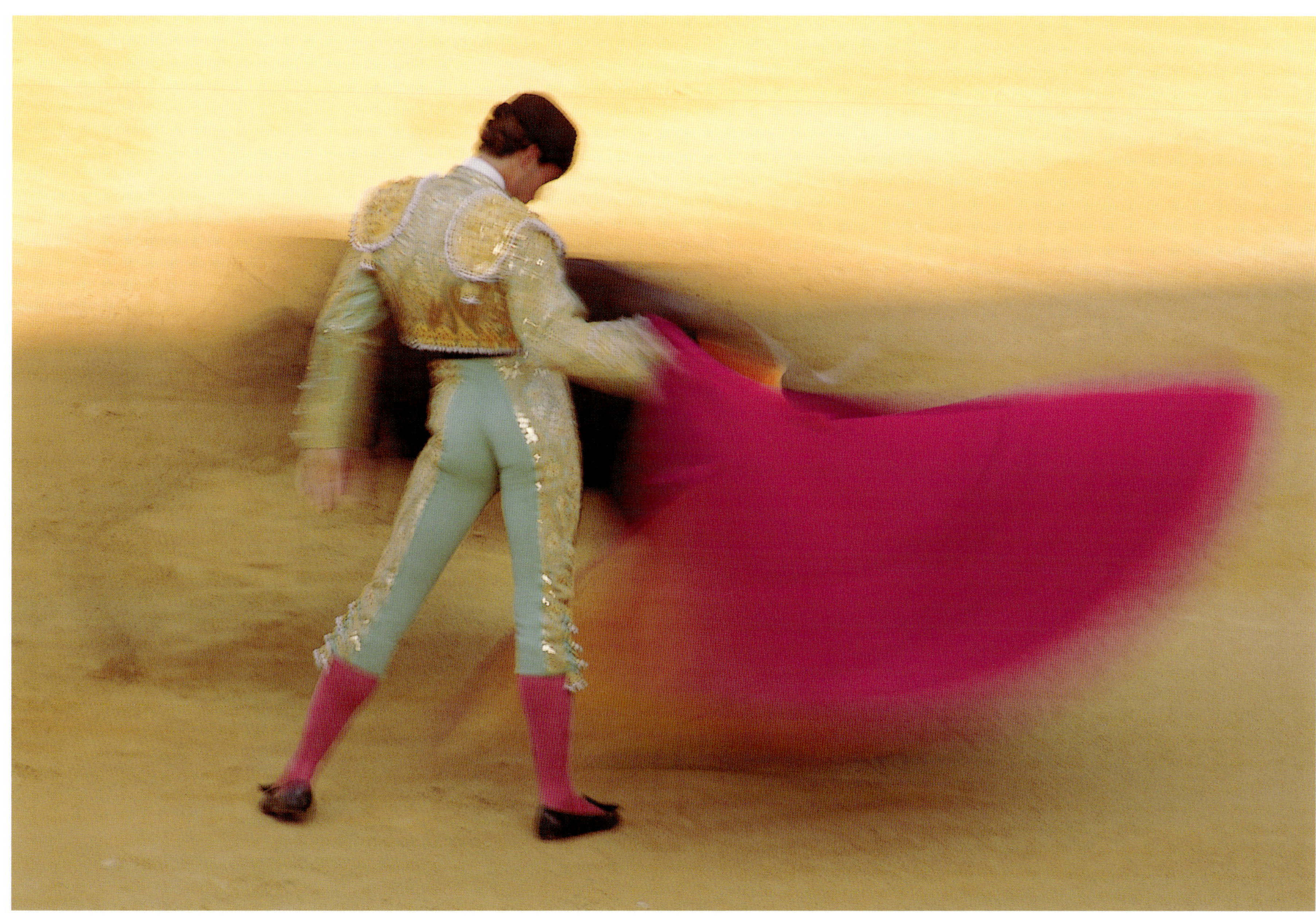

LONG PASS / *Larga*
Manolo Carrión; Valencia; July 22, 1993

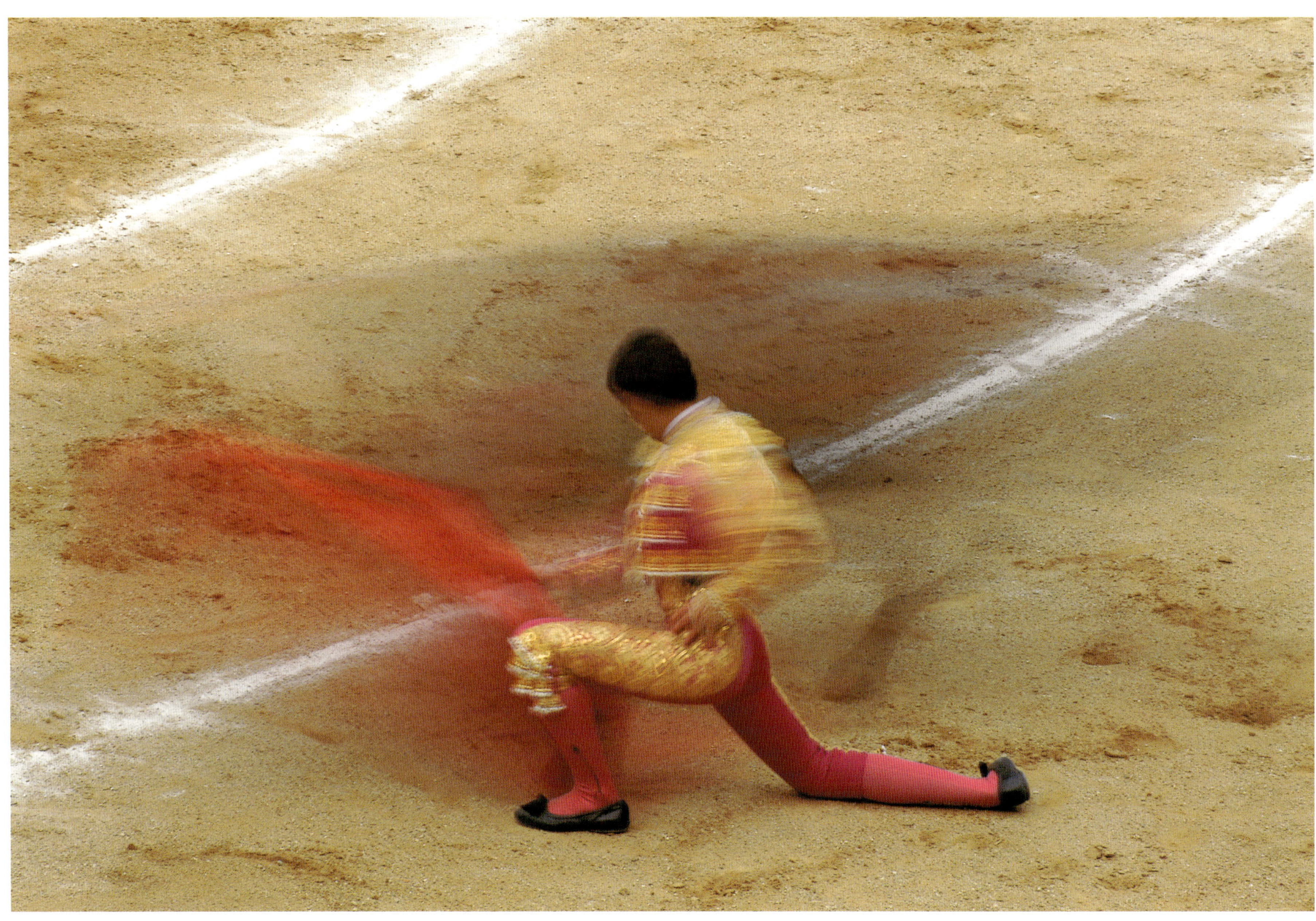

DOUBLING PASS WITH ONE KNEE ON THE GROUND / *Doblón*
Manolo Carrión; Las Ventas, Madrid; July 4, 1993

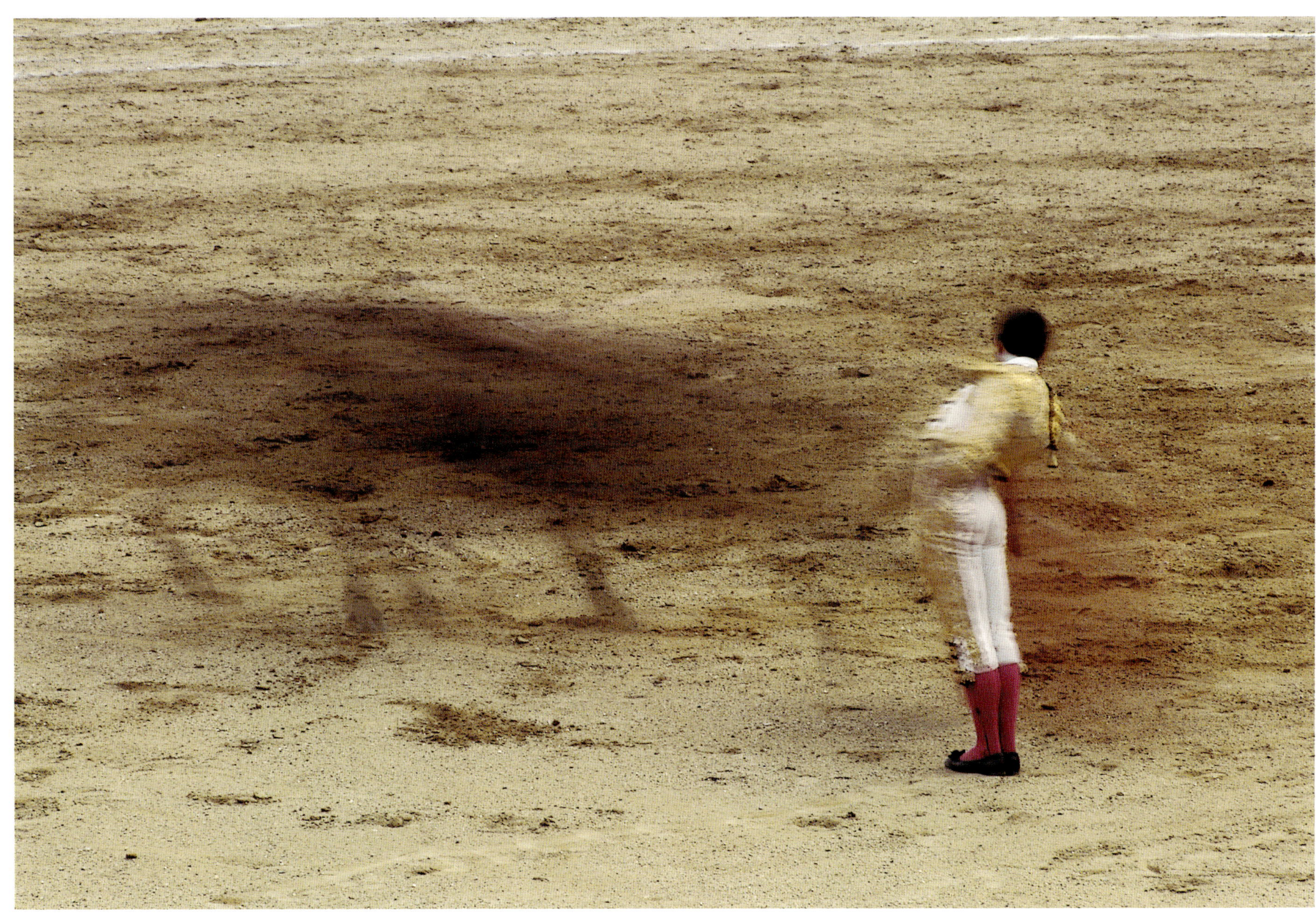

CITING ON THE RIGHT / *Citando a la derecha*
César Rincón; Las Ventas, Madrid; May 22, 1991

"He always wanted to be a bullfighter, but he only made it to 'banderillero.'"

—Pedro Almodovar from his film, "Talk to Her"

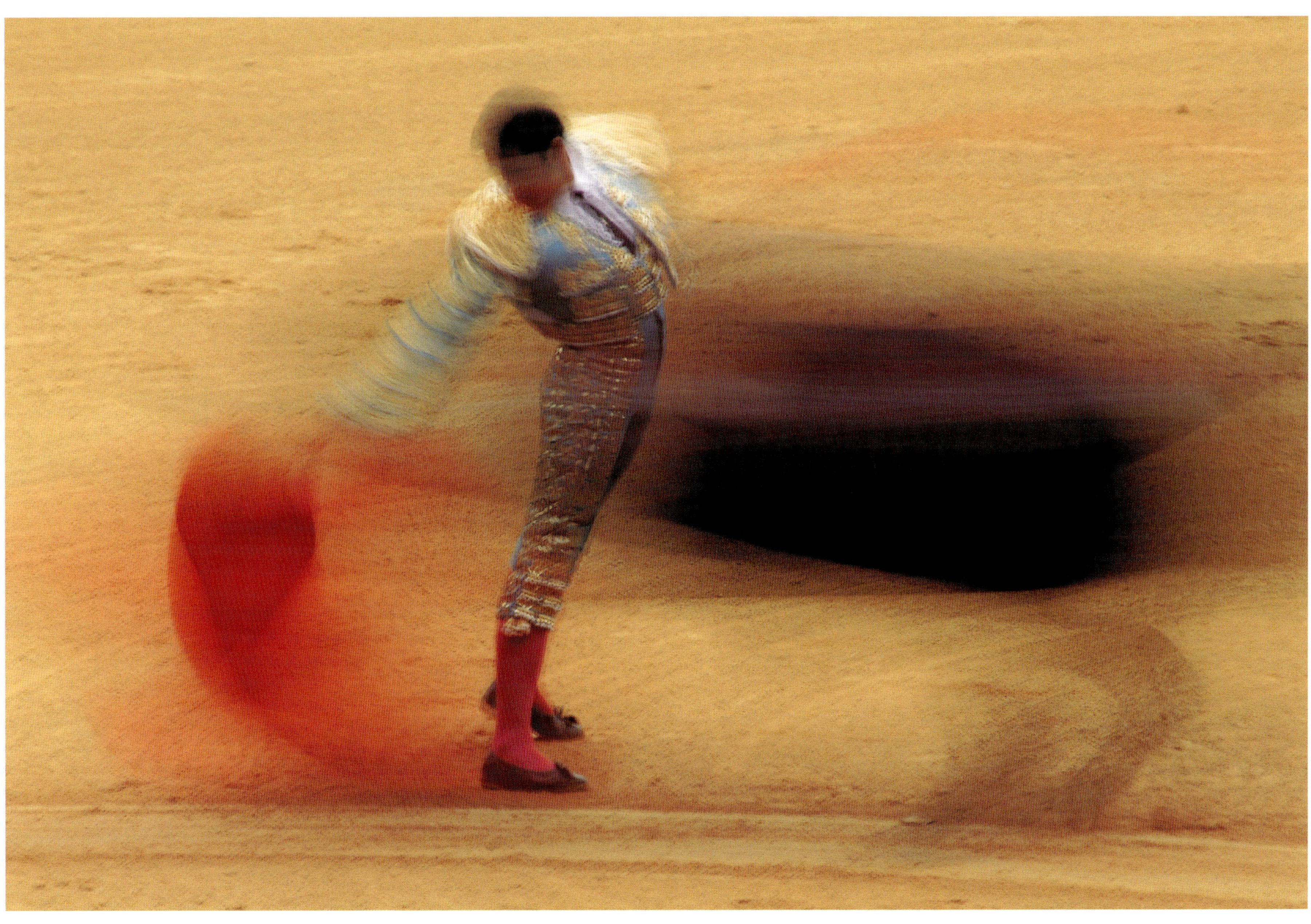

RIGHT-HANDED PASS / *Derechazo*
César Rincón; Real Maestranza, Sevilla; April 26, 1993

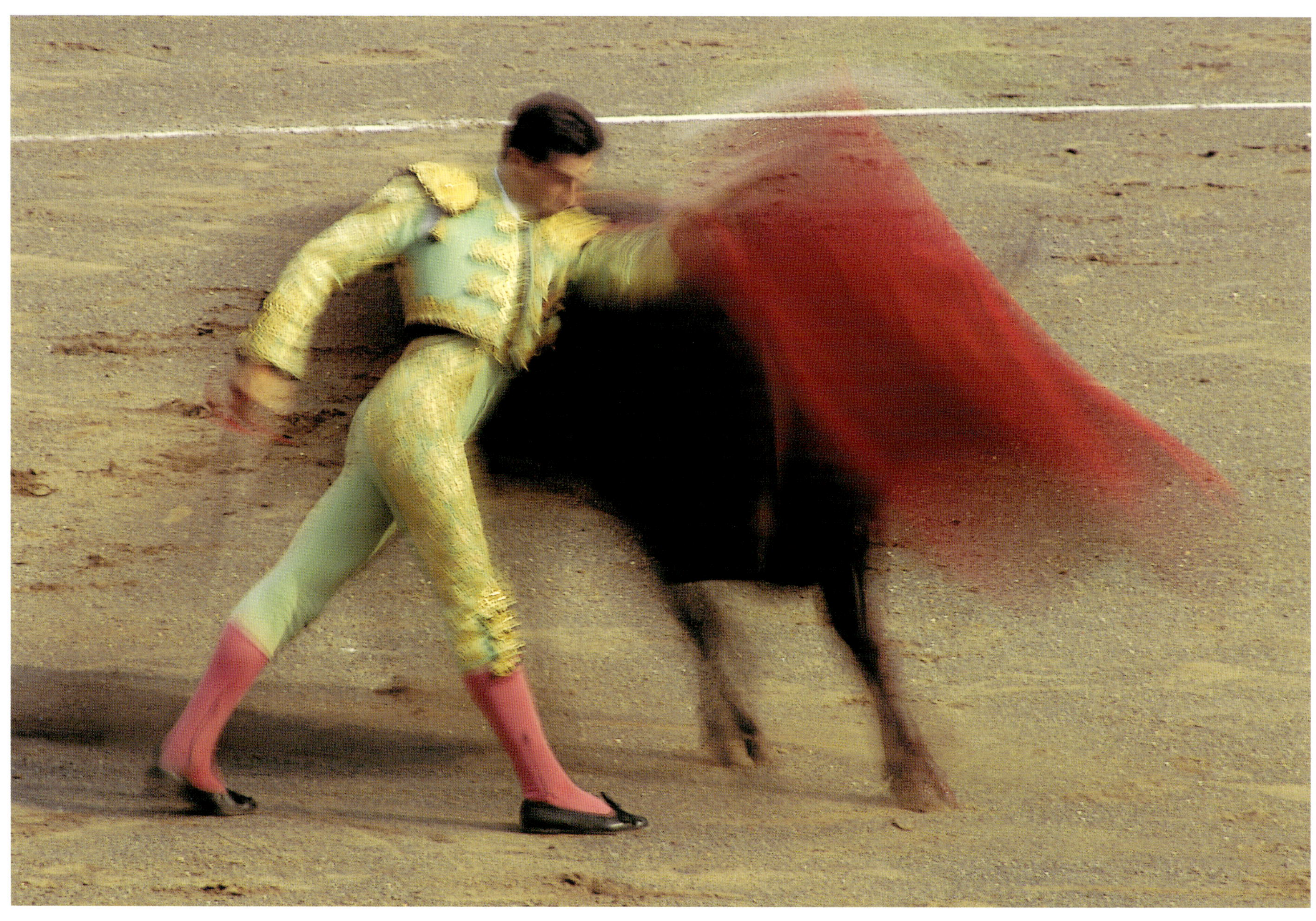

CHEST PASS ON THE LEFT / *Pase de pecho*
Enrique Ponce; Vista Alegre, Bilbao; June 7, 1992

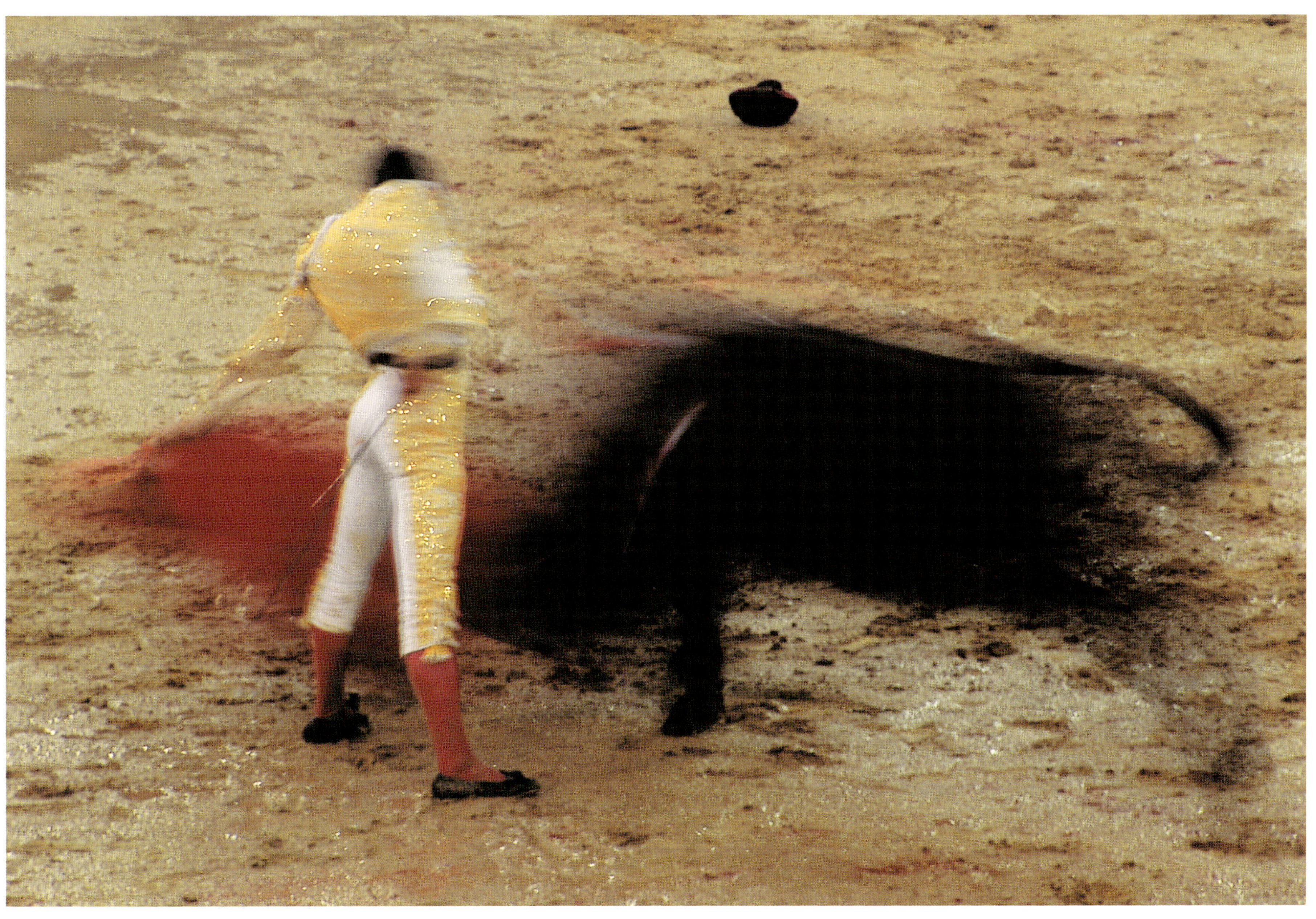

NATURAL PASS / *Natural*
Finito de Córdoba; Las Ventas, Madrid; May 17, 1993

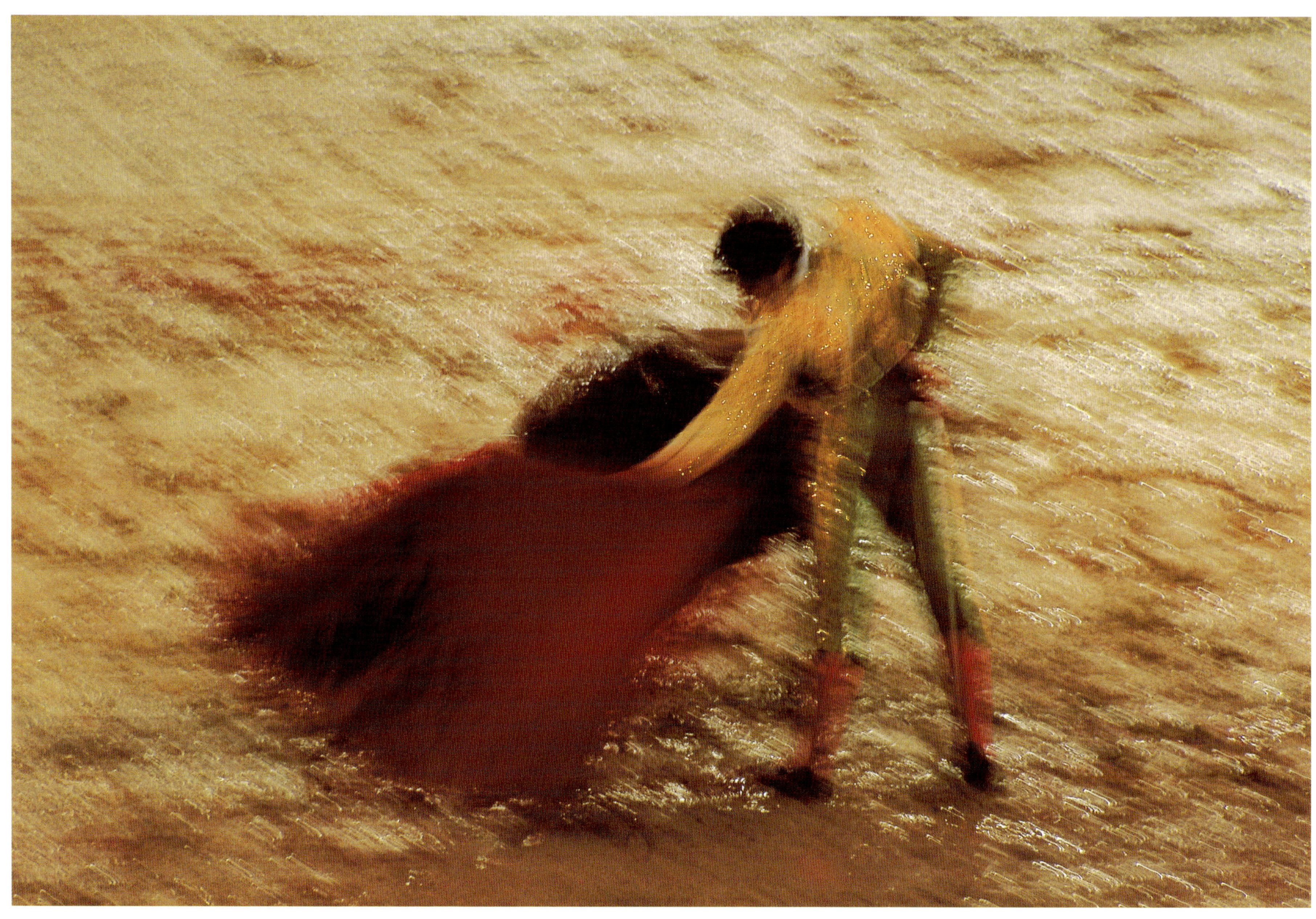

NATURAL PASS / *Natural*
José Tomás; Las Ventas, Madrid; May 15, 1998

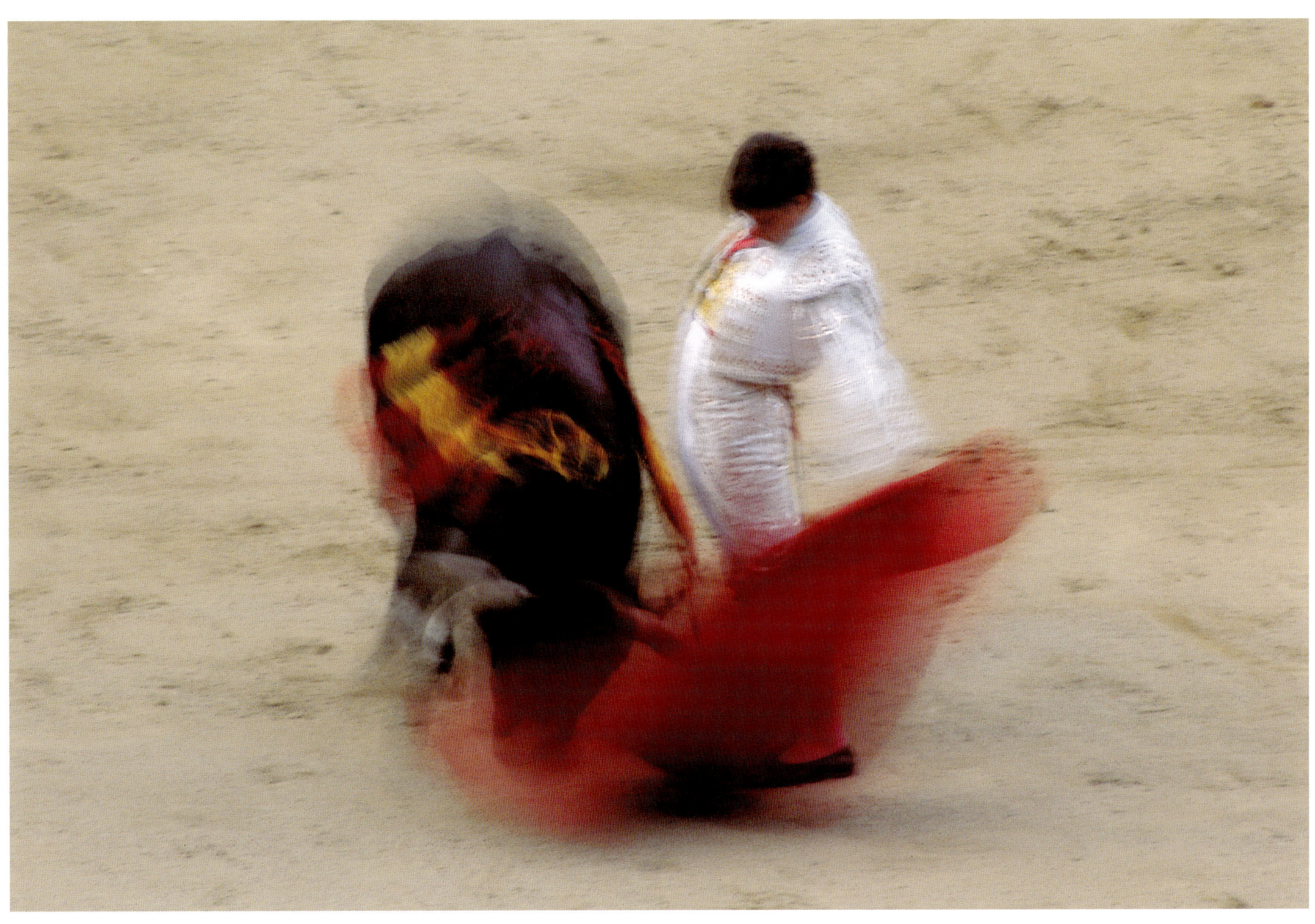

NATURAL PASS WITH FEET TOGETHER / *Natural a pies juntos*
El Juli; Las Ventas, Madrid; June 15, 2000

"The crowd roared, and he saw the bull charge down the ramp, then stop.

Dead still. Like the bull on a wine bottle. Black and huge, and still."

—RODDY DOYLE FROM HIS BOOK *BULL FIGHTING*

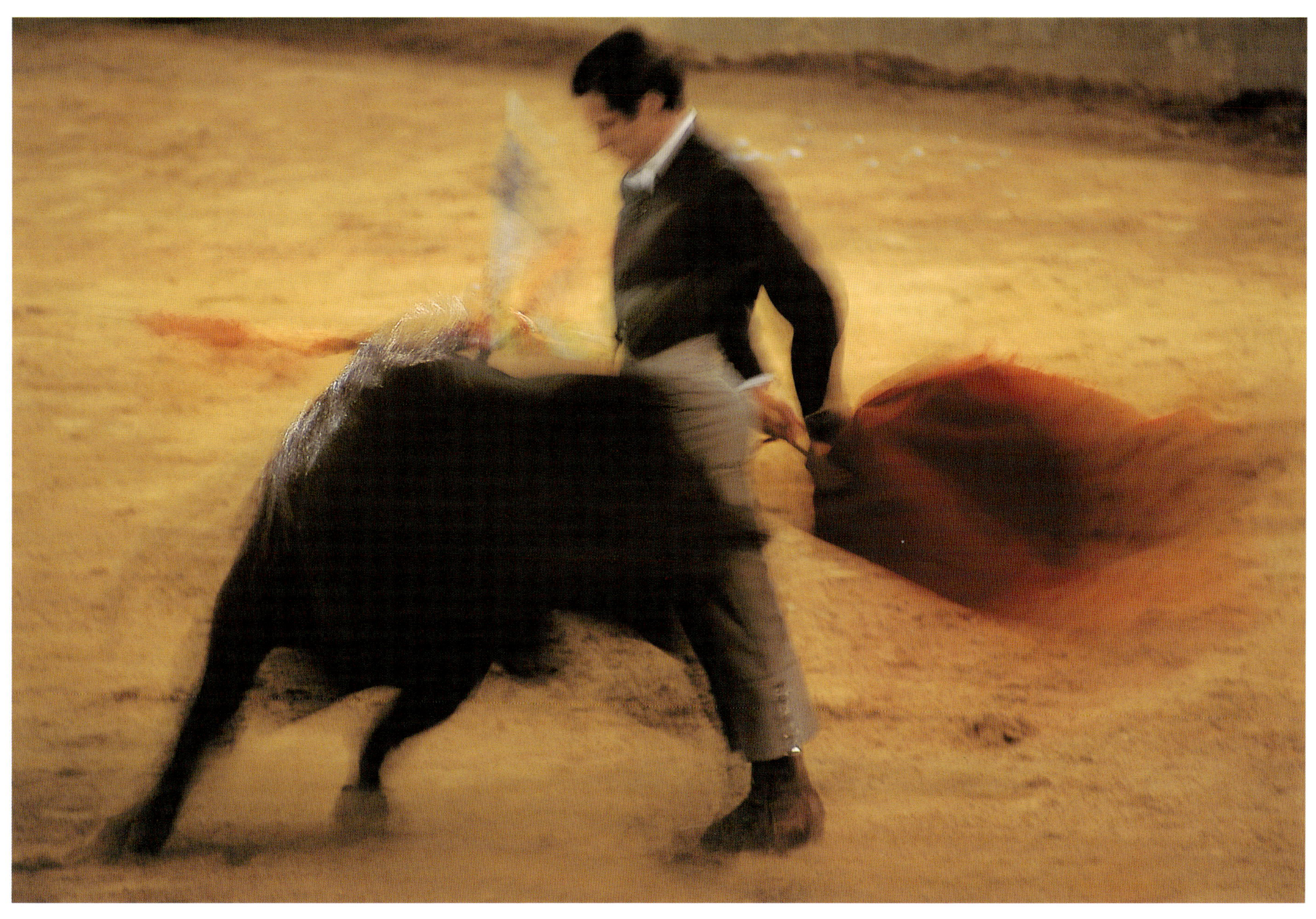

CHANGE OF HANDS BEHIND THE BACK / *Cambio de manos detrás de la espalda*
 Joselito; Las Ventas, Madrid; October 24, 1992

"Apostrophes, cries, and uproar grow to a furor!

 Because it is a celebration of courage!

 It is the celebration of people with heart!"

—from Bizet's opera Carmen, the aria "Toreador"

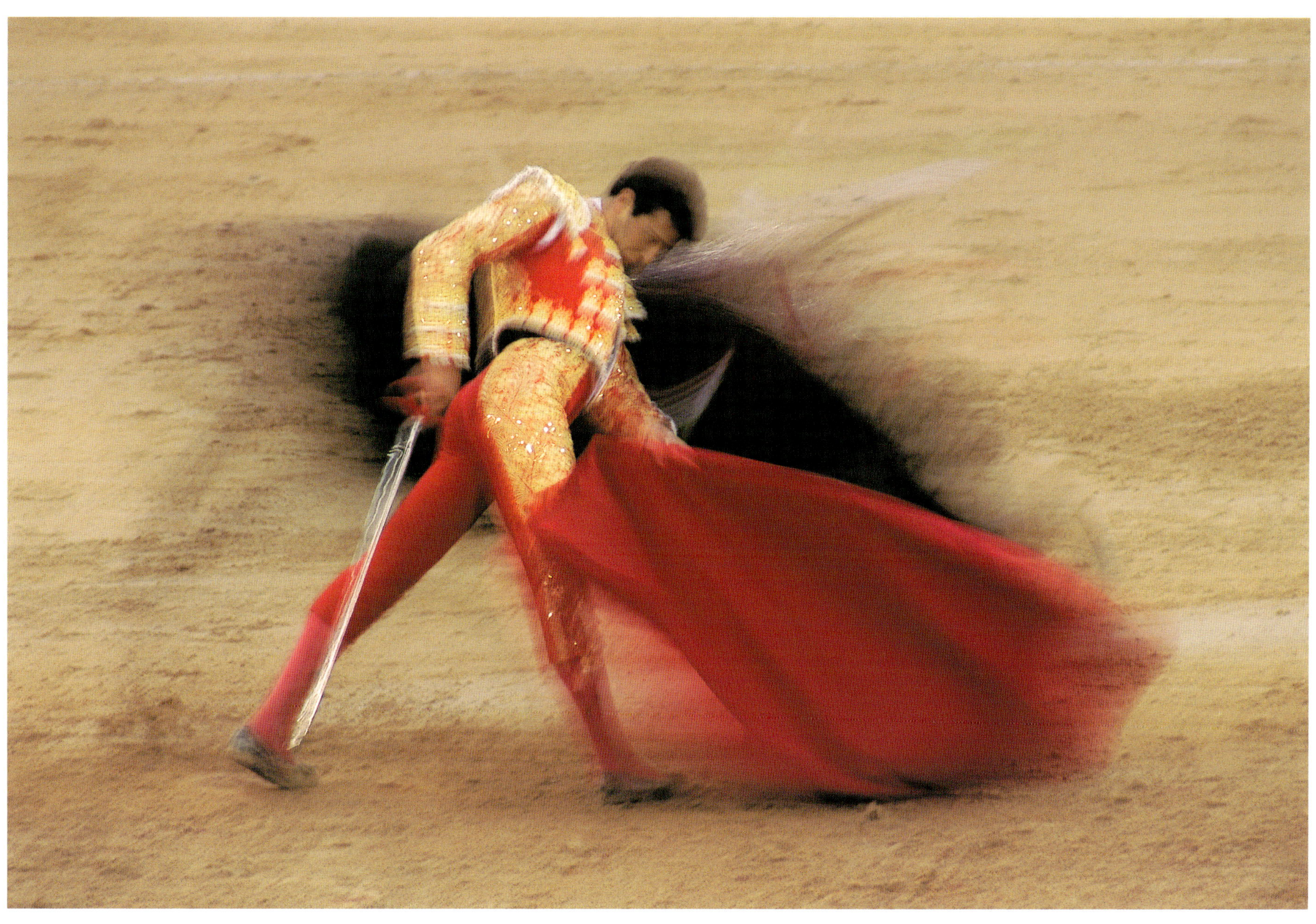

Trincherilla
Enrique Ponce; Las Ventas, Madrid; May 24, 1993

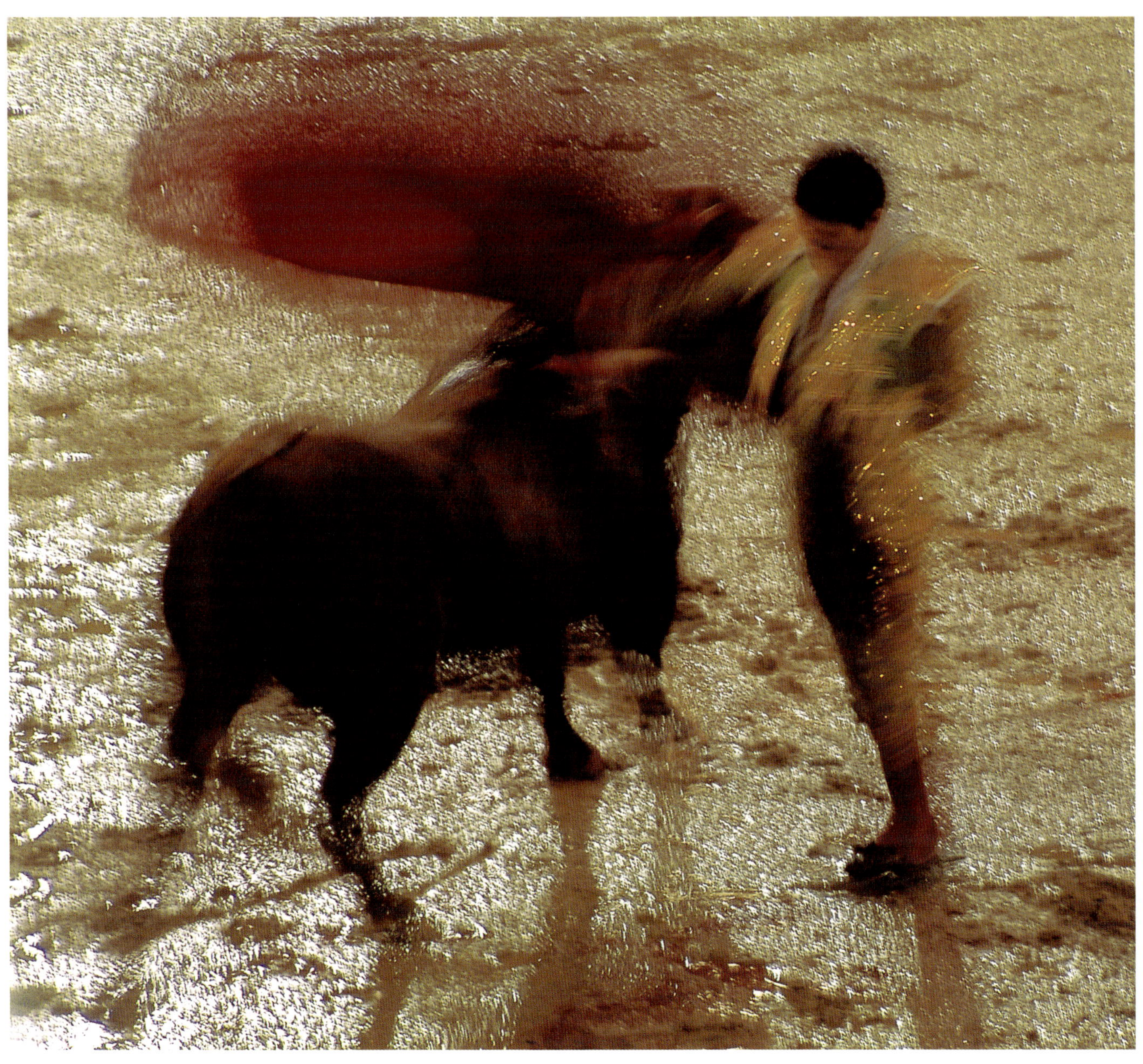

Manoletina
José Tomás; Las Ventas, Madrid; May 15, 1998

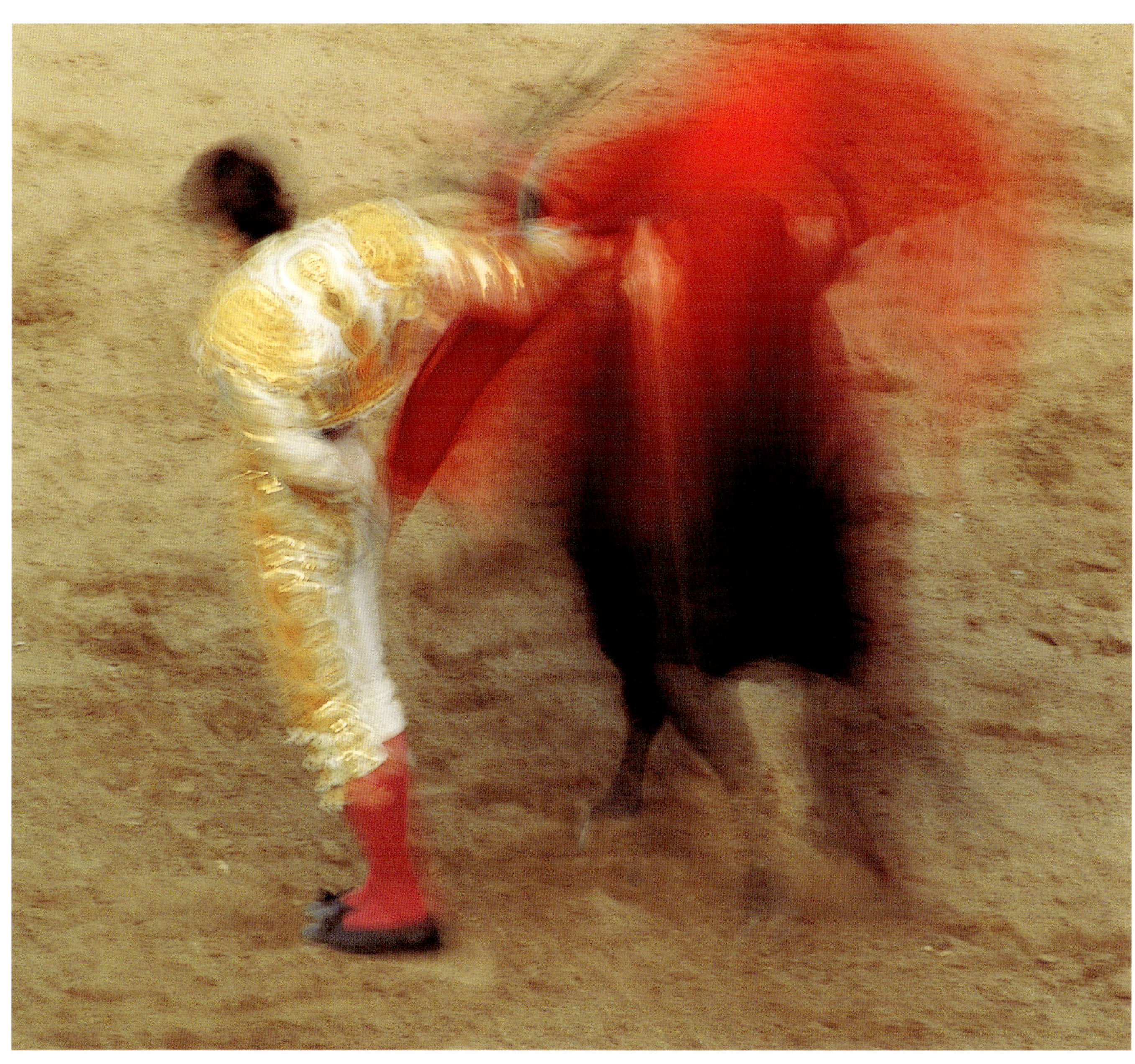

Manoletina
Litri; Guadalajara; September 19, 1992

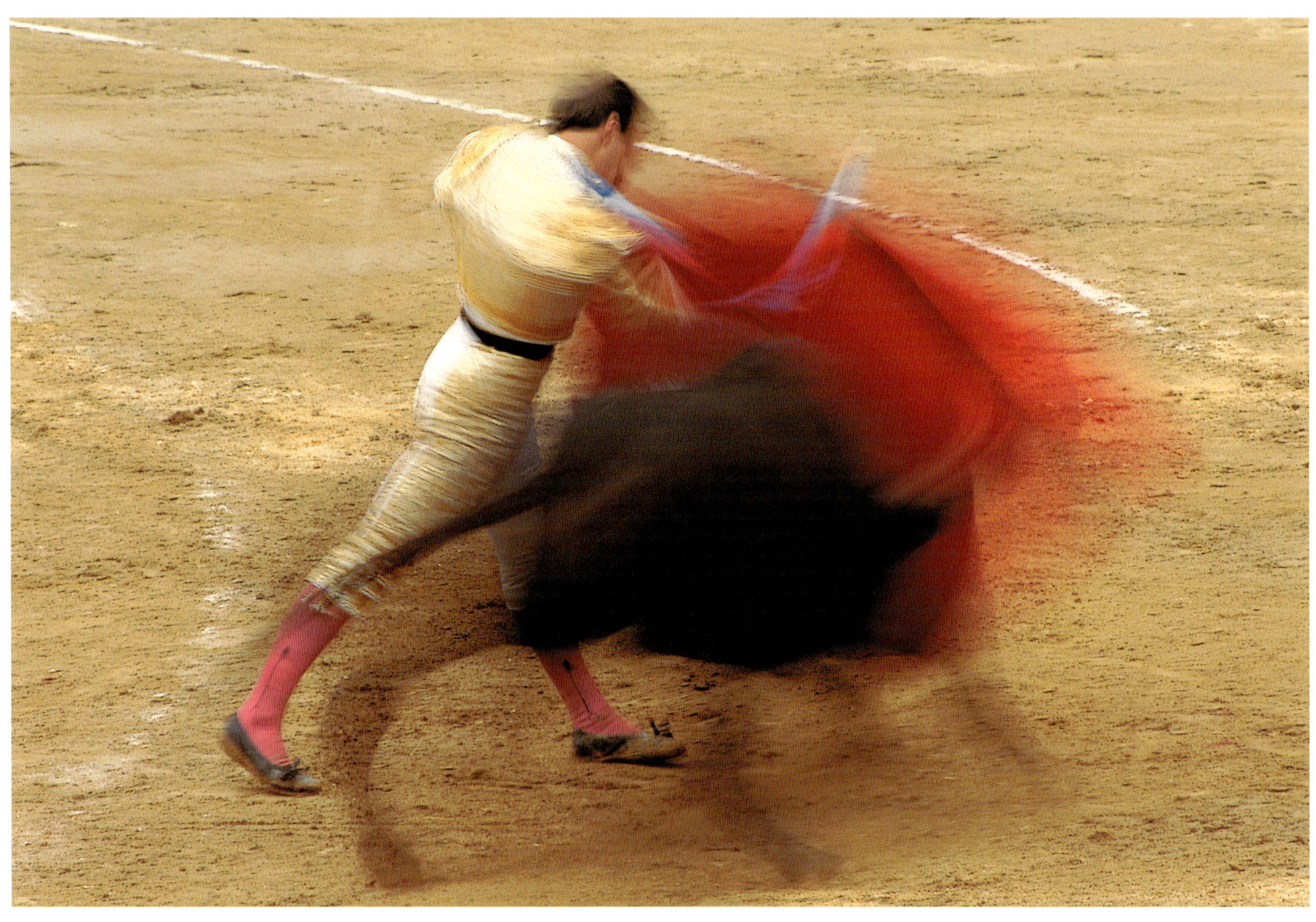

AIDED HIGH PASS / *Ayudado por alto*
Juan Carlos García; Las Ventas, Madrid; September 29, 1993

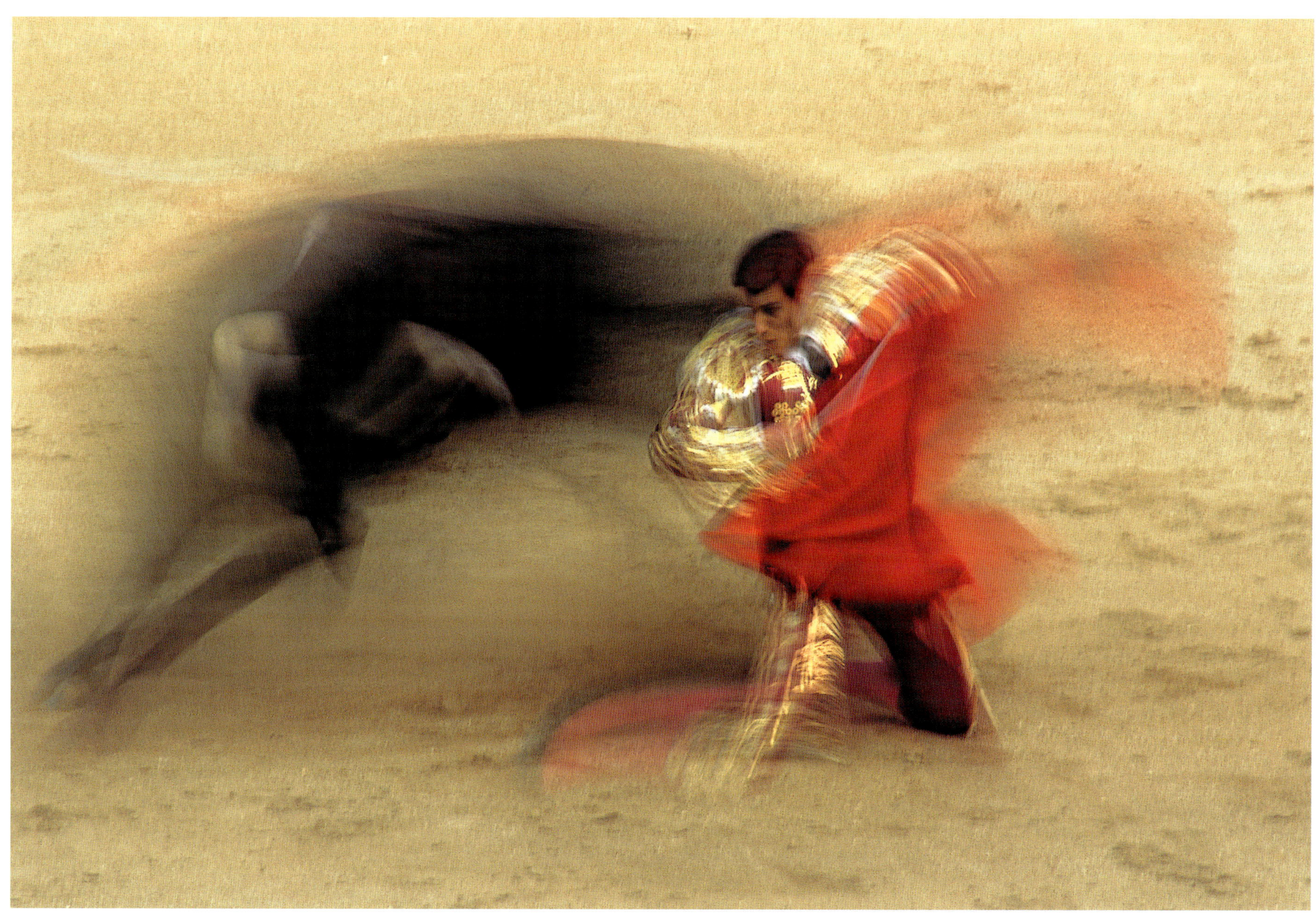

KNEELING WINDMILL PASS / *Molinete de rodillas*
Litri; Las Ventas, Madrid; May 12, 1992

"The bullfighter lives only for and until his next performance in the arena."

—John Willis, narrator in the David L. Wolper 1962 film, "Story of a Matador"

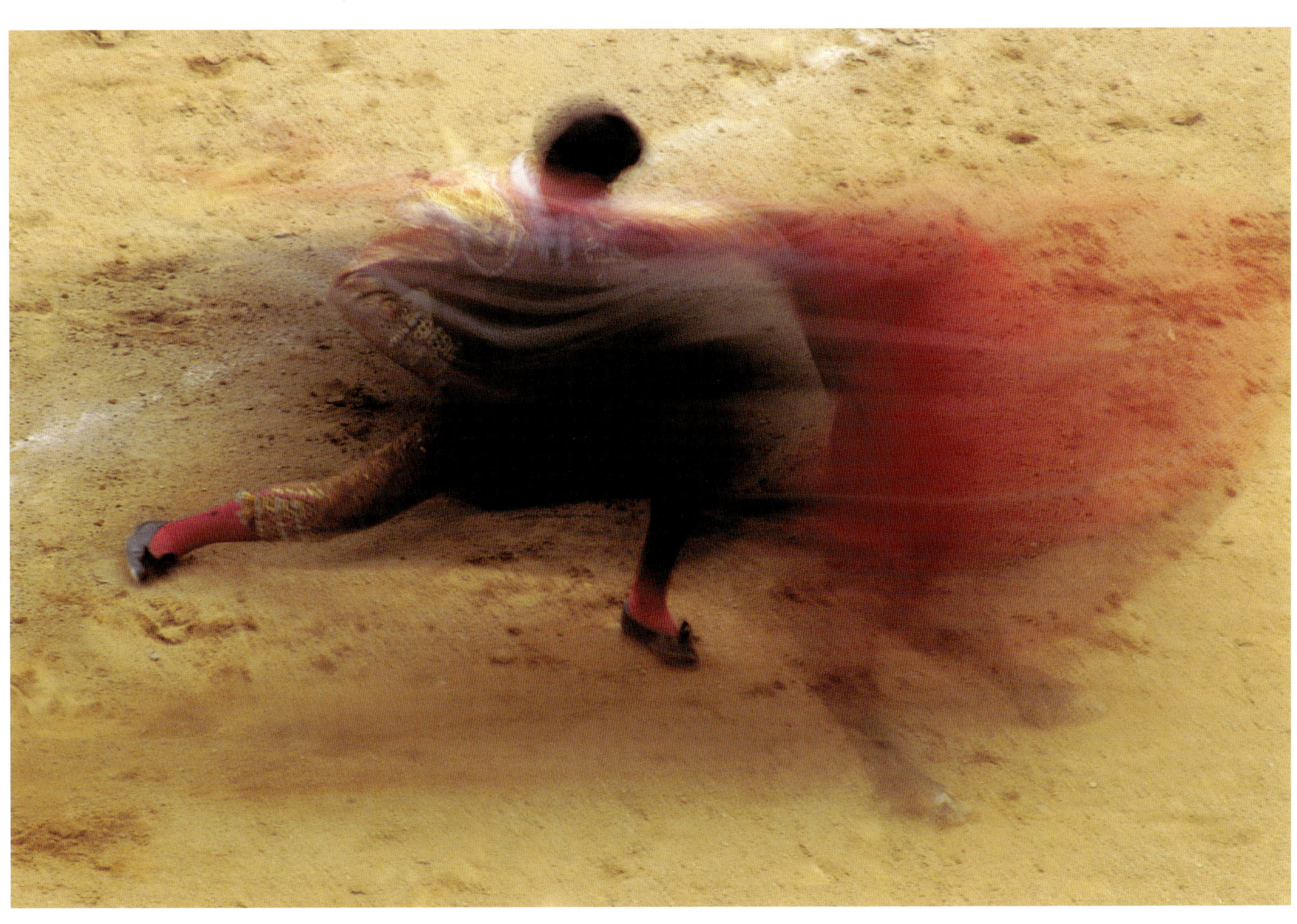

AIDED LOW PASS / *Ayudado por bajo*
Enrique Ponce; Las Ventas, Madrid; June 11, 1992

"It isn't a sport. It's more about creating and inspiring. It's like any other art. A painter doesn't paint because he thinks he's going to sell his paintings for millions. We could have stopped by now. When you start out, you want to be famous. But there has to be something behind that. Or it's not worth it."

—Alejandro Amaya, American-born Mexican bullfighter

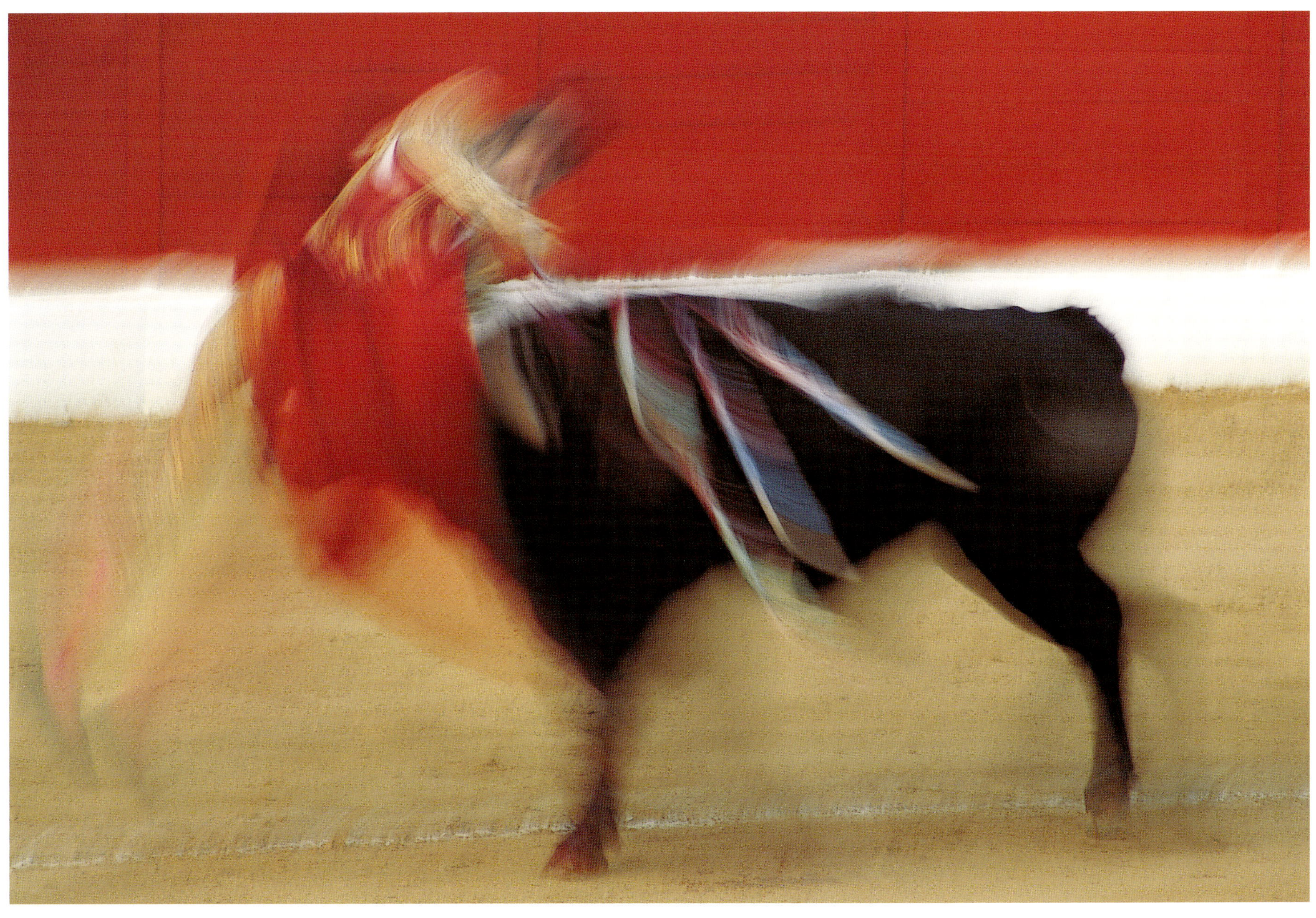

SWORD THRUST / *Estocada*
Enrique Ponce; Alcázar de San Juan, Ciudad Real; September 5, 1992

Sequence Four

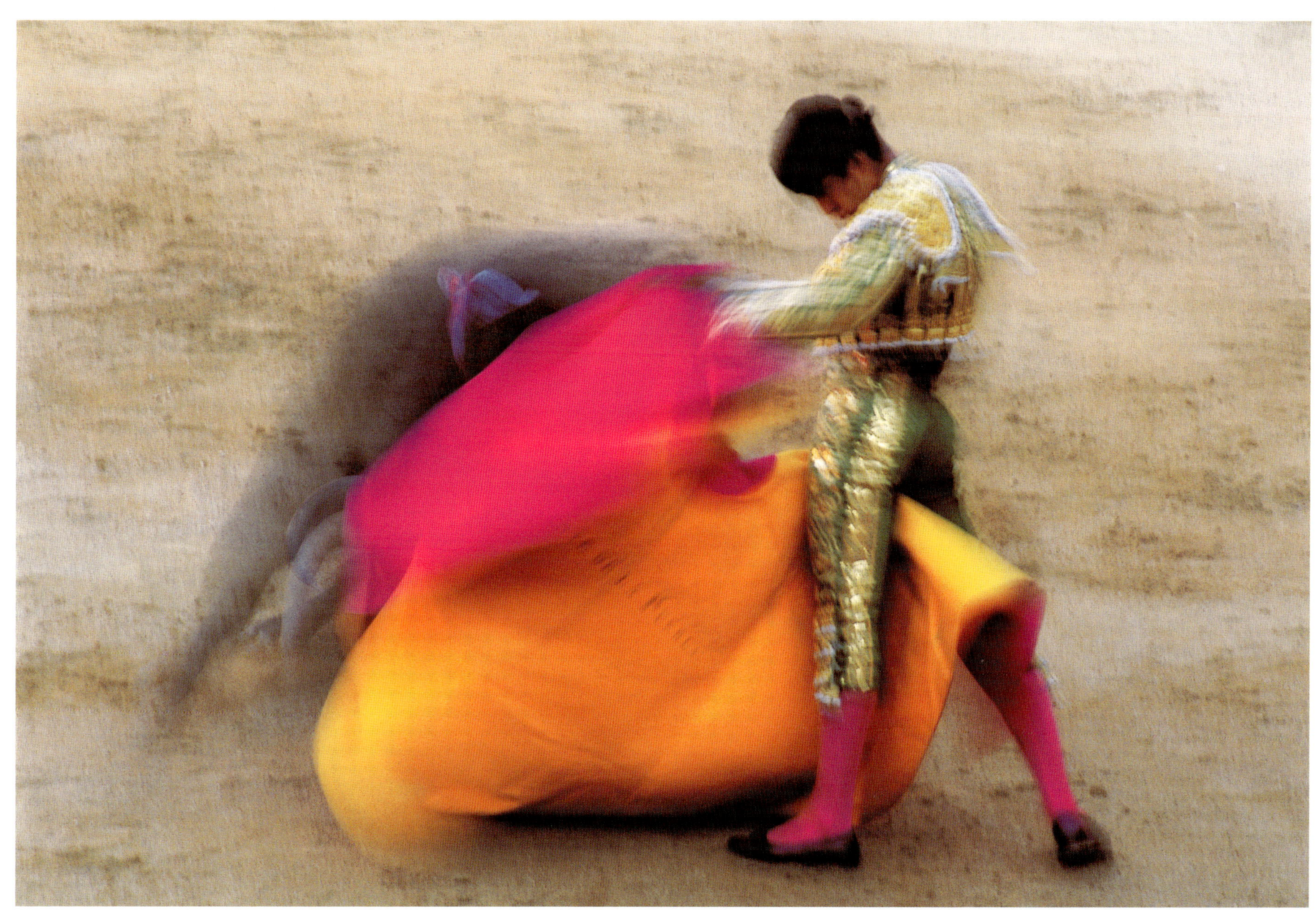

Verónica
Morante de la Puebla; Las Ventas, Madrid; May 29, 2000

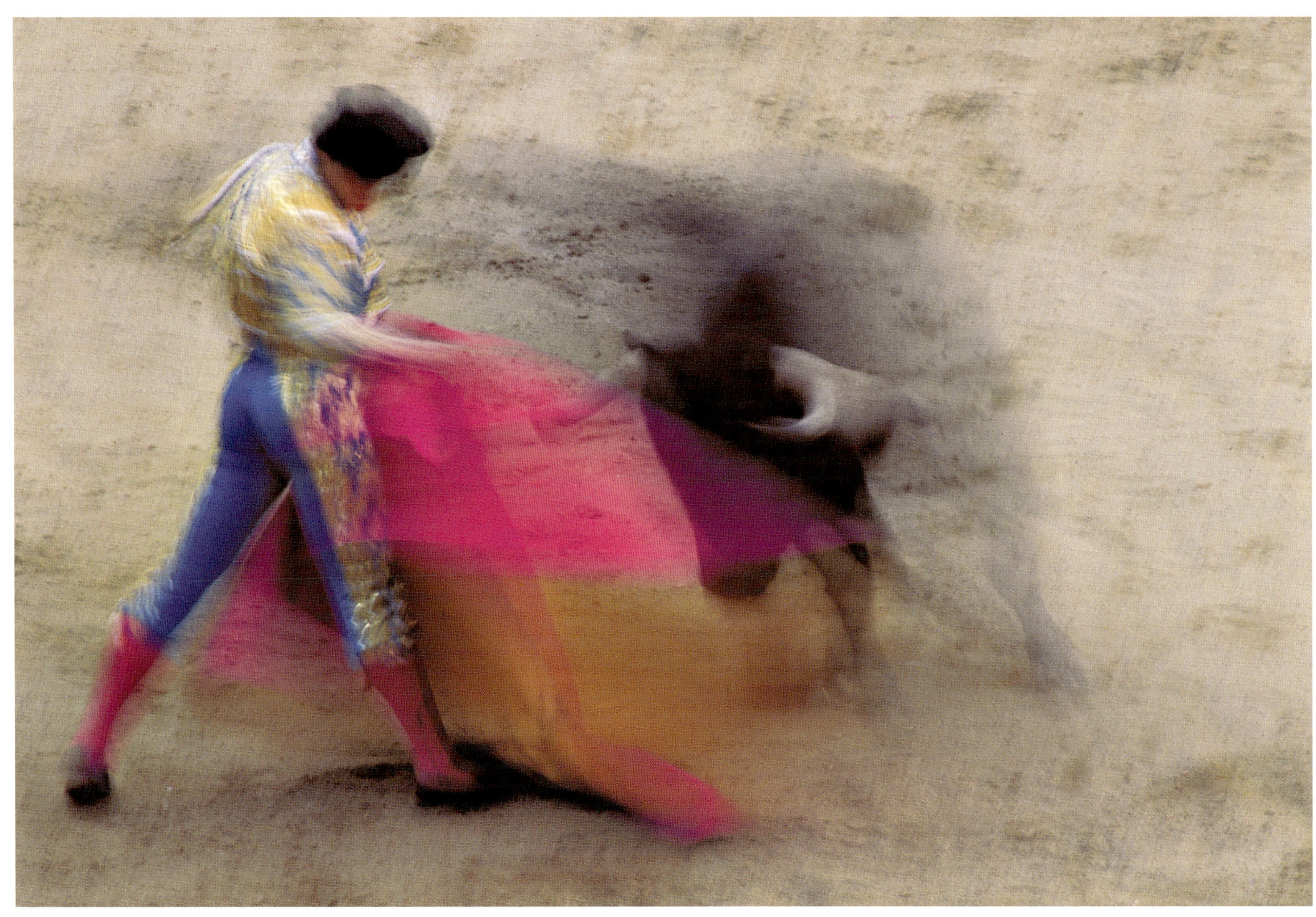

VERONICA / *Verónica*
Víctor Puerto; Las Ventas, Madrid; October 7, 2000

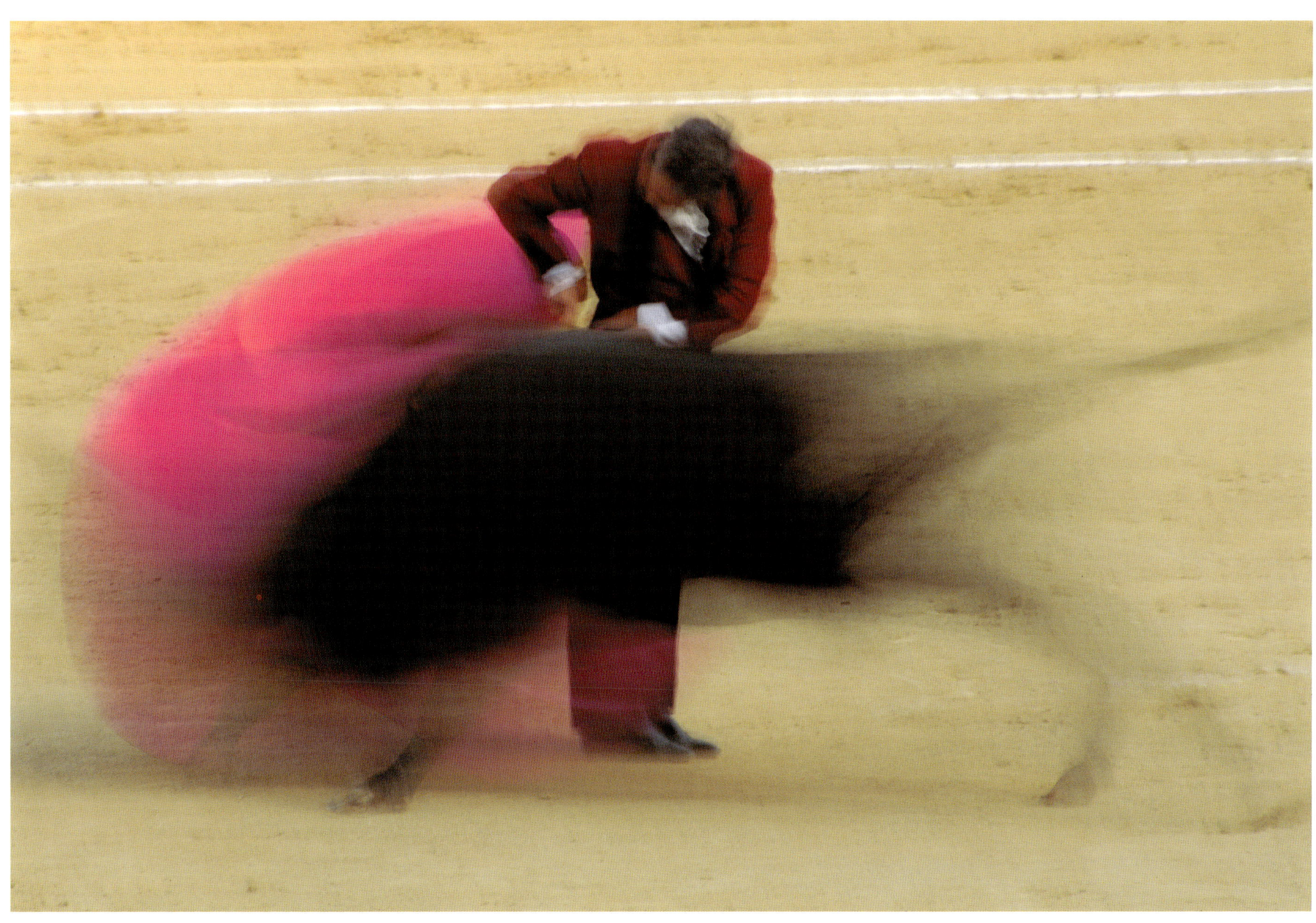

MEDIA VERONICA WITH FEET TOGETHER / *Media Verónica a pies juntos*
Palomo Linares; Las Ventas, Madrid; October 24, 1992

"Groups of silence in the corners

 at five in the afternoon.

 And the bull alone with a high heart!

 At five in the afternoon."

—From the elegy, "Llanto por la muerte de Ignacio Sánchez Mejías"/
"Weeping for the Death of Ignacio Sánchez Mejías," by the poet Federico Garcia Lorca

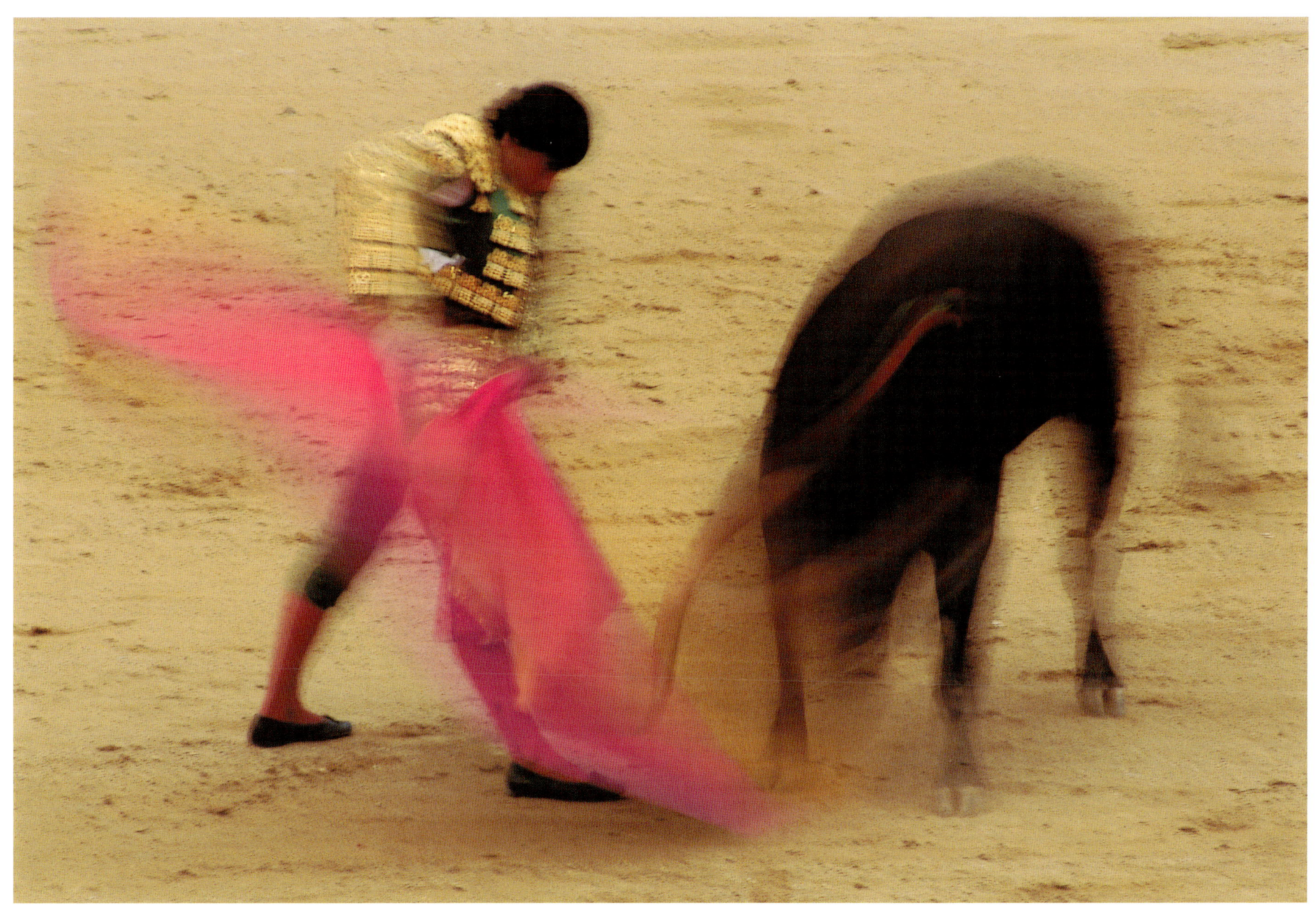

HALF VERONICA / *Media Verónica*
David Luguillano; Las Ventas, Madrid; May 9, 1993

"The cape stands out like sculpted gold; the muleta is like a thread of silk binding the man and the bull together. It is exquisite, the stuff of dreams, and one feels tears in his eyes, a profound exaltation in his heart. You hear the phrase, "he and the bull were one." With Curro it's different. There is no man. There is no bull. There is merely a golden moment…"

—JAMES MICHENER, ON CURRO ROMERO FROM HIS NOVEL *IBERIA*

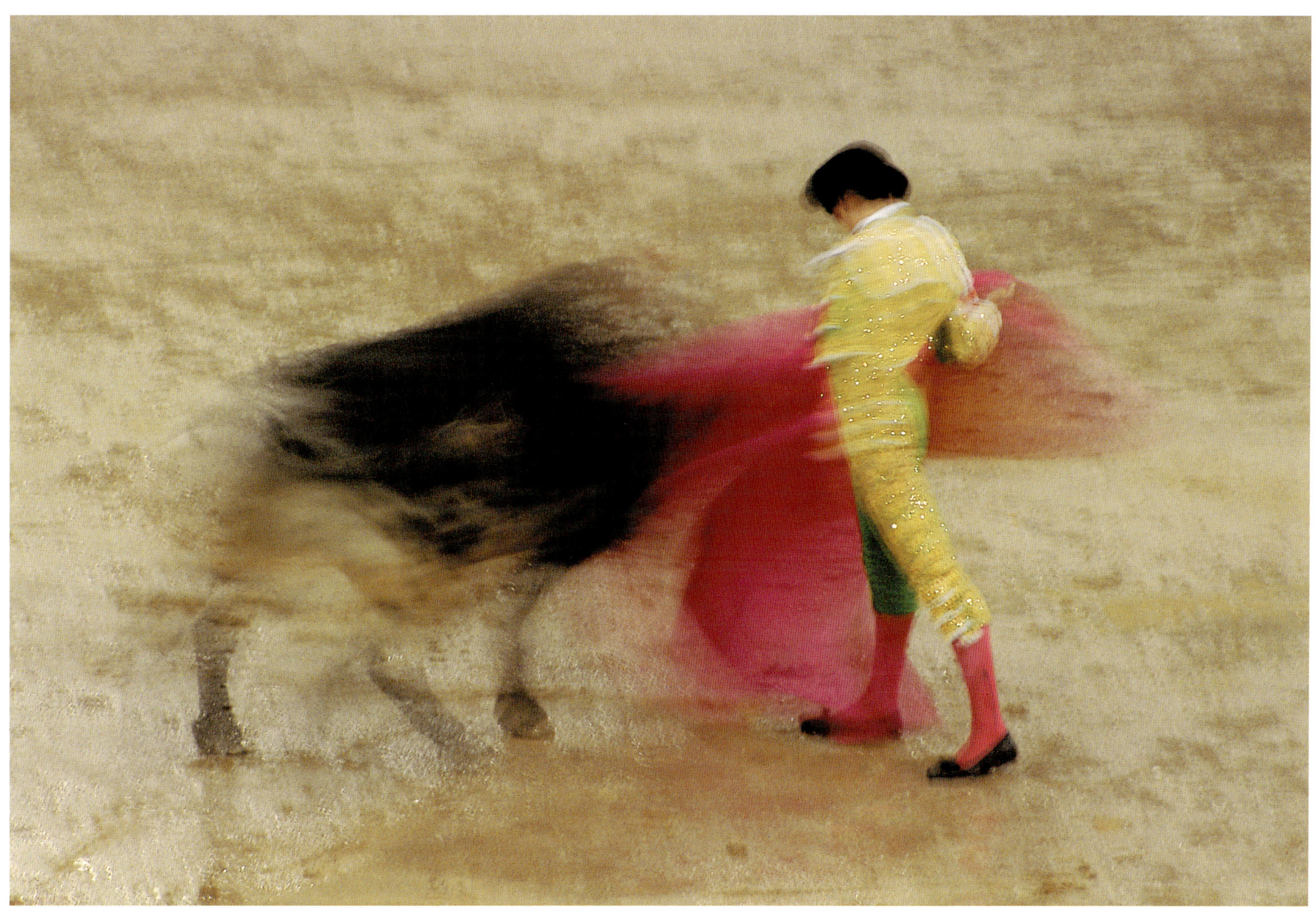

LONG PASS / *Larga*
José Tomás; Las Ventas, Madrid; May 15, 1998

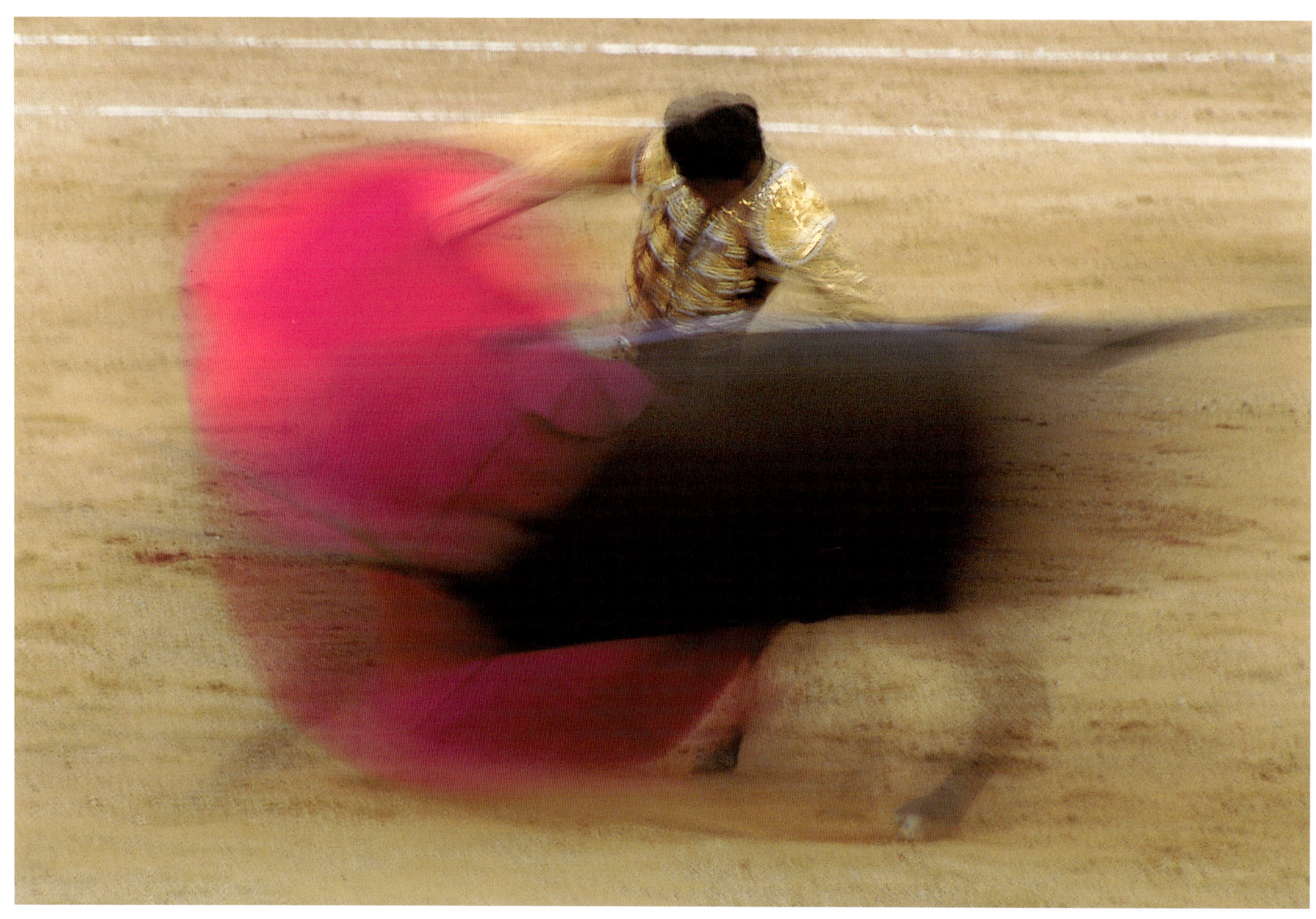

Navarra
Joselito; Las Ventas, Madrid; June 17, 1993

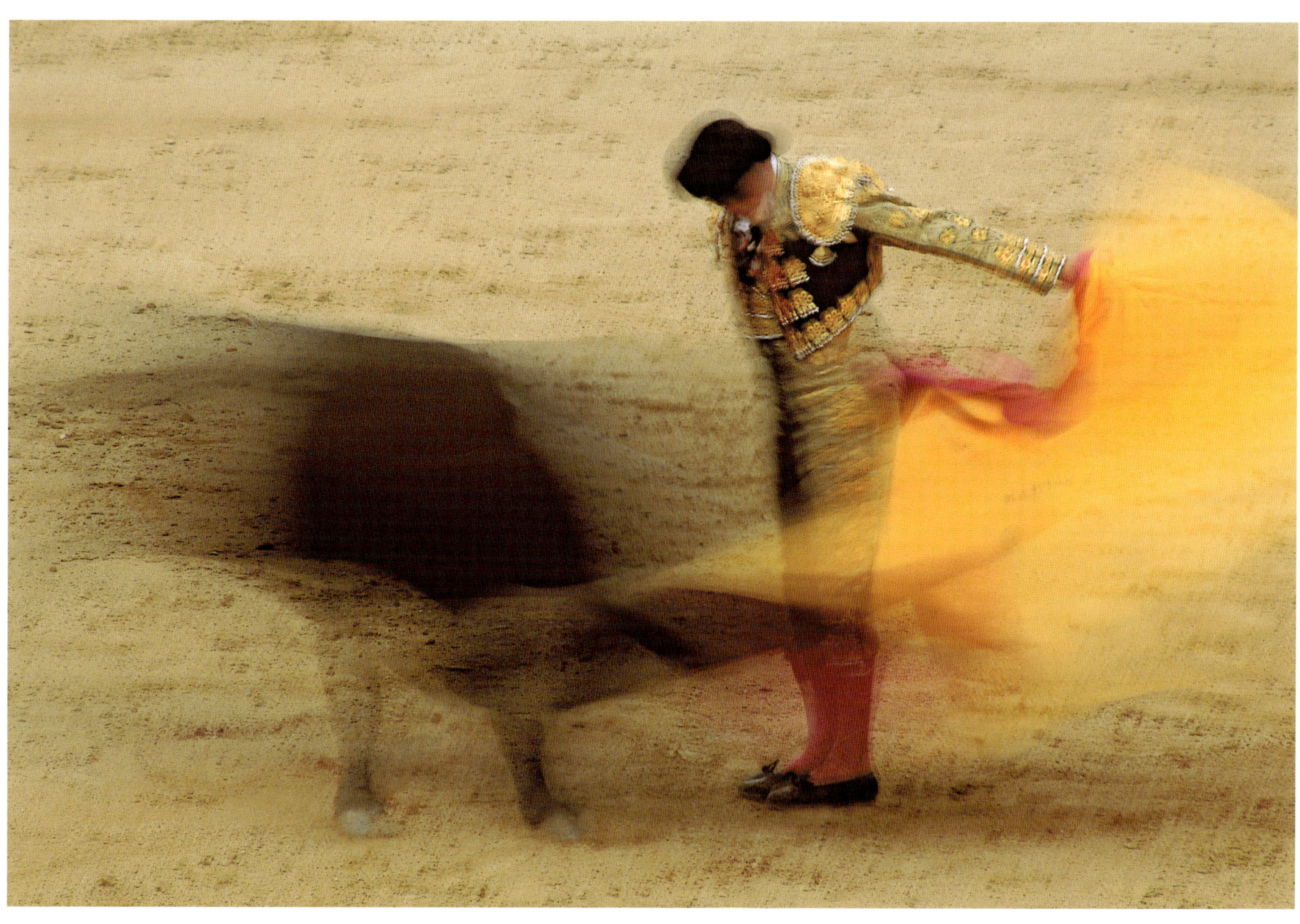

Gaonera
Martín Antequera; Las Ventas, Madrid; May 30, 2000

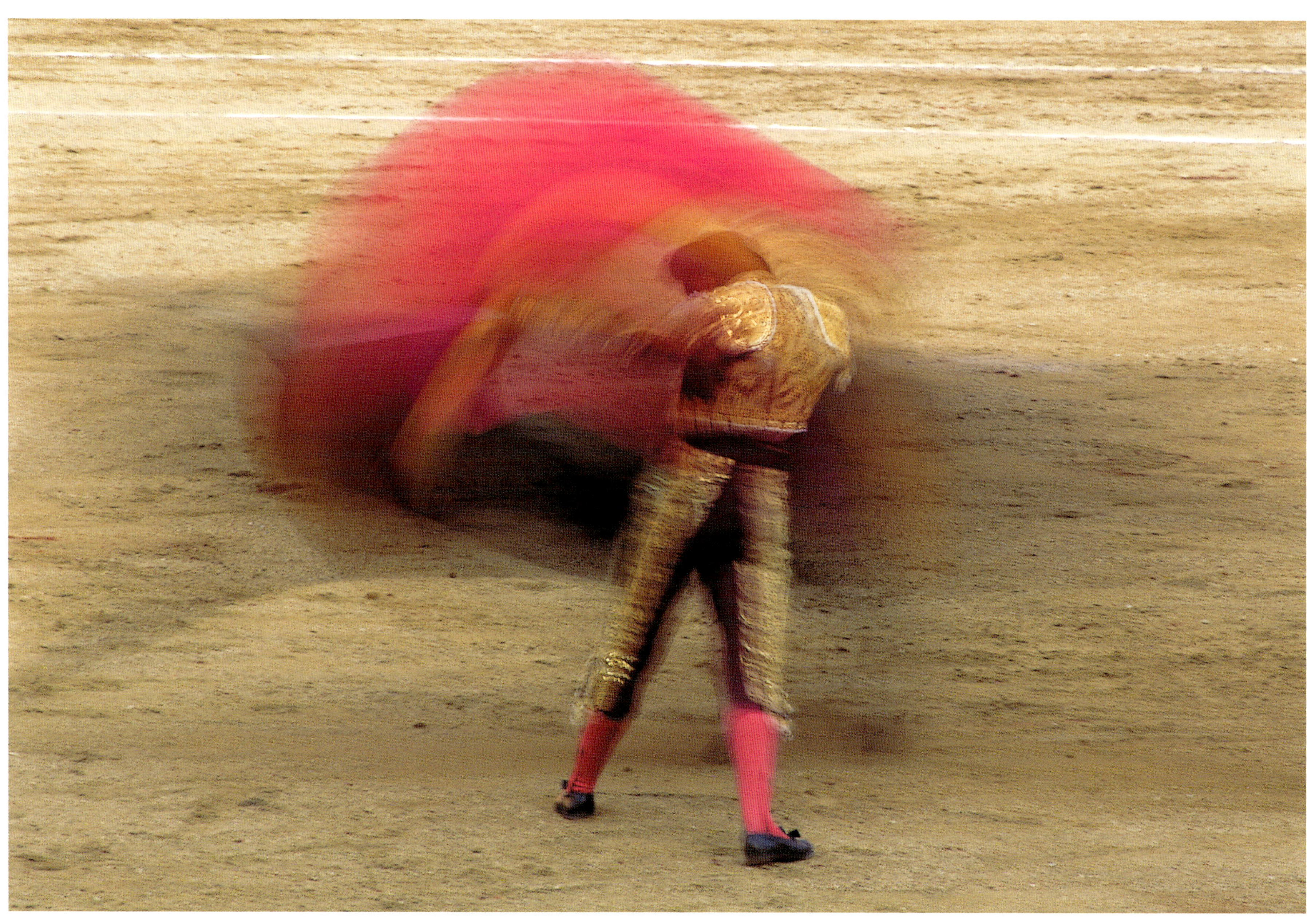

HALF FAROL PASS / *Medio farol*
Joselito; Las Ventas, Madrid; June 17, 1993

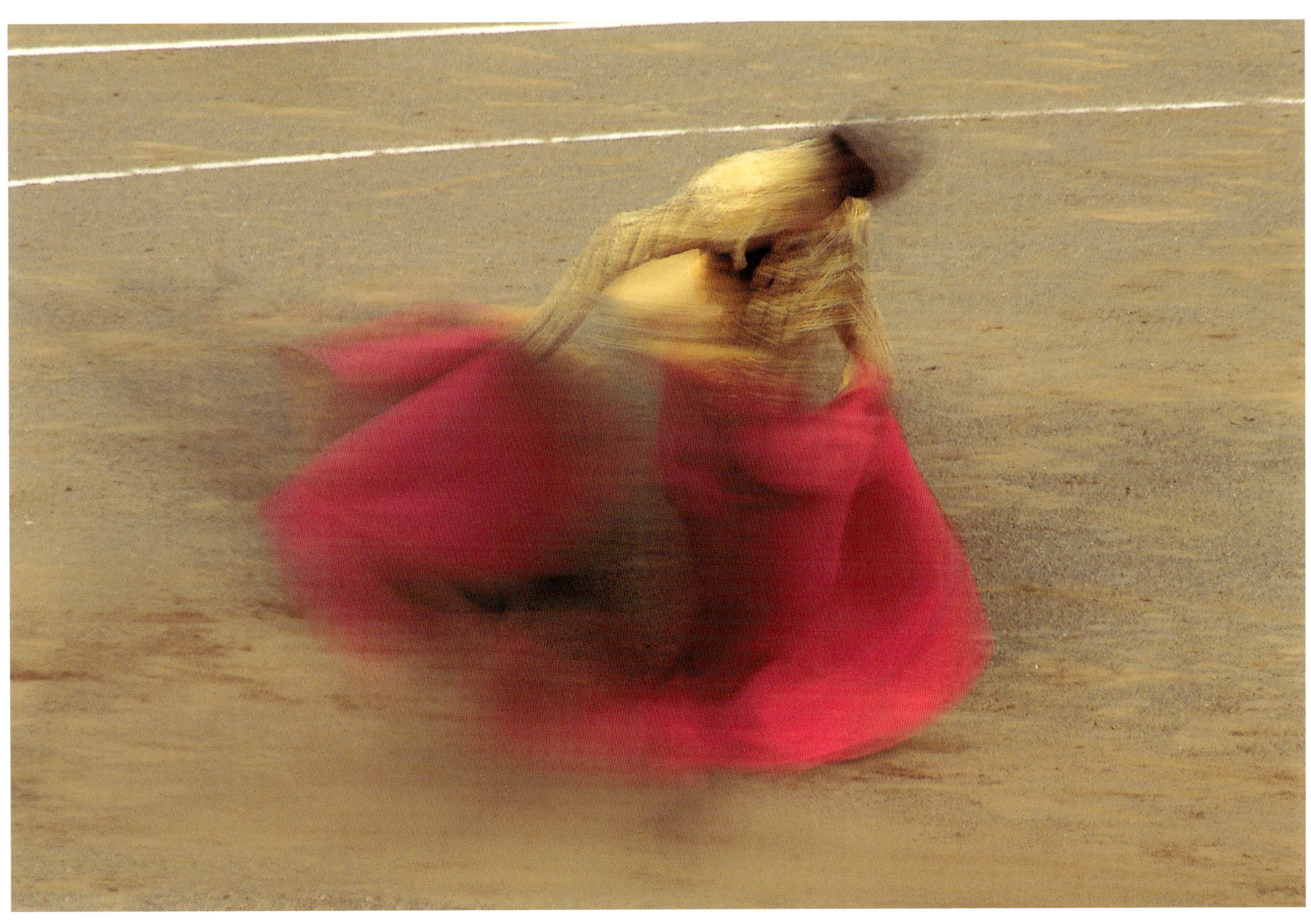

WALKING CHICUELINA / *Chiceulina al paso*
Jose Ortega Cano; Vista Alegre, Bilbao; June 7, 1992

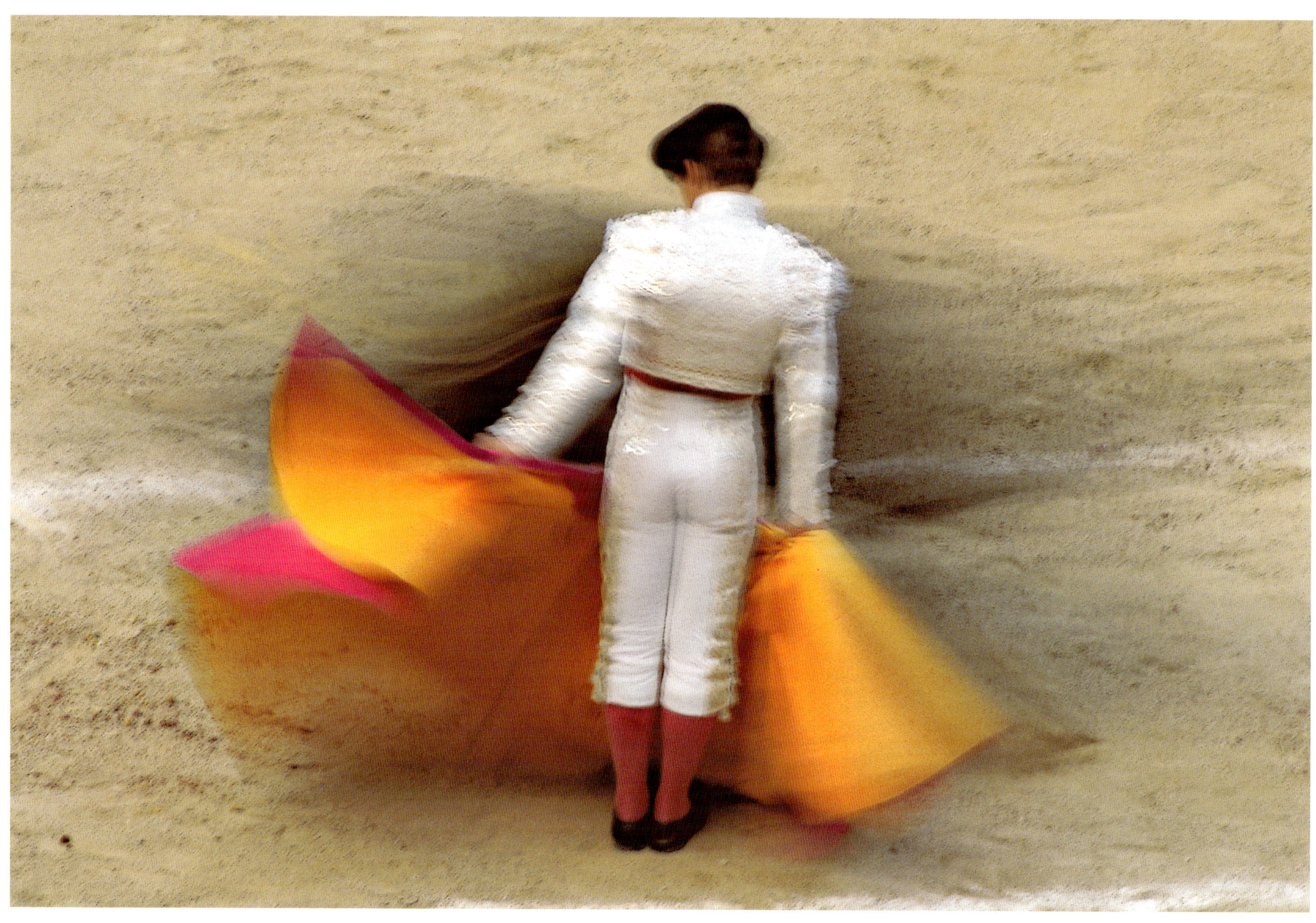

APRON PASS / *Delantal*
El Juli; Las Ventas, Madrid; June 16, 2000

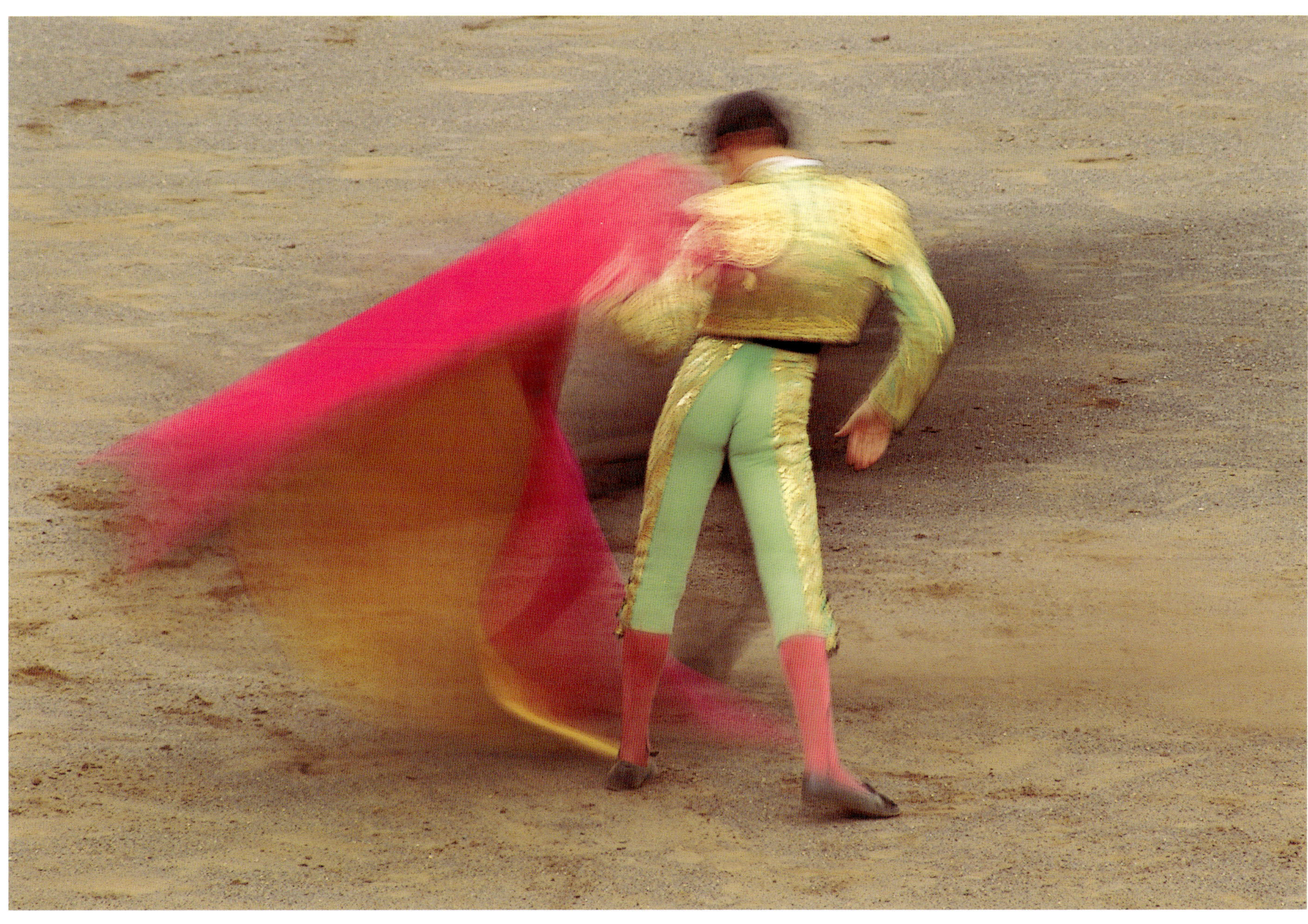

LONG PASS / *Larga cordobesa*
Enrique Ponce; Vista Alegre, Bilbao; June 7, 1992

"The clearest modern encapsulation of that pursuit is bullfighting; for though honor is riskily pursued by pilots and mountaineers, their sphere of action is remote from most of us. The bullfighter brings the pursuit down to earth and reduces it to a pattern. The connection with tragedy is even closer. For example, 'Othello' is a dramatized bullfight if there ever was one. The brave Othello is the courageously blundering bull, lured to his death by the Matador Iago and that maddening handkerchief."

—Kenneth Tynan from his 1955 book, *Bull Fever*

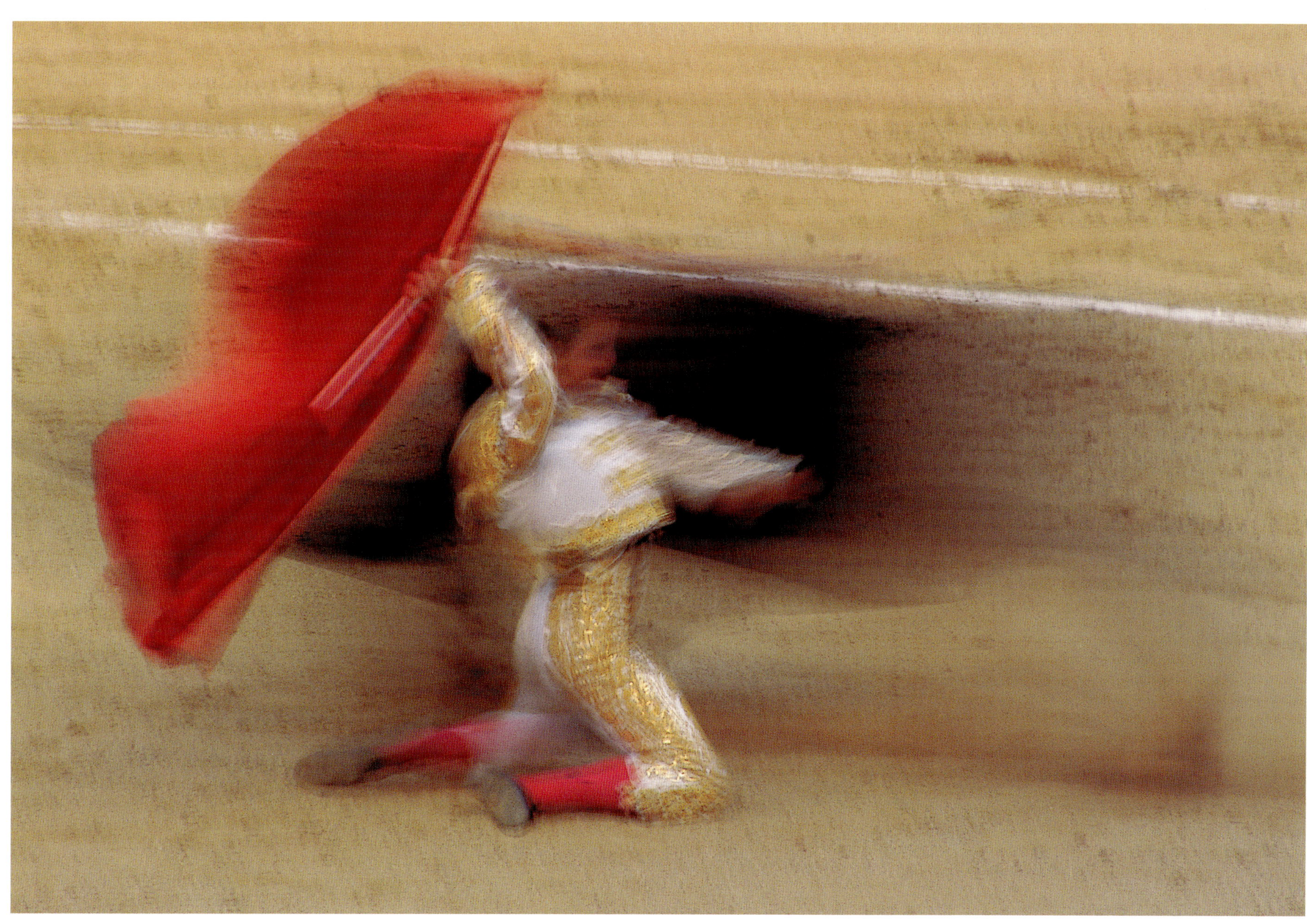

KNEELING FAROL PASS / *Farol de rodillas*
Javier Vázquez; Las Ventas, Madrid; June 29, 1994

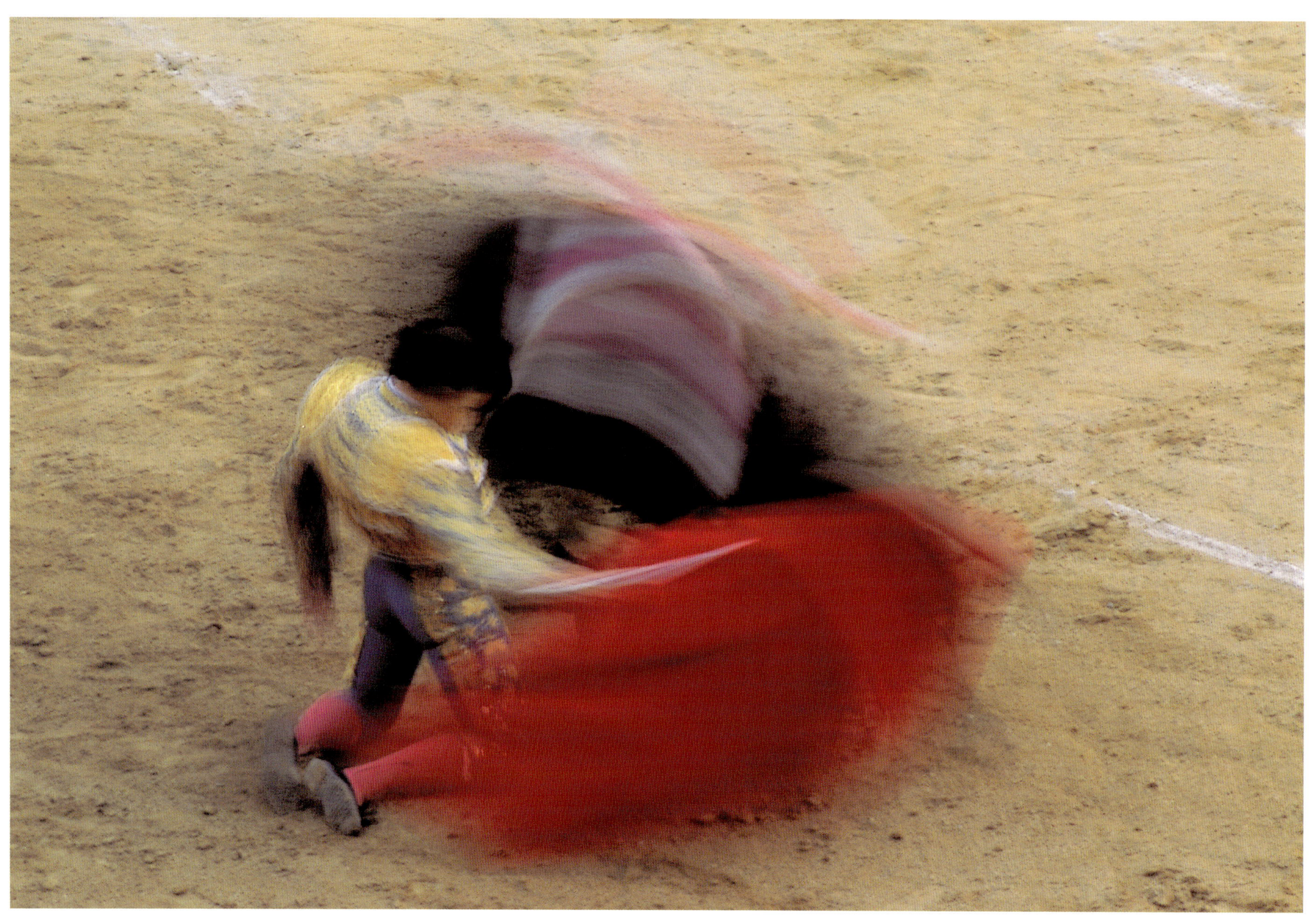

KNEELING RIGHT HANDED PASS / *Derechazo de rodillas*
Víctor Puerto; Las Ventas, Madrid; October 10, 2000

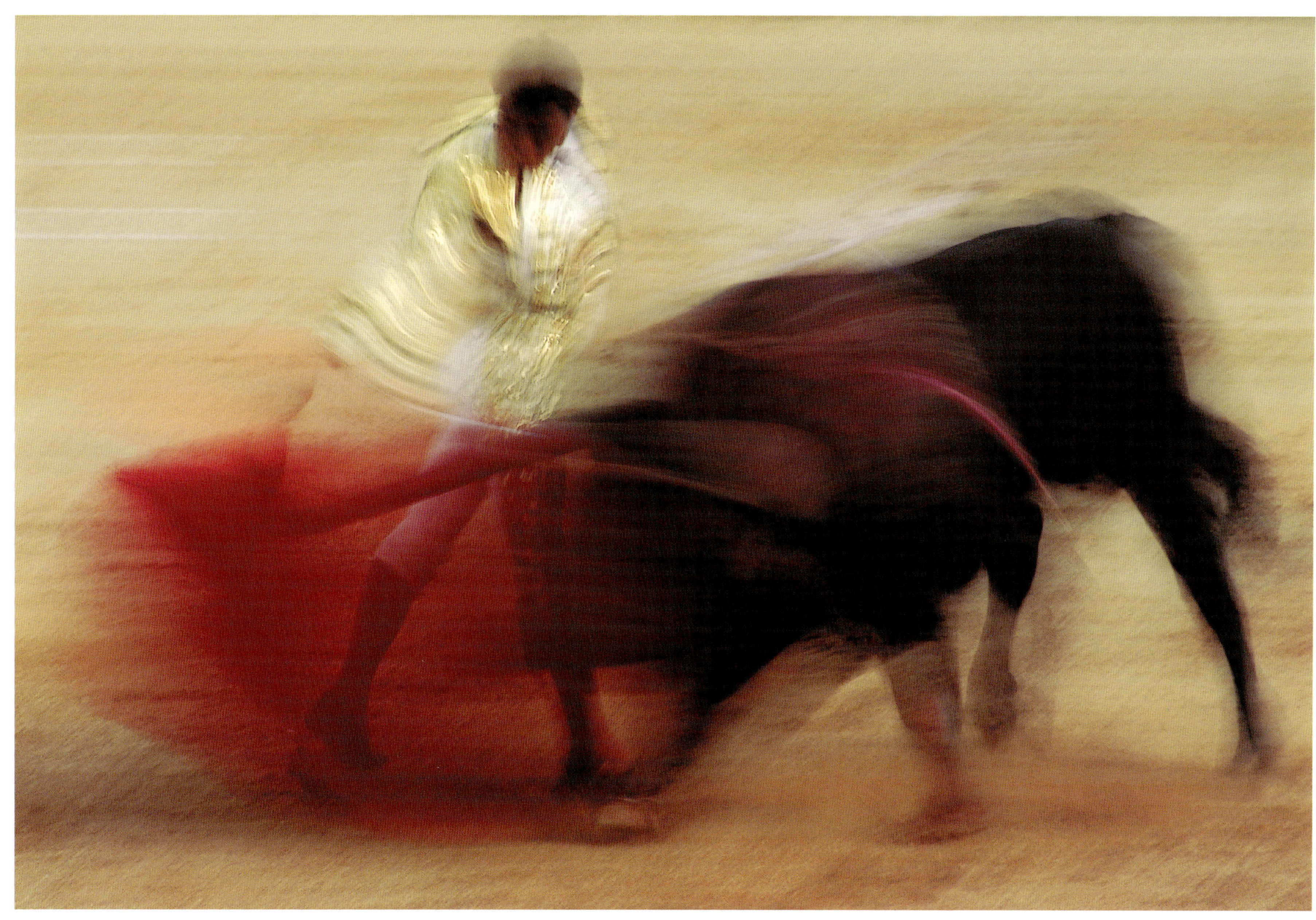

RIGHT-HANDED PASS / *Derechazo*
César Rincón; Alcázar de San Juan, Ciudad Real; September 5, 1992

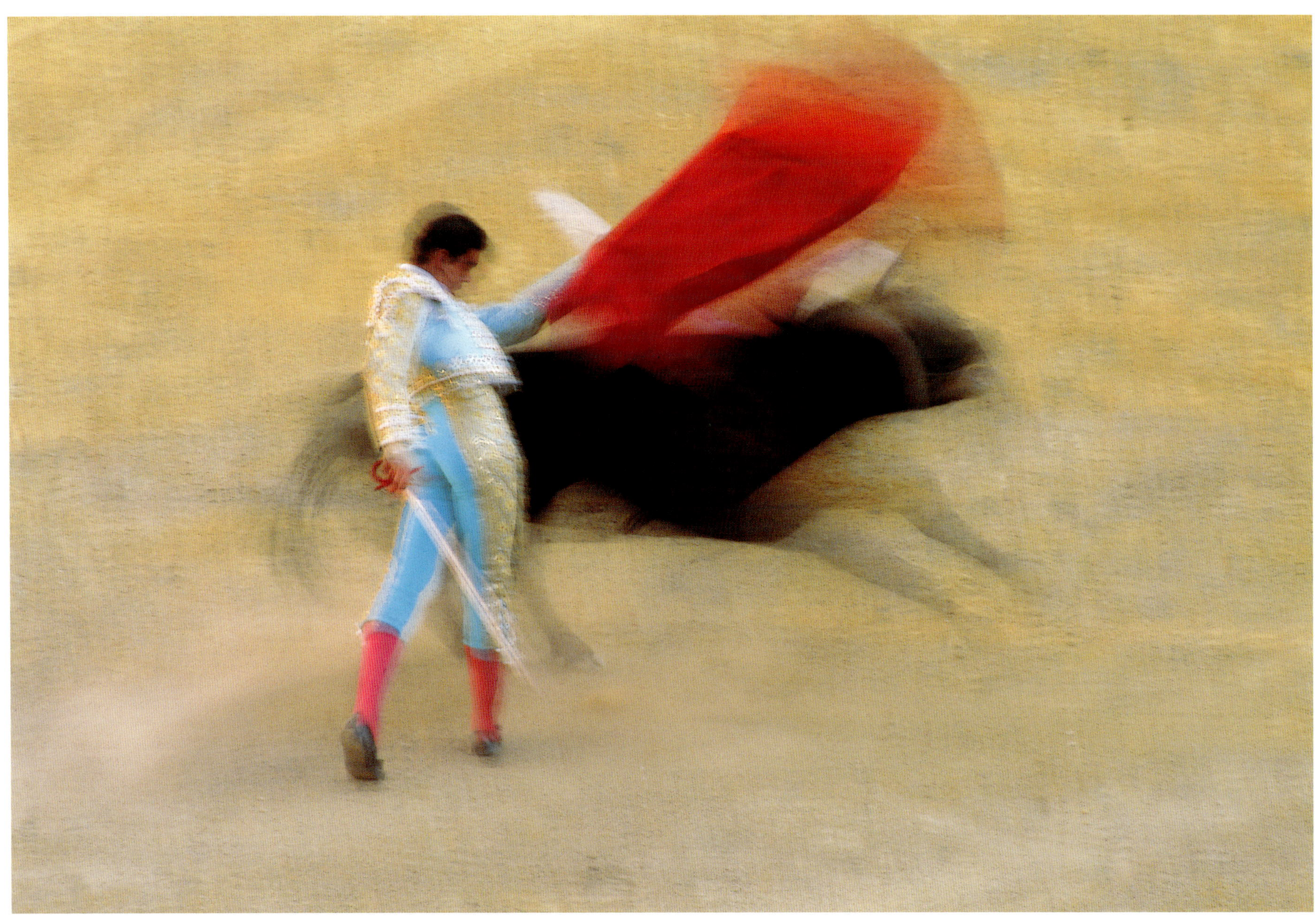

CHEST PASS ON THE LEFT / *Pase de pecho*
José Tomás; León; June 24, 2000

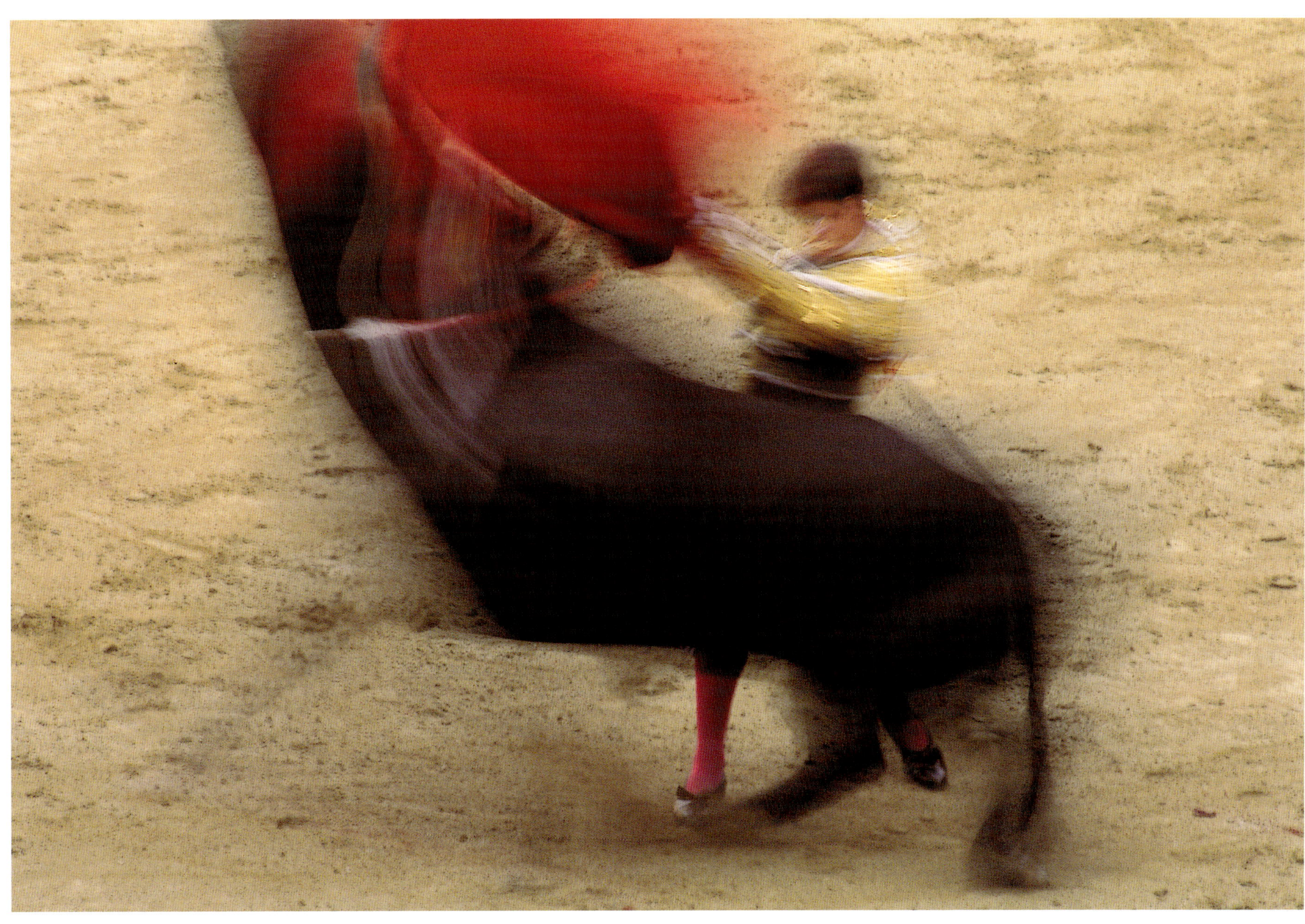

CHEST PASS ON THE LEFT / *Pase de pecho*
El Juli; Las Ventas, Madrid; May 17, 2000

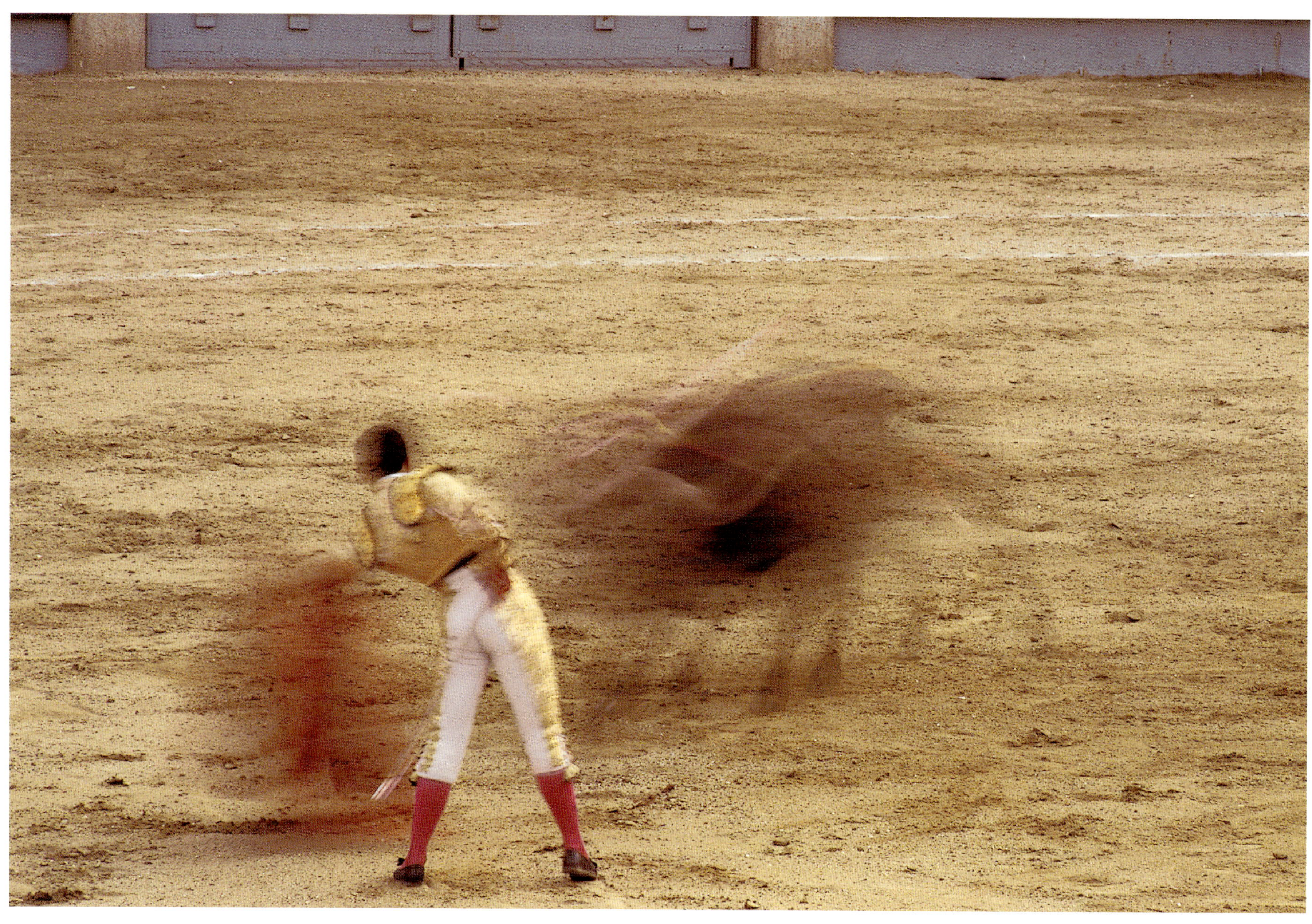

CITING ON THE LEFT / *Citando a la Izquierda*
César Rincón; Las Ventas, Madrid; May 22, 1991

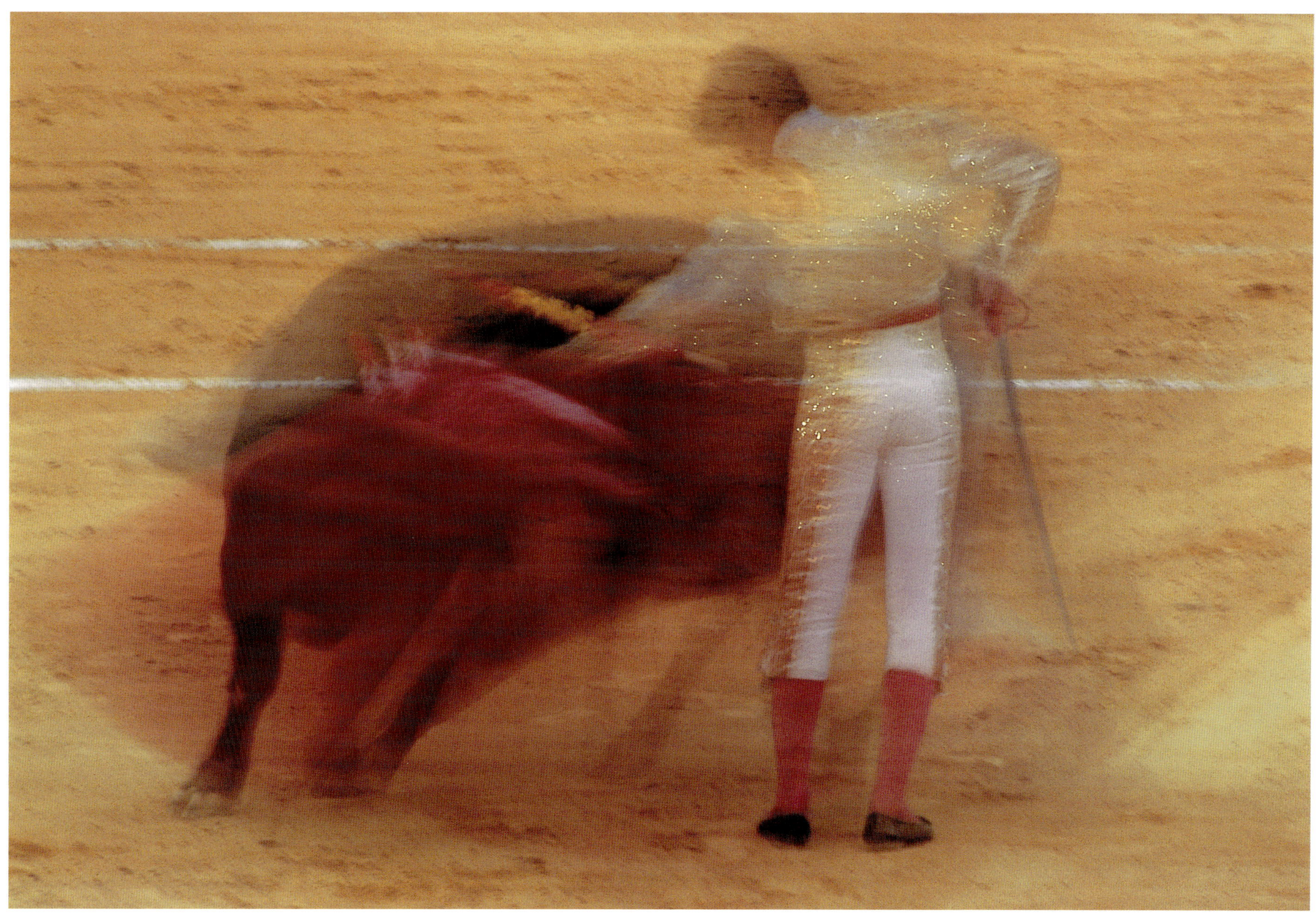

NATURAL PASS / *Natural*
Vicente Barrera; Valencia; July 23, 1993

"Paco Camino is the greatest torero of the past 20 years. He leads the bull with the muleta where the bull does not want to go. That is the most difficult thing in the art of bullfighting, because it involves the total domination of man over beast."

—Antonio Diaz-Canabate, one of Spain's foremost authorities on bullfighting, writing for the Madrid's newspaper, the A.B.C. in 1964

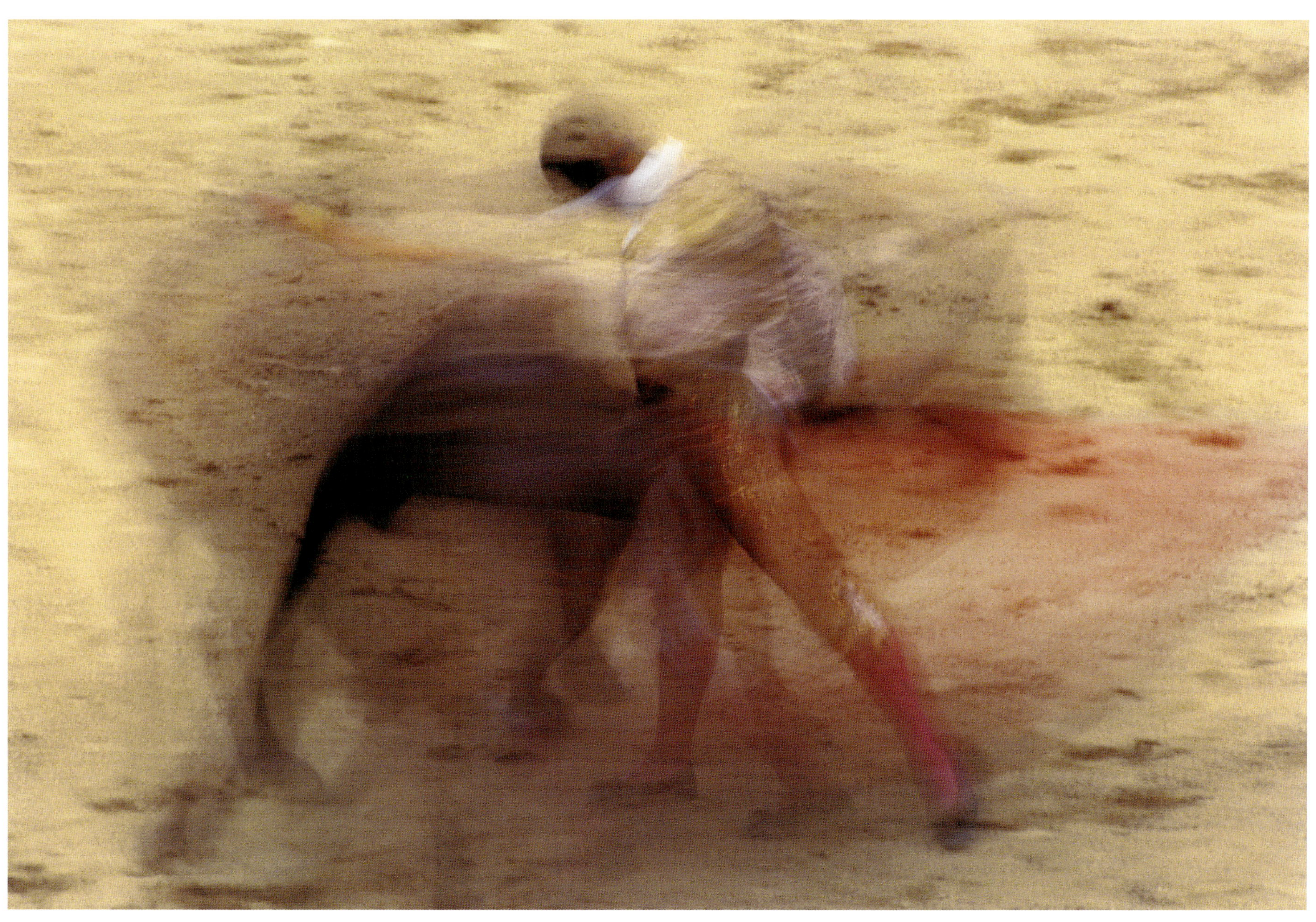

CHANGE OF HANDS BEHIND THE BACK / *Cambio de manos detrás de la espalda*
César Rincón; Las Ventas, Madrid; June 6, 1991

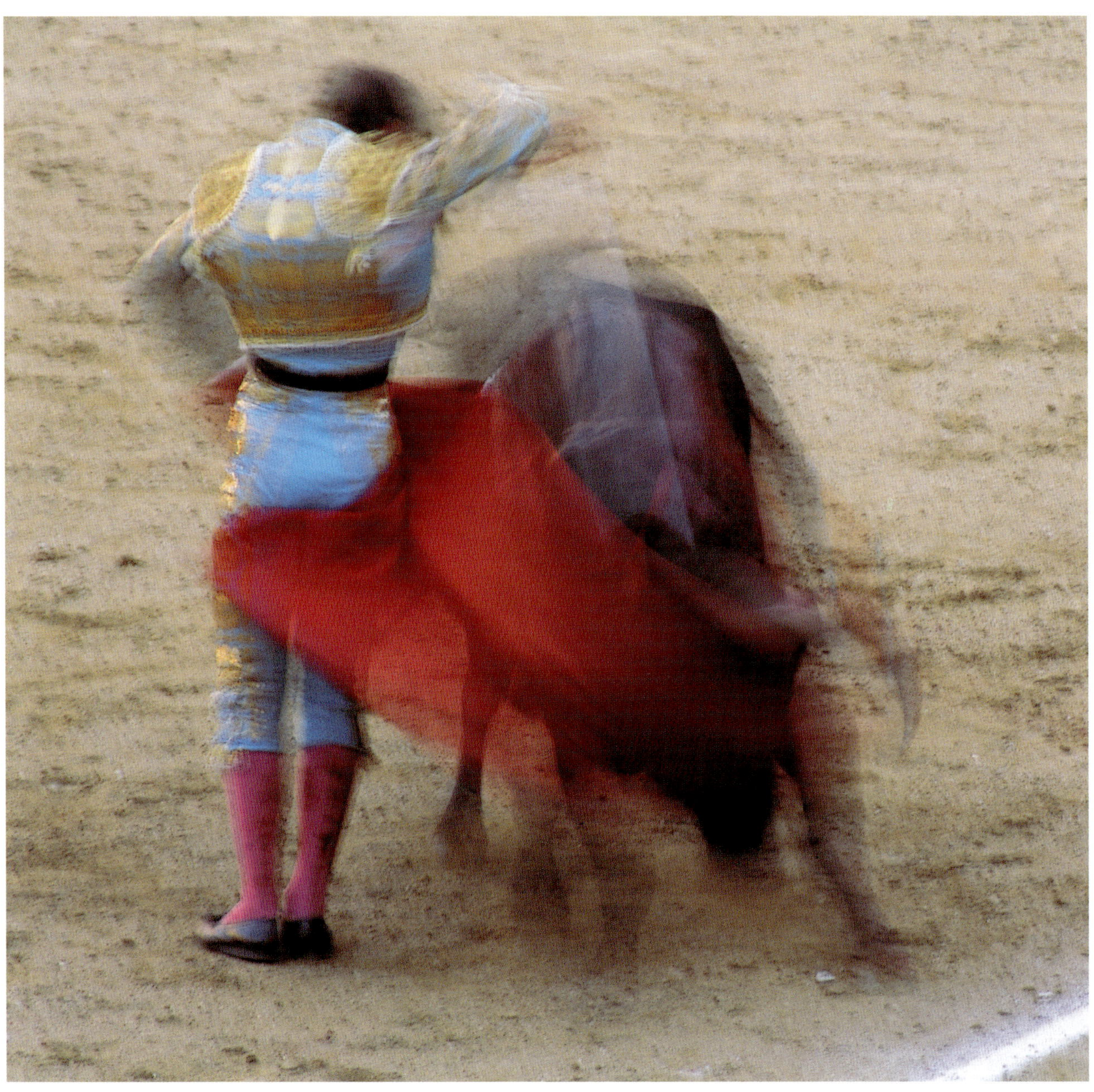

WINDMILL PASS WITH THE LEFT HAND / *Molinete*
Diego Gonzalez; Las Ventas, Madrid; September 18, 1994

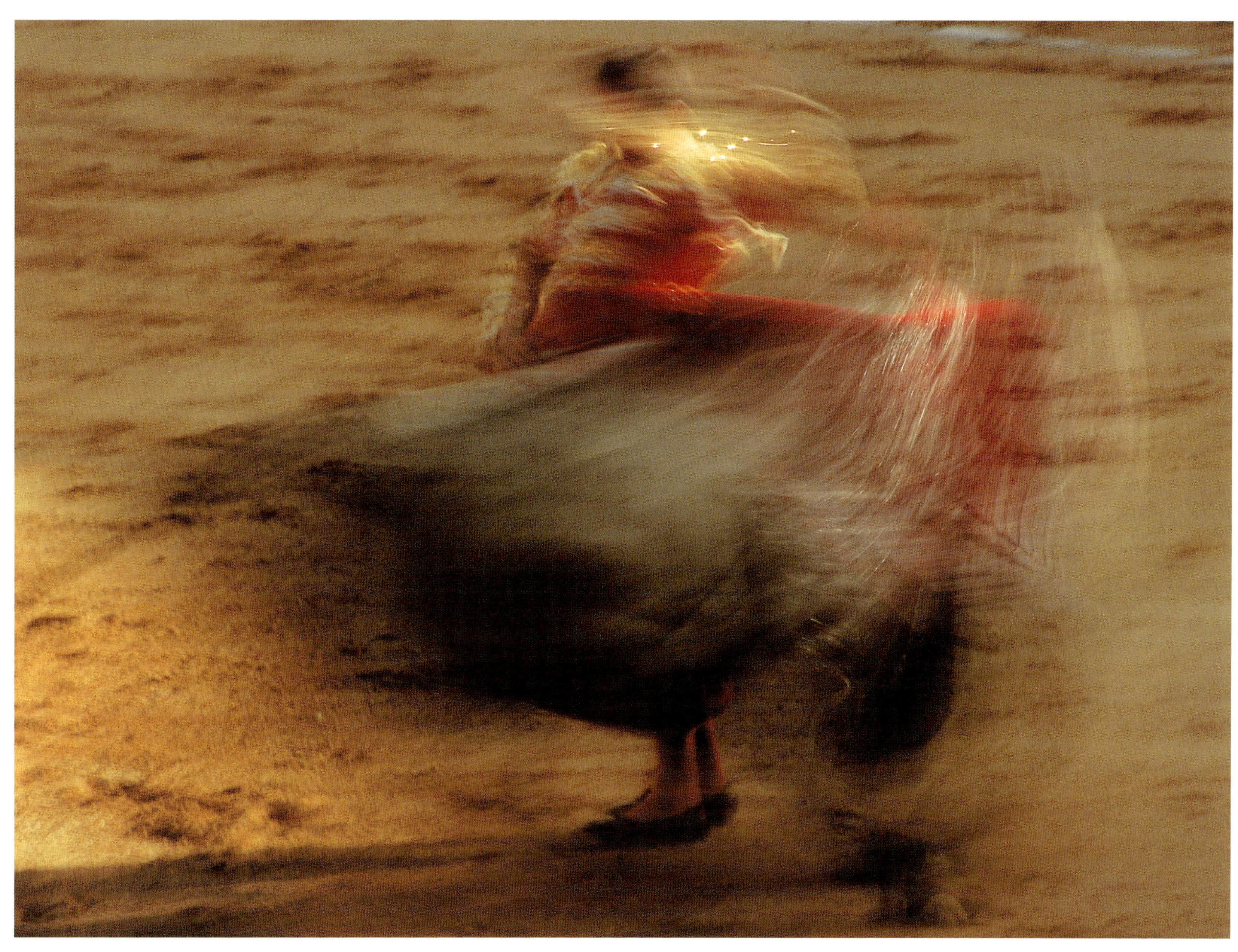

WINDMILL PASS WITH THE RIGHT HAND / *Molinete*
Niño de la Capea; La Glorieta, Salamanca; September 15, 1992

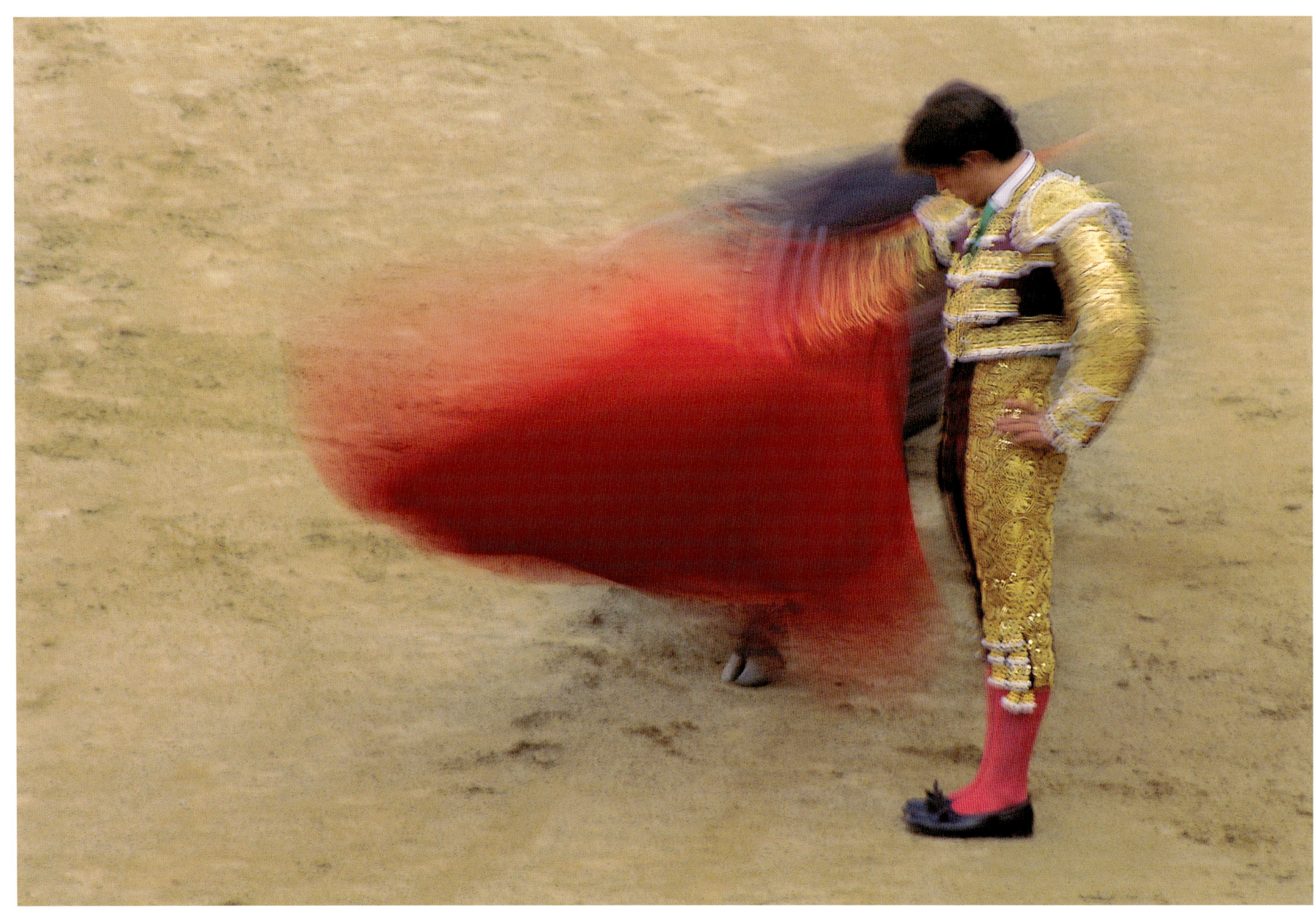

SIDE PASS / *Pase de costadillo*
El Juli; Las Ventas, Madrid; May 17, 2000

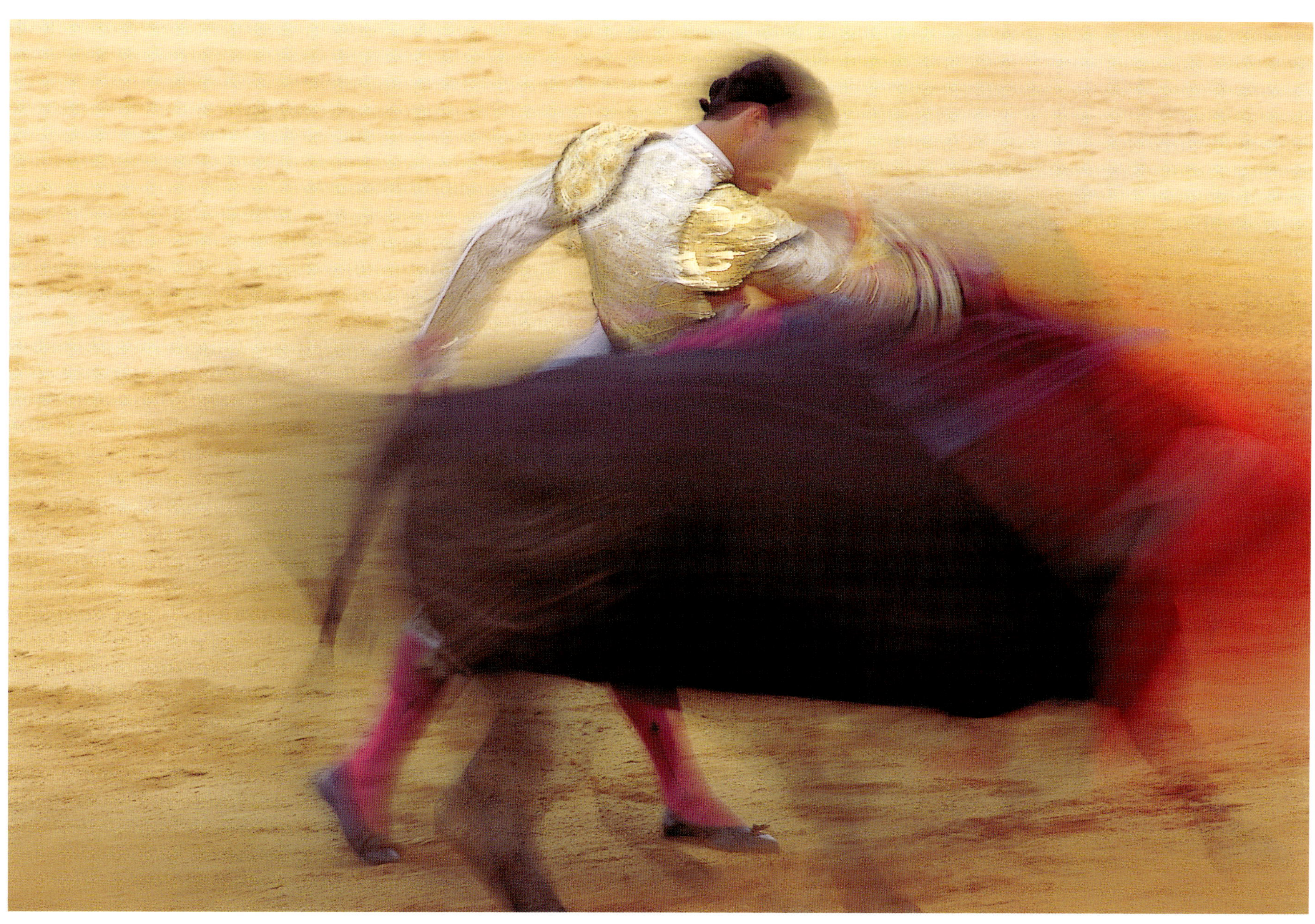

CHEST PASS ON THE RIGHT / *Pase de pecho*
César Rincón; Real Maestranza, Sevilla; April 19, 1992

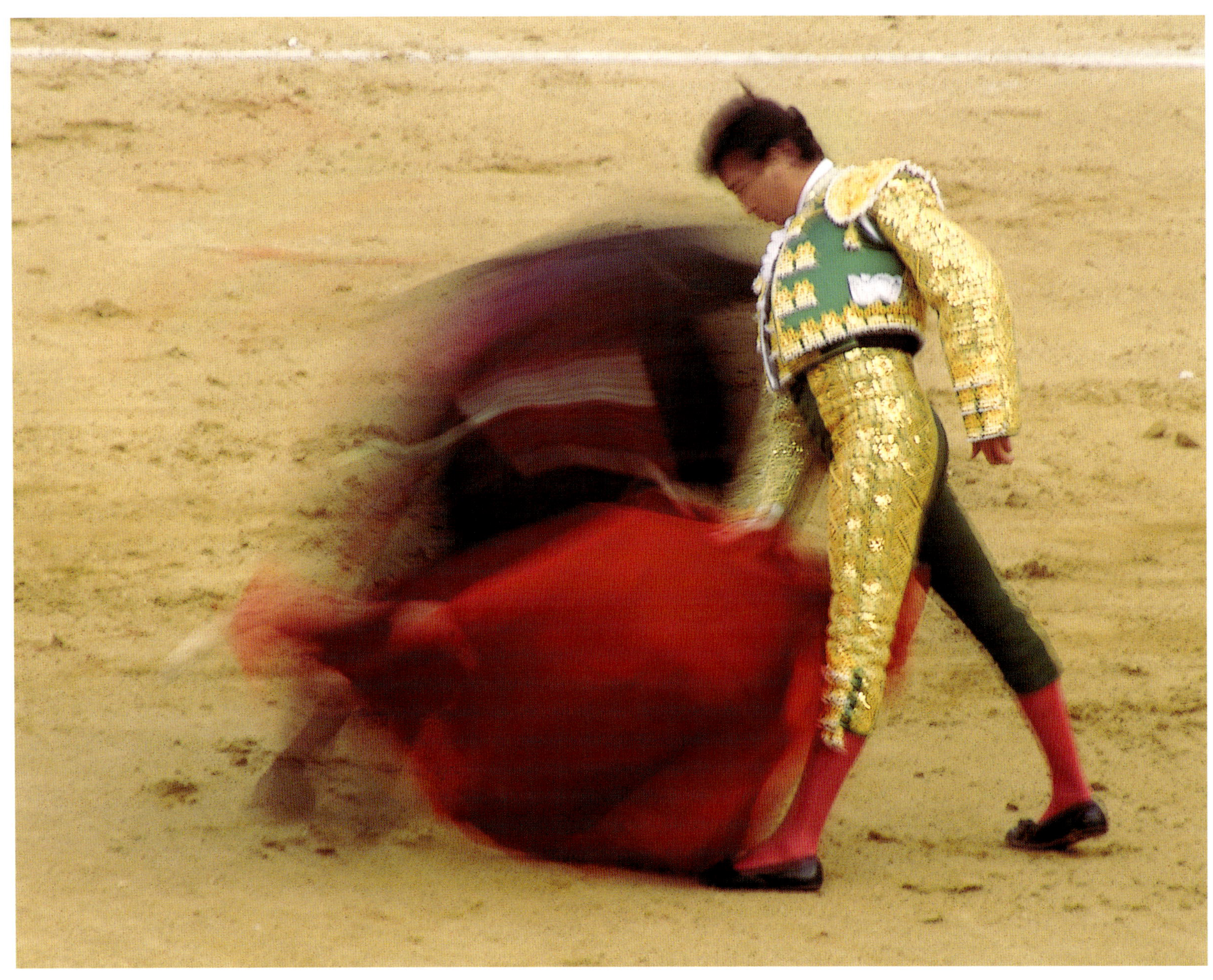

Trincherazo
Armillita; Las Ventas, Madrid; May 29, 1993

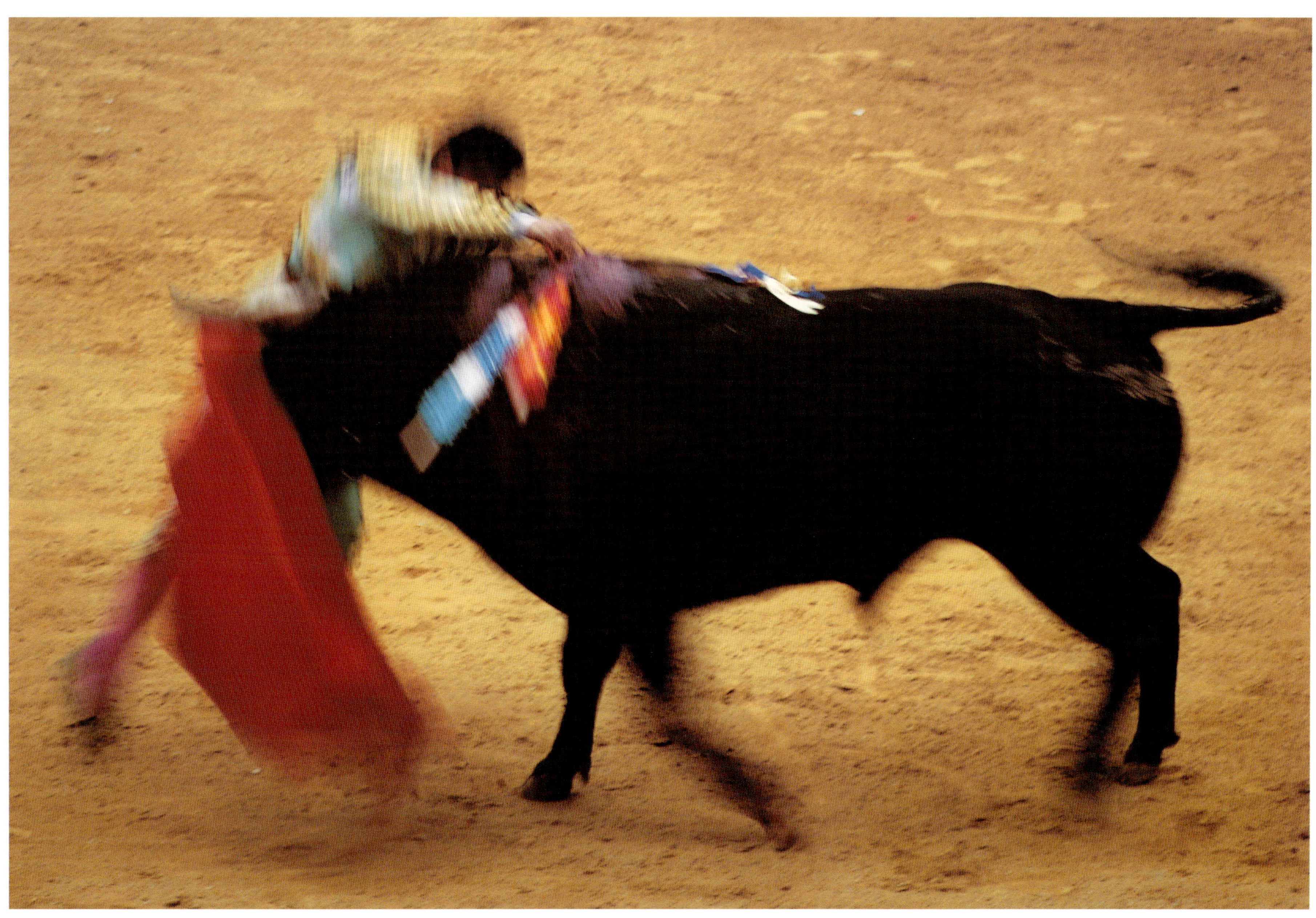

SWORD THRUST / *Estocada*
César Rincón; Granada; June 20, 1992

"It is the paradox of the pass that it never ceases to deceive as it reveals its truth."

—Ricardo B. Sanchez

The photographs for this book have been made during a period of 10 years during which Ricardo B. Sánchez photographed over 160 bullfights in most of the important bullrings in Spain. More than ten thousand images were shot to select these pictures, ninety-eight percet of the material has been recorded on Fuji Velvia film and the remainder on Kodachrome 64. The equipment used was Leica R4 cameras with a Tamron SP 200-500 mm lens or a Tamron SP 300 mm mounted on a Gitzo tripod. These photographs were made at speeds ranging from a second to a fifteenth of a second. In some cases, due to the fact that most of these photographs were made in the shade, the images have been warmed up to eliminate some excessive green and blue tones but otherwise they are true to what the camera recorded on the film.

INDEX

Abellán, Miguel, *75, 119*

Alcázar de San Juan, Ciudad Real, *141, 159*

Almodóvar, Pedro, 124

Amaya, Alejandro, 140

Antequera, Martín, *151*

Armillita, *170*

Ayudado por alto (aided high pass), 41, *98–99, 136*

Ayudado por bajo (aided low pass), 41, *72, 105, 139*

banderillas, 26–27, 40

banderilleros, 36–37, 40

Barrera, Vicente, *60, 66, 163*

Bergamín, José, 62, 70

Bilbao, Vista Alegre, *24, 89, 126, 153, 155*

Bizet, Georges, *Carmen*, 132

Boadella, Albert, 114

Bote, José Luis, *20*

Brionesa, 39, *50*

Buddha, 84

bullfighting

    athleticism of, 46

    as celebration of domination and conquest, 32–33, 35

    costume for, 21, 23, 26, 37

    death's presence in, 54

    essence and seduction of, 27–28

    existentialism and, 29–30

    form in, 30, 32, 35–36, 38

    fundamental elements to, 26–27

    injury risk to bullfighter, 14, 21, 41

    as metaphor for life, 19, 21

    opening ceremony, 37

    as part of culture, 18–19, 35

    sense of self in, 28–29

    Spanish terms, 21

    tercios, 35–37, 40, 92

bulls

    breeding and size of, 35, 36

    color blindness of, 40

Calderón de la Barca, Pedro, 16

Cambio de manos, 41

Cambio de manos detrás de la espalda, *131, 165*

Camino, Paco, 164

Cano, Ortega, *91, 111–12, 153*

cape, 21, 25–27, 37–39, 41

Capeína, 41, *67*

capote, 38

Carrión, Manolo, *121–22*

Cela, Camilo José, *48*

Chamaco, *10*

Chicuelina, 39, *53, 117–18*

Chicuelina al paso (walking chicuelina), *153*

Circular, 41

Circular invertido (inverted circular pass), *102*

Citando a la derecha (citing on the right), *123*

Citando a la izquierda (citing on the left), *162*

Ciudad Real, Alcázar de San Juan, *141, 159*

Cogida (gored or tossed), *20, 31*

cornadas, 19

cuadrilla, 36

Dávila Miura, Luis, 92

deception and illusion, 12–14, 16–18, 21–22, 26–27, 33

Delantal (apron pass), *83, 154*

Derechazo (right-handed pass), *15*, 40–41, *58–59, 89–90, 125, 159*

Derechazo de rodillas (kneeling right-handed pass), *158*

Díaz-Canabate, Antonio, 164

diestro, 13

Doblón (doubling pass with one knee on the ground), *87, 122*

Doblón con Rodilla en Tierra, 41

Doyle, Roddy, 130

El Juli, *82, 85, 129, 154, 161, 168*

El Parque, León, *63, 77*

Espartaco, *68, 100*

Esquivias, Toledo, *58, 93*

Estocada (sword thrust), *73, 141, 171*

Estocada al volapie (sword thrust), 107

faena, 19, 21–22, 40–41

Farol de rodillas (kneeling farol pass), 157

Farol invertida (inverted Farol), *82, 85*

Faroles, 39

Finito de Córdoba, *103, 127*

Frascuelo, *79*

Gaonera, 39, *52, 151*

García, Juan Carlos, *136*

García Lorca, Federico, 106

   "Weeping for the Death of Ignacio Sánchez Mejías," 146

Gonzalez, Diego, *166*

Granada, *171*

Graves, Robert, 88

Guadalajara, *102, 135*

Hemingway, Ernest, 120

   Death in the Afternoon, 35

Joselito, *44, 47, 51, 53, 59, 67, 78, 80, 96, 107, 109–10, 131, 150, 152*

La Glorieta, Salamanca, *71, 91, 95, 101, 167*

La Tercera, San Sebastián de los Reyes, Madrid, *110*

Lance (cape pass with feet together), *78, 112*

Larga (long pass), 39, *121, 149*

Larga a porta gayola, 37, *43, 75*

Larga cordobesa (long pass), *155*

Las Ventas, Madrid, *10, 15, 20, 43, 49–52, 55, 57, 61, 67, 69, 73, 75–76, 78–79, 81–83, 85–87, 97–99, 103, 105, 109, 111–13, 117–19, 122–23, 127–29, 131, 133–34, 136–37, 139, 143–45, 147, 149–52, 154, 157–58, 161–62, 165–66, 168, 170*

León, *160*

   El Parque, *63, 77*

Linares, Palomo, *145*

Litri, *135, 137*

Lopez, Lupita, *34*

Luguillano, David, *147*

Madrid, *96*

   La Tercera, San Sebastián de los Reyes, *110*

   Las Ventas, *10, 15, 20, 43, 49–52, 55, 57, 61, 67, 69, 73, 75–76, 78–79, 81–83, 85–87, 97–99, 103, 105, 109, 111–13, 117, 119, 122–23, 127–29, 131, 133–34, 136–37, 139, 143–45, 147, 149–52, 154, 157–58, 161–62, 165–66, 168, 170*

maestro, 36–38

Manoletina, 41, *66, 134–35*

Manzanares, José María, *90, 98*

Manzanares, Toledo, *65*

María, José, *65*

matador, 13, 36–41

Media Verónica, 39, *147*

Media Verónica a pies juntos (Media Verónica with feet together), *47, 80, 113, 145*

Media Verónica de rodillas (kneeling half Verónica), *111*

Medio farol (half farol pass), *152*

Mendes, Victor, *31*

Michener, James, *Iberia,* 148

Molinete (kneeling windmill pass), *137*

Molinete (windmill pass with the left hand), *166*

Molinete (windmill pass with the right hand), 41, *97, 167*

Mora, Juan, *45, 113*

Morante de la Puebla, *69, 117, 143*

morrillo, 39

mozo de espadas, 36

muleta, 13–14, 21, 25, 27, 38, 40–41

Muletazo sentado en el Estribo (Muletazo seated on the barrera step), *57*

Natural (left-handed pass), 40–41, *63, 65, 93, 95, 127–28, 163*

Natural a pies juntos (natural pass with feet together), *129*

Navarra, 150

Niño de la Capea, *71, 95, 167*

Niño de la Taurina, *118*

Nogales, Manuel Chaves, 25

Ojeda, Paco, *97*

Ortega, Domingo, 88

Pase de costadillo (side pass), *168*

Pase de la firma (signature pass on the left), *103*

Pase de la firma (signature pass on the right), *68*

Pase de pecho (chest pass on the left), 41, *61, 91, 126, 160–61*

Pase de pecho (chest pass on the right), *96, 169*

Pase de pecho con rodilla en tierra (kneeling chest pass), *60*

paseillo, el, 37

pases, 13, 19, 23, 37–41

Paula, Rafael de, 56

Pedresina, 41, *86*

peto, 39

photography, about, 12–14, 16–18, 32–33

picadores, 36, 39

Picasso, Pablo, 94

plaza de toros, 35

Plaza Mayor, Salamanca, *31*

Ponce, Enrique, *24, 72–73, 89, 93, 102, 105, 115, 126, 133, 139, 141, 155*

Puerto, Victor, *76, 81, 144, 158*

Quevedo, Francisco de, 16

quites, 39

Real Maestranza, Sevilla, *44, 47, 59, 68, 90, 100, 107, 125, 169*

Revolera, 39, *49, 79, 115*

Rincón, César, 15, *49–50, 52, 55, 58, 61, 101, 123, 125, 159, 162, 165, 169, 171*

Salamanca

La Glorieta, *71, 91, 95, 101, 167*

Plaza Mayor, *31*

Saltillera, 39, *119*

Sanchez, Ricardo B., 12, 13, 17–18, 23, 46, 172

Savater, Fernando, 54

seduction, 12–14, 18, 21, 28, 30

Segovia, *53, 115*

Sevilla, Real Maestranza, *44, 47, 59, 68, 90, 100, 107, 125, 169*

Story of a Matador (film), 138

suerte, 21

Suerte Suprema, 27, 40–41, *73*

swords, 22, 36, 40–41, 92

Tafallera, 39, *51, 55*

Tafallera (Tafallera with feet together), *81*

Talavera de la Reina, Toledo, *45*

tandas, 40–41

tercio de banderillas, 40

tercio de muerte, 40

tercio de varas, 37

tercios, 35–37, 40, 92

Toledo, *72, 80*

Esquivias, *58, 93*

Manzanares, *65*

Talavera de la Reina, *45*

Tomás, José, *63, 77, 87, 128, 134, 149, 160*

torero, 19, 21–23, 36, 92, 107

toreros de plata, 37

traje de luces, 23, 37

Trincherazo, 41, *71, 100, 170*

Trincherilla, 69, 101, 133

Tynan, Kenneth, *Bull Fever,* 156

Valencia, *60, 66, 121, 163*

vara, 26, 37, 39

Vázquez, Javier, *43, 57, 83, 86, 99, 157*

Verónica, 10, 24, 37, 39, *44–45, 77, 109, 143–44*

Verónica de rodillas (kneeling Verónica), *76, 110*

Vista Alegre, Bilbao, *24, 89, 126, 153, 155*

Wolper, David L., 138